At Risk: Roma and the Displaced in Southeast Europe

Published by
United Nations Development Programme
Regional Bureau for Europe
and the Commonwealth of Independent States

Bratislava 2006

ISBN: 92-95042-53-0

Cover design: RENESANS
The cover design is based on photographs by Andrej Ban and Daniela Rusnok
Layout and print: Miro Kollar and Stano Jendek|Renesans

Report team

Project Coordinator and Lead Author:
Andrey Ivanov

Authors:
Mark Collins, Claudia Grosu, Jaroslav Kling, Susanne Milcher, Niall O'Higgins, Ben Slay, Antonina Zhelyazkova

Contributors:
Erika Adamova, Florin Banateanu, Assen Blagoev, Yassen Bossev, Guy Dionne, Michaela Gulemetova-Swan, Jakob Hurrle, Borka Jeremic, Johannes Kontny, Nick Maddock, Paola Pagliani, Alexei Pamporov, Tatjana Peric, Maria Luisa Silva, Moises Venancio

Foreword

This publication builds on and expands the groundbreaking work first published in *Avoiding the Dependency Trap*, the 2003 regional report by the United Nations Development Programme (UNDP) on Roma in Central Europe. That report offered a deeper, more complex view of Roma exclusion. Using quantitative data from cross-country surveys, it complemented the traditional human rights paradigm with a human development perspective. The report emphasized the importance of integrating the Roma just as the countries of Central Europe were preparing to enter the European Union (EU).

At Risk also appears at an auspicious moment in the EU integration process. Focusing on another group of EU aspirants – the countries of Southeast Europe – the report similarly addresses the situation of Roma using quantitative data from cross-country surveys. But it also focuses this lens on the displaced – refugees and internally displaced persons (IDPs), a significant vulnerable group in this post-conflict region.

There are many dimensions of vulnerability. Vulnerable groups face different types of threats, including poverty and exclusion, and have varying, but generally insufficient, resources to cope with these threats. Based on solid quantitative data and statistics, *At Risk* analyses the determinants of vulnerability as they affect Roma and the displaced. It puts forward a new, integrative approach built on the concept of vulnerability. It attempts to reconcile an approach focused solely on one at-risk group with broader development frameworks that go beyond a single group. This perspective is particularly crucial in the diverse and fragile Balkans.

Development and inclusion – as well as exclusion – take place at the local level, in constant interaction with other groups, with neighbours' passive or active participation. That is why the report addresses the socio-economic status of Roma and the displaced against the background of their 'better-off neighbours', the majority populations living side by side with Roma and the displaced.

Moreover, those majority populations are often vulnerable as well, sharing a similar socio-economic environment. Thus the purpose of providing information on the 'majorities living in close proximity' is not just to offer a control group for statistical calculations. Comparing the status of Roma and the displaced to that of other groups living side by side and sharing similar challenges is key to breaking the circle of exclusion. We must involve, understand and address majorities together with minorities.

The overall picture can outline the common challenges that should be addressed. This approach is particularly relevant for a region like the Balkans, which needs policy interventions that go beyond the group identity that is usually defined along ethnic and sometimes religious lines. The whole logic of the report's analysis – and the set of suggested policy approaches – is therefore built on the concept of *group-sensitive, area-based development*. Understanding the determinants of vulnerability, integrating suitable responses into national-level policy frameworks, and addressing them in an area-based development context is a sustainable way to dealing with the challenges these groups face.

As humanitarian assistance for the displaced is being phased out but appropriately crafted development programmes have yet to come on line, the report also advocates for the creation of a broader framework of international support to address the vulnerability of refugees and IDPs in the region. Like the 'Decade of Roma Inclusion' initiative launched in 2005, a 'Decade of the Displaced' could help mobilize governments to approach these issues in a systematic manner – although I hope that working together, governments, the international community and representatives of the displaced themselves can ensure that it would take less than 10 years to improve conditions for these most vulnerable communities. With their record of successes and failures in the Balkans, international organizations have a moral obligation to embark on a truly integrated approach to development.

I am confident that this report, like *Avoiding the Dependency Trap*, will have lasting impact on thinking about vulnerable groups in the region in general and on policies towards Roma and displaced people in particular. I am very proud of this great intellectual contribution towards social inclusion in our region by lead author Andrey Ivanov, who was also chief author of *Avoiding the Dependency Trap*; author Susanne Milcher; and Ben Slay, who ably assisted with a very strong substantive editing.

Kalman Mizsei
Assistant Administrator and Regional Director
UNDP Regional Bureau for Europe and the CIS

Acknowledgements

This publication is part of a much broader effort to address the dimensions of vulnerability in Southeast Europe. The effort commenced with a large-scale data collection exercise in 2004, spanned numerous discussions on sampling methods and data findings, and culminated in the writing and production of this report. Because of the project's size and longevity, many people deserve to be commended and thanked for their effort.

First and foremost, I would like to thank Kalman Mizsei, Assistant Administrator of the United Nations Development Programme (UNDP) and Director of UNDP's Regional Bureau for Europe and the Commonwealth of Independent States. Together with his management team, he offered unflagging support not only for this project but for the broader concept of vulnerability embraced by this report.

It is easier to list those from UNDP who were not involved in the project than those who were. Thanks are due to most of my colleagues from the UNDP Regional Centre in Bratislava, and particularly to the Poverty Reduction Practice. Eunika Jurcikova and Veronika Krajcirikova were extremely helpful managing the administrative aspects of the project.

Given the regional nature of the project, many colleagues from UNDP country offices were involved, as well as participants in meetings and conferences where the data and findings were discussed. Two events particularly influenced the report – the Data Experts Group Meeting held in Bratislava in 2004 and the conference on Roma and Vulnerability organized jointly with Friedrich Ebert Stiftung in Brussels in 2005. Both events provided extremely valuable input and ideas that later influenced the final analysis.

A great team of authors contributed to the report: Mark Collins, Claudia Grosu, Jaroslav Kling, Susanne Milcher, Niall O'Higgins, Ben Slay and Antonina Zhelyazkova. I would like to thank all of them for their hard work and creativity. Since the workload was never distributed equally, I am particularly grateful to Susanne, Mark and Ben who invested a great deal of time, effort and energy.

Special thanks are due to colleagues who contributed their expertise to the report or who participated in the revision and consultation process: Erika Adamova, Florin Banateanu, Assen Blagoev, Yassen Bossev, Guy Dionne, Michaela Gulemetova-Swan, Jakob Hurrle, Borka Jeremic, Johannes Kontny, Maria Luisa Silva, Nick Maddock, Paola Pagliani, Alexei Pamporov, Tatjana Peric and Moises Venancio.

At the final stage of the report, a peer group of experts reviewed the text and contributed valuable comments. This group consisted of Nato Alhazishvili (*UNDP Bratislava Regional Centre*), Reza Arabsheibani (*London School of Economics*), Nadja Dolata (*UNDP Bratislava Regional Centre*), Arancha Garcia del Soto (*Refugee Initiatives, Solomon Asch Centre for the Study of Ethno-Political Conflict*), Walter Kälin (*Representative of the Secretary-General on Human Rights and Internally Displaced Persons*), Katrin Kinzelbach (*UNDP Bratislava Regional Centre*), Nikolay Kirilov (*Roma Foundation – Lom*), Ivan Krastev (*Centre for Liberal Strategies*), Dennis McNamara (Director of the *Inter-Agency Internal Displacement Division, United Nations Office for the Coordination of Humanitarian Affairs*), Massimo Moratti (*International Committee for Human Rights*), Sarah Poole (*UNDP Turkey*) and Dena Ringold (*The World Bank*).

Communicating the report to the public is no less important than producing it. Special thanks are therefore due to our colleagues from the communications team – Denisa Papayova, Peter Serenyi, Zoran Stevanovic and Sonya Yee. Pierre Harzé and Claire Roberts from UNDP's Brussels office were particularly instrumental in preparing the launch of the report.

Andrey Ivanov
Project Coordinator and Lead Author

Bratislava, June 2006

List of abbreviations

CARDS	Community Assistance for Reconstruction, Development and Stabilization
CEI	Central European Initiative
CGAP	Consultative Group to Assist the Poor
CIS	Commonwealth of Independent States
CRR	Centre for Retirement Research
EC	European Commission
EU	European Union
ERRC	European Roma Rights Centre
GDP	Gross Domestic Product
IDP	Internally Displaced Person
ILO	International Labour Organization
IDMC	International Displacement Monitoring Centre
IOM	International Organization for Migration
IRU	International Romani Union
KLA	Kosovo Liberation Army
MDGs	Millennium Development Goals
NATO	North Atlantic Treaty Organization
NGO	Non-governmental Organization
NRC	Norwegian Refugee Council
NSHC	Novi Sad Humanitarian Centre
OCHA	United Nations Office for the Coordination of Humanitarian Affairs
OECD	Organization for Economic Cooperation and Development
OHCR	Office of the High Commissioner for Human Rights
OLS	Ordinary Least Squares
OSCE	Organization for Security and Cooperation in Europe
OSI	Open Society Institute
PPP	Purchasing Power Parity
RBEC	Regional Bureau for Europe and the CIS
SFRY	Socialist Federal Republic of Yugoslavia
SMEs	Small- and Medium-sized Enterprises
UN	United Nations
UNECE	United Nations Economic Commission for Europe
UNESCO	United Nations Educational, Scientific and Cultural Organization
UNDP	United Nations Development Programme
UNHCR	United Nations High Commissioner for Refugees
UNICEF	United Nations Children's Fund
UNMIK	United Nations Interim Administration Mission in Kosovo
SAP	Stabilisation and Association Process
SUTRA	Sustainable Transfer to Return-related Authorities
WB	World Bank
WHO	World Health Organization

Contents

List of boxes

Introduction

Vulnerability as a human development challenge

Eradicating poverty and overcoming social exclusion are global challenges, and are not solely issues for developing countries. Poverty pockets and excluded and/or marginalized groups exist in the new member states of the European Union (EU) as well, and irrespective of the level of overall national development, whole communities in these countries are deprived of opportunities for equal participation in development. Countries in Southeast Europe now preparing to join the EU face similar problems. The impacts of transition vary widely amongst different socio-economic groups in these countries, and some vulnerable communities are in danger of being left behind. Roma, internally displaced persons (IDPs), and refugees, as well as segments of `majority´ communities, often face levels of exclusion and poverty equal to those found in developing countries.

Addressing the needs of vulnerable communities is critically important for maintaining social cohesion in these societies—some of which are still bearing scars from the conflicts that accompanied Yugoslavia's violent dissolution. The social inclusion of Roma, IDPs and refugees is critical to Southeast European countries' prospects for discharging the responsibilities of the European Social Charter, as well as the requirements of EU accession. These include the design and implementation of the joint inclusion memoranda, and the national action plans for social inclusion. More broadly, addressing the challenges of social inclusion is central to these countries' prospects for implementing the EU's Lisbon Strategy to combine increased competitiveness with social inclusion.

Vulnerable groups and the United Nations Development Programme (UNDP)

The social inclusion of Roma, IDPs, and refugees is critically important to UNDP, which has been underscoring the importance of inclusion and equality for sustainable human development since the publication of its first *Human Development Report* in 1990. The concept of human development recognizes that people are the true wealth of nations, and sees them as both the means and ends of development. To develop their human potential, people must be able to make choices about their lives in a way that helps them be productive, creative and satisfied.

The adoption of the Millennium Development Goals (MDGs) at the Millennium Summit in September 2000 was also critical for prospects for the social inclusion of vulnerable groups in Europe. The MDGs, which represent a comprehensive human development agenda (with its poverty alleviation goals linked to time-bound targets and quantitative indicators to assess performance in reaching these targets), were accepted by all United Nations (UN) member states, including the new EU member states and countries in Southeast Europe now aspiring for membership.

Because pockets of severe poverty are present even in developed countries, adapting the MDG targets and indicators to national circumstances and monitoring progress towards their implementation is necessary even for developed countries. All the countries covered in this report have elaborated their national MDG reports and MDG monitoring frameworks. Complementing national MDG frameworks with disaggregated quantitative indicators and vulnerability analysis is a pragmatic answer to the poverty challenges in the region. It is also an underpinning idea of this report.

The last decade has seen increasing attention paid to socio-economic vulnerability in the new EU member states and countries of Southeast Europe. UNDP in 2002 conducted extensive survey research on Roma vulnerability in Bulgaria, the Czech Republic, Hungary, Slovakia and Romania. The resulting regional human development report (*Avoiding the Dependency Trap*) analyzed the status of Roma from a human development perspective in these

Addressing the needs of vulnerable communities is critically important for maintaining social cohesion in Southeast Europe

Complementing national MDG frameworks with disaggregated quantitative indicators and vulnerability analysis is a pragmatic answer to the poverty challenges in the region

Box 1: **The MDG framework**

The Millennium Development Goals originate from the Millennium Declaration that was signed by 189 countries, including 147 Heads of State, at the United Nations' Millennium Summit in New York in September 2000. The eight MDGs provide time-bound quantified indicators to help governments and other actors measure progress in reducing poverty and social exclusion. Goal 1 calls for halving the number of people living in absolute poverty (defined in general as $1/day in purchasing-power-parity (PPP) terms, and for more developed countries like those in Southeast Europe PPP $4/day) by 2015. Goal 2 envisages reaching 100 per cent primary school completion by 2015. Goal 3 supports gender equality, empowering women and eliminating gender disparities in primary and secondary education. Goal 4 calls for reducing child mortality by two thirds by 2015. Goal 5 aims to reduce maternal mortality by 75 per cent. Goal 6 deals with combating HIV/AIDS, malaria, tuberculosis, and other communicable diseases. Goal 7 addresses environmental aspects of poverty, while Goal 8 calls for stronger global partnerships for development. Specific targets and quantified indicators are associated with each of these goals.

Poverty pockets and the social status of vulnerable groups, however, are often hidden in developed countries by national averages. This is why the real challenges in meeting the spirit of the MDGs lie in redressing the development obstacles facing marginalized and vulnerable groups. Meeting MDG targets in Southeast European countries therefore means addressing the needs of vulnerable groups like Roma.

http://www.undp.org/mdg

Many countries experience fatigue from narrow group-focused approaches

countries.[1] The report argued that the problems facing Roma are primarily issues of underdevelopment, poverty and social exclusion. Discrimination is both a cause and a consequence of inadequate development opportunities; as such, the enforcement of anti-discriminatory legislation is a necessary but not sufficient condition for addressing the hardships experienced by Roma in these countries. Without development opportunities for Roma, legal guarantees of Roma equality will remain hollow, and in the long run could even promote further exclusion. Roma should be involved in all levels of the development process as partners. Both communities, Roma and non-Roma should have the opportunity to develop and implement a common policy that underlines European diversity (cultural, ethnic, religious) as a way of removing segregation, apathy and aversion to Roma civil society.

The report's recommendations to monitor poverty and other MDG-related targets relevant for vulnerable groups and Roma in particular were broadly confirmed by the 'Decade of Roma Inclusion' initiative, which was launched in 2003 by the participating governments of eight countries in Central and Southeast Europe, the World Bank, the Open Society Institute (OSI), and other organisations including UNDP. The 'Decade' grew out of the conference 'Roma in an Expanding Europe: Challenges for the Future', hosted by the Government of Hungary in June 2003.[2] At this conference, five prime ministers and high-level representatives from eight countries – Bulgaria, Croatia, the Czech Republic, Hungary, Macedonia, Romania, Serbia and Montenegro, and Slovakia declared addressing Roma development challenges to be a priority policy concern. National action plans for meeting these priorities were subsequently designed, and in February 2005 the Decade was formally launched in Sofia where these countries' prime ministers pledged to close the gaps in welfare and living conditions between Roma and the non-Roma in their countries, and to break the vicious circle of poverty and social exclusion. At the practical level, the Decade can be seen as an endeavour for meeting the MDG targets for Europe's most vulnerable group – the Roma.

The Decade of Roma Inclusion has been associated with the targeting of policy support for vulnerable groups. Three years after the idea of the Roma Decade was first mooted (and following a long record of targeted focus on different vulnerable groups' problems in various forms and approaches), there is now abundant evidence that targeted attention to vulnerable groups is not sufficient to lift them out of poverty and exclusion. A survey on the perception of the Decade of Roma Inclusion and its priorities conducted by the World Bank and OSI in late 2005 shows that 'Roma-only' measures are not perceived favourably either by Roma or by other communities.[3] Deeper analysis suggests that this is not a commu-

---

1 Using comparable quantitative data developed from more than 5,000 interviews (1,000 in each of the five countries), *Avoiding the Dependency Trap* provided the public and policy makers with a more complete picture of the hardships facing Roma communities. In this way, *Avoiding the Dependency Trap* paved the way for fuller consideration of new policies for Roma integration.

2 http://www.romadecade.org.

3 The national reports and the regional summary of the survey are available on-line at. http://www.worldbank.org/roma.

nication problem, but rather an indicator of broader fatigue from narrow group-focused approaches (see Box 2). Because group-focused interventions increasingly fail to receive broad public support, they should wherever possible be reformulated into policies that focus on vulnerable groups and the areas in which their communities are found. The concepts of 'vulnerability' and 'vulnerability risk' are paramount in this regard—which is another major hypothesis underpinning this report.

> Box 2: **The Decade of Roma Inclusion – targeting Roma and majorities alike?**
>
> For the Decade of Roma Inclusion to succeed, political commitment alone is not sufficient. The magnitude of the challenge requires broad social support.
>
> Revealing the extent to which the objectives and priorities of the Decade are understood and supported by Roma and majority communities was the purpose of a regional study conducted by the World Bank and Open Society Institute in late 2005. Focus groups with Roma and majorities addressing the same set of issues were conducted in all countries of the Decade (Bulgaria, Croatia, the Czech Republic, Hungary, Macedonia, Romania, Serbia and Montenegro, and Slovakia).
>
> The results reveal that, while all parties agree on the importance of the Decade of Roma Inclusion, there is still some scepticism and disbelief among both non-Roma and Roma communities about its feasibility. Perceptions of possible causes of the problems Roma are facing differ between the two groups. However, the belief that policy should not discriminate against people who face similar social and economic conditions is broadly shared by all respondents. Both Roma and majorities share the view that measures exclusively targeting Roma are likely to deepen their social exclusion, raising new issues instead of solving the existing ones. Respondents believe that measures favouring one ethnic group over others are not widely accepted, and may be perceived as a threat to majority communities—alienating in this way vulnerable groups that face challenges similar to those of Roma communities.
>
> Fearing hostility from other communities, Roma—even those who find themselves marginalized—do not particularly favour preferential social protection and economic opportunities vis-à-vis the majority. Such ambivalence towards 'positive discrimination' may be reinforced by the rise of nationalism and xenophobic trends that exploit negative social stereotypes about Roma.
>
> On the other hand, this survey suggests that targeted assistance for Roma is welcomed—when matched by equal measures for other vulnerable groups. When applied in a given region or locality, this is the philosophy of area-based development (see Box 3).
>
> Box based on *Current Attitudes Towards the Roma in Central Europe: A Report of Research with non-Roma and Roma Respondents*. The national reports and the regional summary of the survey are available at http://www.worldbank.org/roma.

Approaches to vulnerability

While 'vulnerability' is a commonly used concept, it can be subject to various interpretations. It is also in need of operationalization, particularly in terms of proper definitions of the target group.

The major idea behind the concept is the many dimensions of vulnerability. Individuals and/or groups can be vulnerable in various ways; they can face different types of threats and have different resources to cope with the threats. Different vulnerability determinants can coincide and interact in certain environmental and group settings, making some more vulnerable than others.

Poverty and the risk of falling into poverty are usually the first common criterion for determining vulnerability. The poor most often have low levels of education, and live in small, sub-standard apartments/houses in poor neighbourhoods, settlements, and regions. In addition, the poor often have no savings, subsist on poor quality diets, and can have difficulty affording even the most basic healthcare services. Because of their poverty they usually experience multiple disadvantages, which distance them not only from employment, income and education, but also from social and community networks. Extreme poverty means that not even basic food needs can be met. Extreme poverty in the Western Balkans may be more prevalent than national data suggest, since the official poverty statistics do not always capture the status of the poorest groups that live in segregated poor settlements.

Apart from poverty, people may find themselves in vulnerable positions due to a lack of educational opportunities, inadequate personal (physical) security, poor housing, or poor access to health care. Displaced status is another major determinant of vulnerability, often correlating with the other factors listed above. The same may apply to ethnicity or religious affiliation, physical, mental, or emotional disability, age or family status (e.g., single parents). Hence a list of vulnerability determinants can be assembled and applied to both individuals and groups.

Seen from this perspective, the concept of vulnerability is closely related to that of 'human security'. This concept was first introduced in the UNDP's *Human Development Report* of 1994 as an attempt to move from state-centred emphases on national security towards more people-centred approaches. The report listed seven areas of potential insecurity (economic, food, health, environment, personal, community and po-

The concept of vulnerability is closely related to that of 'human security'

Human security seeks to conceptualize contemporary security threats in an integrated, multi-dimensional, comprehensive way

litical insecurity). In its 2000/2001 *World Development Report,* the World Bank identified the following risk categories: natural, health, social, economic, political, environmental (specifying whether the risks are to individuals, households, communities, regions, nations, etc.). Human security seeks to conceptualize contemporary security threats in an integrated, multi-dimensional, comprehensive way. By focusing on individuals and communities, human security looks beyond the security of borders and states. By not distinguishing between 'freedom from fear' and 'freedom from want', human security complements state security, supports human rights and strengthens human development. In its 2003 *Human Security Now* report, the United Nations' Commission on Human Security paid special attention to 'downturns with security' in order to help protect poor individuals and communities from the negative impact of economic downturns and political upheavals.

Human security reflects a multitude of economic, social, and political risk factors. Socio-economic risk pertains to security of employment and income or access to such public services as health care, adequate housing and education. This dimension is generally associated with the 'supply side' of societal systems, and with 'freedom from want' in a broad sense. It can also be estimated using quantitative data. Personal security risk is generally associated with the integrity of the individual, and with 'freedom from fear'. For example, the fear of losing access to medical care during health care reform, or the fear of losing one's job during enterprise restructuring contributes to this insecurity. The same applies to crime – individuals do not need to become victims themselves to feel insecure. Unlike the socio-economic dimension, personal security is difficult to quantify; measuring it relies more on qualitative data or proxies for estimating risks and fears. Both personal and socio-economic dimensions have important gender aspects, as is apparent in gender-based and domestic violence. The personal security risks that women face are often different than those facing men.

Unlike most human security monitoring examples, vulnerability analysis focuses on status and less so on its perception

Personal and socio-economic risks are attributable more to the individual and household, while the other three human security risks are attributable rather to territory or groups and their interaction. The first of these are environmental risks (e.g., pollution and man-made or natural disasters such as floods and earthquakes), political risks and risk due to random hazards. These risks can be estimated on the basis both of quantitative and qualitative data. Risk of pollution for example can be monitored using both data on the status of the environment and people's perception of its deterioration. The same applies to political risk – the risk of civil or human rights violations, including those violations occurring due to international conflicts, civil wars and ethnic violence. In broader terms the political dimension can also include freedom from such arbitrary behaviour as corrupt civil service, institutional unpredictability, poorly functioning judiciaries, or poor contract enforcement. And these are areas that are difficult to quantify. Risk due to random individual hazards (fires, traffic accidents) could result from inadequate physical infrastructure or capacity of state officials, and can be measured using proxy indicators.

These different threats may interact to create individualized profiles of human insecurity, which can be measured as the capacity to identify and avoid threats or attenuate their consequences. What distinguishes the concept of human security from vulnerability analysis is the dynamic nature of the latter and stronger reliance on quantitative measurements. It can be applied to groups and individuals to outline both the magnitude of vulnerability and its determinants in comprehensive vulnerability profiles. Based on this, policies addressing the determinants of vulnerability can be designed and implemented and progress in decreasing vulnerability can be monitored. Unlike most human security monitoring examples, vulnerability analysis focuses on status and less so on its perception.

In this context the concept of vulnerability is closely related to 'social exclusion', a concept developed in industrial countries (Saith, 2001). The term was first used to describe the position of low-skilled people who faced increased difficulties in gaining access to the labour market. In contrast to more traditional concepts like inequality and poverty, social exclusion does not primarily deal with material deprivation (which should be secured by the welfare state) but stresses the importance of social networks for inclusion. As its antithesis, exclusion is a multidimensional concept and is linked, among others, with employment, housing, culture and institutional representation. Social exclusion has been defined in European documents such as the 1992 Second Report of the EC Observatory on National Policies to Combat Social Exclusion, "in relation to the social rights of citizens…to a certain basic standard of living and to participation in the major social and occupational opportunities of society". Other definitions focus on the difference between voluntary and non-voluntary exclusion. Individuals are socially excluded if they are residents in society, but cannot participate in normal social activities for reasons beyond their control, even though they would like to participate. (Other approaches suggest that groups should be considered socially excluded if they are denied opportunities for participation, irrespective of whether they actually desire to participate or not.) Opportunities for individual participation are in turn central to the concept of human development.

In the Balkans, groups that stand out as especially at risk of poverty and exclusion are Roma, the displaced, the unemployed, the less educated and women. Gender can further exacerbate vulnerability: Roma women, having fewer job opportunities and weaker access to income than Roma men, face more and different obstacles to escaping poverty due to constraints hampering their ability to influence their own lives. In some countries, households with many children and elderly households are also at particular risk of falling into poverty. In rural areas and in underdeveloped regions, poverty is more widespread.

The 1990s in Southeast Europe 'produced' additional vulnerability dimensions related to the collapse of former Yugoslavia. In many of these countries, independence was regarded as the final outcome of national struggles for self-determination and anti-communist emancipation. This process dramatically affected various minorities and particularly those without a nation-state to protect them (like Roma). Violent conflicts in the Western Balkans produced streams of refugees and IDPs, among them also Roma – a new phenomenon for post-World War II Europe.

The modern emergence of ethnically defined nation-states redefined the concept of 'minorities', with direct implications for different groups in the Balkans. Starting with the 1918 Treaty of Versailles, which set standards for the protection of minorities in the newly established nation-states after World War I, the legal framework for the protection of ethnic and national minorities developed during the 20th century into an important branch of international law. In practice, this framework was 'designed' to manage the challenges (and political tensions) stemming from the scattered diasporas of Europe's nation-states.

Integrating risk analysis and asset vulnerability

The concepts of human development and human security are therefore closely linked to vulnerability analysis. People who are facing human security risks, who are in deep poverty, or are socially excluded, are vulnerable. People lacking freedom of choice are vulnerable. However, a dose of discipline is required here. The overlaps of these various concepts can give rise to excessively 'flexible' uses of the term 'vulnerability'. As a result, different practitioners attach different meanings to the term 'vulnerable groups' (Hoogeveen et al., 2004). According to the World Bank, the 'vulnerability' concept most appropriately refers to the relationship between poverty, risk and efforts to manage risk (Alwang, Siegel, Jørgensen, 2001). The World Bank sees poverty as a forward-looking concept that measures the probability (risk) of experiencing some future reduction in household welfare. In particular, household vulnerability is affected by uncertain events, vulnerability to which depends on the characteristics of the risk and the household's ability to respond. The poor and the near poor tend to be vulnerable due to their limited access to assets and limited abilities to respond. Vulnerability is therefore closely linked to asset ownership (or control).

In the Balkans, groups that stand out as especially at risk of poverty and exclusion are Roma, the displaced, the unemployed, the less educated and women

Assets are a key link between economic growth and vulnerability. While originally applied to the reassessment of urban poverty reduction strategies (Moser, 1998), the broad concept of asset vulnerability can be used in other contexts as well, particularly for groups identified according to other vulnerability criteria. Within this framework, vulnerability can be defined as insecurity in individual, household and community welfare in the face of a changing environment. Analyzing vulnerability involves identifying threats as well as prospects for responding to threats, in terms of exploiting opportunities, or in recovering from the negative effects of a changing environment. Assets are central to resisting these threats or responding to their consequences.

Analyzing vulnerability involves identifying threats as well as prospects for responding to threats

Asset vulnerability frameworks generally classify assets in terms of labour (ability of household members to generate income), human capital (including education, skill

Box 3: **Area-based development**

Area-based development can be defined as programming or policies in a defined geographical area that seeks to address certain special problems or needs, or the development potential, of a given area. The notion implies that (1) policies and programming at the national level may be inadequate or less effective than tailored solutions within a well-defined region or locality; and (2) the development challenges to be addressed have a multi-sectoral character, and as such require an integrated, consistent response. Local problems are often associated with tensions, fissures or conflicts in local communities, particularly along ethnic or religious lines. This can make policies and programming that focus on group identity and affiliation quite risky.

The area-based development concept has evolved from the integrated rural development approach popular in the developing world, and particularly in Africa, during the 1970s and 1980s. This approach emphasized comprehensive multi-sectoral responses to the development challenges of a defined geographic area, often with a strong agricultural emphasis. Typical focus areas were locally oriented agricultural research, extension services and irrigation, as well as marketing, health, education, water supply and sanitation, and roads. Because sectoral ministries were believed to be unable to provide services in a coordinated manner, fragmentary development patterns were the feared results. Underpinned by donor finance, integrated rural development was designed to correct this.

The area-based development paradigm typically replaces the rural development emphasis with crisis prevention or post-conflict recovery themes. It retains, however, the multi-sectorality and the geographic (as opposed to thematic) developmental focus. Also in common with integrated rural development is the use of sub-national management arrangements in the areas concerned. The support and active involvement of local communities are often seen as both a precondition for success and an important outcome of area-based projects.

Vulnerability is not about ethnicity or group affiliation: it is a matter of facing certain vulnerability risks

sets and health characteristics), access to physical assets (including residential ownership), and household relations (including household composition and cohesion, internal hierarchies and other aspects of household relations). This component has strong links to the gender dimensions of social exclusion and poverty, as women tend to have poorer access to assets than men, which affects their position within households and communities. Social capital – reciprocity within communities and between households based on trust deriving from social ties – can deplete or magnify the productivity of household assets. All these factors determine a household's ability to respond to vulnerability shocks.

This report defines 'vulnerability' as a high level of human insecurity, quantified, monitored and analyzed at individual and household levels through the lens of assets and, more broadly, capabilities (Sen, 1992, in Robeyns, 2000). It addresses Roma and displaced persons' exposure to various vulnerability risks. It analyses the magnitude and determinants of those risks compared to similar risks faced by the majority control group.

Roma and displaced persons are chosen not because they are Roma and displaced *per se*, but because they face particularly unpleasant combinations of vulnerability risks. Vulnerability is not about ethnicity or group affiliation: it is a matter of facing certain vulnerability risks. Most Roma are vulnerable, but not all vulnerable are Roma; most people in majority communities are not vulnerable, but not everyone who is economically and socially secure belongs to a majority community. This common sense logic gets lost when group determinism is applied; proper policy targeting is only possible on the basis of appropriate vulnerability analysis.

This report seeks to promote pragmatic, common-sense analysis and policy formulation. Putting vulnerability status and determinants first – and group affiliation second – makes it possible to identify and support those most in need. This is what group-sensitive policies within an area-based approach are all about.

Outline of the report

The starting point of this report was the comprehensive data collection exercise performed by UNDP's Vulnerable Groups Survey, conducted in October 2004 in eight countries of Southeast Europe and the UN-administered Province of Kosovo (herein referred to as Kosovo). This survey focused on three populations: Roma, displaced persons (refugees and IDPs), and respondents living in majority communities located in close proximity to Roma and displaced (IDPs and refugees). The data collected from the Vulnerable Groups Survey are the basis of this analysis and report for Albania, Bosnia and Herzegovina, Bulgaria, Croatia, Macedonia, Montenegro, Romania, Serbia and Kosovo in Southeast Europe.[4] Since quantitative data cannot capture all aspects of an issue as complicated as the levels and determinants of vulnerability, this dataset was complemented with references and boxes based on qualitative research and work conducted by organizations working directly with these vulnerable groups.

The methodology used here allows us to merge the national samples into three big re-

4 The survey was also carried out in the Czech Republic, Hungary and Slovakia.

gional databases: for Roma, for displaced persons, and for residents of majority communities living close to these vulnerable groups. This study is based on the premise that the socio-economic conditions and the development challenges in the different Southeast European countries are sufficiently similar so as to make such an aggregation sensible. The large numbers of observations that result make possible the in-depth statistical analysis that is needed to investigate the determinants of vulnerability—something that is not possible (or at least prohibitively expensive) at the national level. Having outlined certain correlations and relationships at the regional level, the results can be tested and applied nationally by policy makers seeking to decrease vulnerability and social exclusion. Important tools in this regard are UNDP's national vulnerability reports, which are being elaborated on the basis of national datasets generated in the framework of the regional survey. The national vulnerability reports, together with this regional vulnerability report, constitute a comprehensive package on vulnerability in Southeast Europe. The compact disk attached to this publication contains the regional dataset, the national datasets, and those national reports that have been elaborated to date. In addition, country snapshots of Roma vulnerability based on major MDG indicators were published in February 2005 in the *Faces of Poverty: Faces of Hope* brochure. The country snapshots, the datasets, and the reports that are still to come will be available online at http://vulnerability.undp.sk.

This publication goes beyond providing a snapshot: it offers in-depth analysis of the determinants of vulnerability affecting Roma and the displaced in Southeast Europe. These determinants of vulnerability are analyzed in an 'area-based context', against the background of majority communities living in close proximity to Roma and the displaced. Since people live and interact at the local level, within their close communities, majority-in-proximity samples (rather than national averages) are used as control groups in the analysis. This approach does not attempt to guarantee that national majority communities are fully represented. Indeed, because their circumstances may not be completely dissimilar to those of the Roma and the displaced, the majority-in-proximity sampled may share some of their neighbours' vulnerability determinants, and thus may be more vulnerable than the national averages.

This 'majority-in-proximity sample' approach was chosen over a 'nationally representative sample' approach for several reasons. First, the majority-in-proximity approach reflects the area-based development paradigm. Vulnerable groups' development challenges often have spatial characteristics (e.g., a Roma settlement, a collective centre, a city or region that had been contested during a period of armed conflict) that should be explicitly addressed by policies and programming. Seen from this perspective, it is the status of the adjacent majority communities (not national averages) that matter in defining and addressing vulnerability.

The second argument for using 'adjacent majorities' as control groups is of an analytical nature. Nationally representative samples can be difficult to align with regional (trans-national) samples without a complex system of weights – and the regional database was necessary for in-depth analysis of vulnerability determinants and correlates. Third, because the sampling instruments used are methodologically compatible with those of such official national surveys as labour force and household budget surveys, part of the data obtained and the profiles of majorities in proximity based on these data are comparable to official national indicators (as are the profiles of the other two groups). Such comparisons provide additional information on the distance between those groups and populations overall, and make possible estimates of the time and resources necessary for vulnerable groups to reach certain national benchmarks.

The structure of the report reflects the area-based logic outlined above. Using quantitative data on various aspects of vulnerability generated by the survey, the analysis builds detailed vulnerability profiles of Roma and displaced persons and outlines the specific determinants of vulnerability for each of the groups. Because of differences in the challenges the two groups are facing, the report is divided into two major sections – one devoted to Roma, and one devoted to the displaced. Each section begins with a separate introduction that describes the challenges facing each of the groups in the Balkan context. Within each section, specific sectoral issues (poverty, education, employment, health and security threats, etc.) are addressed, reflecting the specific characteristics of each group. These chapters outline the major correlates of vulnerability, identify its determinants, and summarize

Proper policy targeting is only possible on the basis of appropriate vulnerability analysis

major findings and recommendations. The report's final chapter presents a set of recommendations – specifically relevant for Roma, for the displaced, and for any group facing increased vulnerability risk.

Each chapter starts with a brief summary of the main findings. Detailed information about the statistical analysis as well as other relevant data is provided in the Statistical Annex. Information about the research methodology, the sampling process, and the survey instrument is detailed in the Methodological Annex. The source data as obtained from the survey (by countries and aggregated for the region) are presented in the Data Annex.

Part I.

Roma

CHAPTER 1.1

Roma in the Balkan context

Clearly defining the scope of research and the identity of the population studied is particularly important in the case of Roma, especially when talking about the impact of conflict on the Roma communities and the size of these communities. While Roma may or may not be 'Europe's largest minority'[5] the 'Roma universe' is so diverse that it is sometimes difficult to agree who, exactly, is the subject of different political statements, documents and projects.

Major approaches to Roma identity

So who are the Roma (or the Gypsies, as they are often called by majority communities, and often by themselves as well)? Currently there are several major views on Roma identity, ethnicity and nationhood, each of which is supported (and promoted) by different organizations in the context of their specific political agenda.[6] These include:

- The Roma as ethnos and ethnic minority, by the International Romani Union (IRU);
- Roma intellectuals, who suggest that the Roma nation is currently undergoing a process of creation, and that this is the period of the Roma Renaissance;
- Nikolae George's idea of Roma as a trans-European nation without its own territory, alienated from the continent as a whole;
- Roma sometimes define themselves as a nation without a state or non-territorial European nation, a vision developed during the 2000 IRU Congress in Prague. The Congress adopted a declaration demanding that international institutions grant them the status of nation without a state;
- The classical idea of Roma as a cultural minority, migrants etc.; and
- The version of the Roma as a social minority, underclass or in general as a socially vulnerable group is usually proposed by outside experts (Szelenyi, 2000).

The concept of an institutionally represented non-territorial European nation receives perhaps the broadest support, including from the EU. In practical terms, the claim for acceptance as a *nation without state* translates into demands for *representation* in the political bodies of the EU and its member states. The most prominent example is the European Roma Forum accepted by the Council of Europe with a Partnership agreement on 16 December 2004.[7]

The variety of approaches shown above suggests caution in choosing terms to describe Roma, because these terms can influence policies and social attitudes. The inclusion of Roma *en bloc* among the socially vulnerable (along with refugees, disabled persons etc.), creates the danger of social marginalization, deprivation or dilution of cultural self-identity, deprivation of the right to posses or enjoy group ethnic characteristics.

The inclusion of Roma en bloc among the socially vulnerable creates the danger of social marginalization, deprivation or dilution of cultural self-identity

---

5 Roma are not the 'largest ethnic group' in Europe. But they are one of the 'largest ethnic groups residing outside of nation-state borders', because Roma do not have a nation-state of their own. The numbers of Turks, Hungarians and other groups in such a position in Europe (living outside their state's borders) is almost certainly smaller than Roma. More Russians may live outside Russia (in Europe) than Roma – if 'Europe' is defined as the geographic expanse from the Atlantic to the Urals. But since many (perhaps most) Russians are not vulnerable, the statement that 'Roma constitute Europe's largest vulnerable minority' is robustly defensible.

6 This classification has been developed by Ilia Iliev, an anthropologist at Sofia University. "St. Kliment Ohridski" (unpublished paper by Ilia Iliev, presented at a working group on Roma integration within the Open Society Institute-Sofia (13 January 2006). See also Tomova, 2005.

7 The Forum, as its official site states, "is, at heart, a body of community leaders and policy experts who shall be elected by Roma and Traveller institutions across Europe". The sequence of tenses is important – the Forum is legitimized by the Council of Europe as an international counterpart, but is still to be legitimized by Roma populations. Legitimization mechanisms and electoral procedures (for example, the procedures for composing electoral lists) are still to be decided.

The debate over the size of the Roma population is a direct consequence of the lack of clarity regarding Roma identity. 'Counting the Roma' is not easy (if possible at all) given the flexible (or different) meaning ascribed to the term 'Roma' and the diversity of the 'Roma universe'. This is why it is only possible to talk about estimates. Estimates indicate that between 6.8 and 8.7 million Roma live in Europe, 68 per cent of whom live in Central and Eastern Europe and the Balkans. [8]

Roma populations in the countries covered in this report have been estimated as follows:

- Albania. For political reasons, questions to identify respondent ethnicity were omitted from the 2001 census. Out of a population of 3.3 million, estimates of the Roma population vary from 10,000 to 120,000 people (ERRC, 1997). Expert estimates (Liégeois, 2006) put the number at between 90,000 and 100,000.
- Bosnia and Herzegovina. Expert estimates suggest minimum 40,000 and maximum 50,000.
- Bulgaria. Official data (from the 2001 census[9]) report 370,980 people of Roma identity or 4.68 per cent of the population. Expert estimates suggest minimum 700,000 and maximum 800,000.
- Croatia. According to official data (from 2001), 96.12 per cent of the 4.8 million population claim Croatian as their mother tongue, 1.01 per cent Serbian, other languages (Albanian, Bosnian, Hungarian, Slovene, Serbo-Croatian, and Romany) being the mother tongue of between 0.1 per cent and 0.33 per cent of the population for each group. The number of Roma in this census was 9,463 (0.21 per cent). Estimates range between 30,000 and 40,000 (National Programme for Roma).
- Macedonia. Official data from the 2002 census state that Roma number 53,879 or 2.66 per cent of the total population (2,041,467). Expert estimates suggest minimum 220,000 and maximum 260,000.
- Montenegro. Official data from the 2003 census state 2,601 people to be of Roma identity. Approximately 20,000 Roma, Ashkali and Egyptians (RAE) are estimated to live in Montenegro (World Bank, 2005b).
- Romania. Official data from the 1992 census count 409,723 Roma, or 1.8 per cent of the population. Data from the 2002 census suggests 535,250 Roma (2.5 per cent of the total population). Expert estimates suggest minimum 1,800,000 and maximum 2,500,000, making this group the largest Roma population in Europe and possibly the world.
- Serbia. According to the 2002 population census there are 108,000 Roma in Serbia, but unofficial estimates put the figure at between 450,000 and half a million (World Bank, 2005b; Antic, 2005), including 250,000 Roma living in 'mahalas' (illegal settlements) in the suburbs of the larger cities.
- Kosovo. Two per cent of the population (between 36,000 and 40,000 are estimated to be Roma (Living Standard Measurement Survey by the Statistical Office of Kosovo, 2000).

Roma – like other ethnicities in contemporary Europe – possess multiple identities, particularly in terms of vulnerability

However, behind the numbers – whatever the estimates are – is the patchwork of various Roma groups defined differently by cultural criteria, heritage and level of integration. Furthermore, Roma – like other ethnicities in contemporary Europe – possess multiple identities, particularly in terms of vulnerability. Roma can also be refugees, internally displaced persons, disabled, unemployed, illiterate or all of these together. They can also be politicians, scholars or professionals. Roma in various countries, regions, municipalities, and subgroups display different social roles and positions, with different opportunities and social perspectives.

The most general distinction among Roma communities is the one between Muslims (Xoraxane Roma) and Christians (Dasikane Roma), who are divided into more or less autonomous groups within each community. Examples of subdivisions, differentiated according to various features (linguistic, skills, etc.) include the Erli, Gurbeti, Gabeli, Kovachi, Chergara, Romtsi, etc. in the countries of former Yugoslavia; Erlia, Dzambazia,

[8] One of the credible estimates of the Roma population is provided by Jean-Pierre Liégeois in Liégeois, 2006. Unless stated otherwise, the 'estimates' quoted in the paragraphs below and used later in the report are based on this publication.

[9] http://www.nsi.bg/Census/Census.htm.

Kalaydzia, Kalderashi, Chilingiri, Vlaxoria, etc. in Bulgaria; Kaburdzi, Mechkara, Kurtofi, etc. in Albania; Leyasha, Kalderara, Ursari, Rumungari in Transylvania, Rudara etc. in Romania (Marushiakova and Popov, 2001b; Akim, V. 2002). Some of these groups appear in several countries, contributing to the belief that Roma are a 'trans-state entity' (like Kalderari and Vlahichki, ursari in Bulgaria and Romania; or Erlija, Valahi, Egyptian who appear in Serbia, Bulgaria and Hungary).[10] Classification of these groups under an all-encompassing 'Roma umbrella' could deprive them of their distinct ethnic and cultural identities. All this makes general statements about the size of Roma populations extremely difficult (if impossible).

Historical roots

In the Ottoman Empire, Roma could move relatively freely because of their status outside of the two main population categories (Muslim or Christian). A great many of them continued in their nomadic ways within the boundaries of the Empire or out of its confines until the late 19th century. Others settled voluntarily and even took up agricultural activities in villages and big farms between the 16th and 19th centuries (Marushiakova and Popov, 2001a).

In the case of the Austro-Hungarian Empire, Roma were free to move around until Maria Theresa's attempts to settle them in the 18th century. After 1758 the Austro-Hungarian Empress issued a number of decrees to transform Roma into 'Újmagyarok' or 'New Hungarians'. Specially constructed sheds were to replace the tents where they used to live; travelling on horses or horse trading was forbidden. Roma children were forcibly separated from their families so they could be adopted by Hungarians. Joseph II, Emperor from 1765, continued the policy of forced Roma assimilation. He prohibited the Roma languages and traditional Roma dress. Roma music was allowed to be played only on holidays. Education and school attendance were made obligatory. (These forced assimilation policies were subsequently softened in the face of resistance from the Roma communities.)

Kosovo was a special case. Some Roma communities settled in the ethnic quarters of towns or villages; others continued their semi-nomadic way of life (seasonal nomadism) in various traditional or modernized modes. Roma communities there included the Romany-speaking Arli, Kovachi, Gurbeti, Gabeli (coming mainly from Bosnia) and Serbian speaking Gjorgjovtsi. Many scholars who study Roma issues consider Egyptians and Ashkali to be a separate subdivision of the larger Roma community: they are thought to be Roma who lost their Romany language and subsequently began to change their identity. After living as a distinct group, they tried to assimilate as Albanians (on the basis of a common language) and then rediscovered their ancient origins and distinct, non-Romani identity (Marushiakova and Popov, 2001a; Marushiakova et al, 2001).

Even before World War II, Nazi Germany adopted several decrees classifying Roma as inferior persons. During the first year of Nazi rule they were treated as socially alien persons. At that time Roma were equated with beggars, prostitutes, persons suffering from contagious or mental diseases or homosexuals. In 1943 they were designated a threat to the nation and were subject to sterilization and isolation in concentration camps (Fraser, 1992; Kenrick and Puxon,1995).

Roma under socialism

State policies adopted towards Roma during the socialist period should be considered in the context of wartime legacies (the Nazi attempts to exterminate Roma as an inferior ethnic group), of the dominant ideology and political context. The major elements of the latter were (1) consolidation of the state around the Communist Party; and (2) the forced change of social class structures through rapid industrialization and the creation of a modern 'proletariat'. The response to the unfavourable demographic trends that began to take hold in many of these countries during the 1980s also has had a dramatic effect on Roma communities.

State policies towards Roma during the socialist period should be considered in the context of the forced change of social class structures through rapid industrialization and the creation of a modern 'proletariat'

Their status as victims of Nazi persecution meant that Roma were afforded the 'socially progressive strata' distinction by commu-

[10] It should be noted, however, that this is a far-from-complete list of groups and sub-groups. Only in Bulgaria alone, for example, there are more than 90 distinct groups and sub-groups. The purpose of this outline is not to provide a comprehensive list of groups, but just give an idea of the diversity of the 'Roma universe', which is often perceived as homogeneous.

Assimilationist pressures also reflected attempts at state consolidation through rigid political and administrative controls

Minorities are often among the first casualties of war, and the wars of Yugoslav succession were no different in that respect

nist ideology. This distinction was, however, applied selectively: individuals (rather than Roma in their entirety, with their cultural specifics) were supported by the official ideology. Roma individuals were encouraged to become educated and participate in the social and political structures linked to the Communist Party, as well as to the new socialist proletariat. They were assigned the role of 'transmitting new thinking' to their communities, to help them adapt to the official two-class (proletariat and rural agricultural workers) division of society. Roma individuals may have been considered progressive, but not Roma groups with their traditional culture.

Assimilationist pressures also reflected attempts at state consolidation through rigid political and administrative controls that were incompatible with nomadism. There were also consequences of social engineering projects and of policies to integrate national minorities. Deliberately or not, the socialist states often replicated Maria Theresa's assimilationist policies, reflecting similar objectives of consolidating the empire. The tools applied – forced settlement, obligatory education, and state-supported 'religion' (in the form of communist ideology) – were also similar.

The socialist system's emphasis on equality led Roma to work together with members of majority and other minority communities. They spent their holidays together, visited the same sanatoria, and sent their children to the same schools. Universal, nominally free health coverage was available for all, regardless of ethnic or religious affiliation. Survey results not surprisingly show a strong nostalgia for the socialist past among elderly Roma respondents, reflecting the memories of an era when unskilled Roma workers could afford to vacation with engineers; their children studied and played together; doctors distributed contraceptives and provided family planning consultations free of charge; kindergartens supported the raising of small children; and conscription into the so-called construction corps of the army[11] helped young Roma men receive the professional training needed for subsequent employment. Roma children from distant border or mountain areas and children of socially disadvantaged families lived and studied together in school dormitories. Roma children could not drop out of school because laws on compulsory education until the age of 16 were strictly enforced.[12] In short, state socialism provided development opportunities for Roma, particularly in terms of access to employment, health care and education.

Of course, these elements of socialist reality had their ugly face. Being dominated by Roma children, dormitories often turned into instruments of segregation. The construction corps witnessed drastic abuses and exploitation of their conscript labour. Services provided by socialist welfare states were least likely to reach the isolated rural settlements where many Roma lived. Still, from the perspective of today's marginalization, patterns of socialist integration that collapsed during the first years of transition were not without redeeming qualities.

Roma and the conflicts in the Balkans

History shows that minorities are often among the first casualties of war, and the wars of Yugoslav succession were no different in that respect. The status of Roma as a huge 'diaspora without a state behind it', without state resources, religious or educational institutions, meant that Roma were generally victims of the military initiatives of other ethnic protagonists. As such, they were subjected to merciless ethnic cleaning at the hands of virtually all warring parties. In Bosnia and Herzegovina, Roma communities were smashed among the combat forces of Serbs, Muslims and Croats. After the cleansing of Kosovar Albanian settlements before and during the events of 1999, Serbian security and military forces permitted Roma to pillage property and bury the dead without observing the appropriate funeral rituals. The Kosovo Roma then fled from Kosovo together with the Serbs after the intervention of North Atlantic Treaty Organization (NATO) forces, and now face the prospect of

---

[11] The engineering units responsible for maintenance and construction of military infrastructure were often used as a source of cheap labour on various construction sites. These units were dominated by ethnic minorities, whose first months of service were devoted to professional education and vocational training.

[12] This is exactly the pattern applied in countries like the United States where 'individual democratic rights' are not interpreted as 'the right to forego a basic education'.

long-term conflicts (even blood feuds) with Kosovo Albanians. Roma from Kosovo and to some extent from Bosnia therefore find themselves in particularly difficult situations, more so than in Croatia or other Balkan countries (Marushiakova et al. 2001).

The first wave of refugees took place in March of 1999, when hundreds of thousands of Albanians were expelled *en masse* from Kosovo. Many were pushed into refugee camps in Macedonia and Albania; from there certain groups were sent to Central and Western Europe, to the United States and to Australia. Many Rom, Egyptians and Ashkali also shared this refugee wave. A second, much larger wave of Roma refugees took place in July 1999, when most of the non-Albanian population of Kosovo left (again *en masse*) for Serbia, as well as for Montenegro, Macedonia or Western Europe. The vast majority of them live today as IDPs. In 2000, the United Nations High Commissioner for Refugees (UNHCR) registered 27,419 Roms and Egyptians as IDPs in today's State Union of Serbia and Montenegro. Roma organizations assess that up to 80,000 live as IDPs (including about 8,000 - 10,000 in Montenegro), and about 6,000 in Macedonia. There are also about 150-300 Roma refugees from Kosovo in Bosnia and Herzegovina.[13]

Reports from international organizations (mostly UNHCR) suggest that some 30,000 - 35,000 Roms, Ashkali and Egyptians live in Kosovo in different administrative units and some IDP camps. In Prishtina, for example, out of more than 10,000 only 140 remain; in the southern part of Mitrovica out of around 10,000, a few hundred Roms and Ashkali might remain; in Gjilan 350 persons remain out of an earlier figure of 6,500 (UNHCR/OSCE, 2000; UNHCR/OSCE, 2001).

Perhaps the heaviest burden felt by displaced Roma is the rejection they experience from neighbouring communities. Residents of many localities have spent a decade or more accepting refugees and IDPs, and in many places displaced Roma are victims of a double stigmatization. Facing this hostility, displaced Roma often seek shelter with other Roma, living with relatives or friends in some of the poorest parts of the Balkans. The construction of temporary accommodations (*bidonvillas*) next to the dilapidated homes of their hosts is not uncommon. However, because outsiders do not notice these additions to the Roma ghetto (which was 'always there'), they can easily fall outside of the scope of efforts to address the problems of the displaced.

Their status as a 'diaspora without the state behind it' means that for Roma international and European minority protection frameworks cannot be automatically invoked on their behalf. This contrasts with the case of other refugees and IDPs—whose very definition hinges on the existence of at least titular nation-states. In fact, the more comprehensive application of minority protection standards to the Roma began only in the late 1990s. Since Roma were not recognized as an ethnic or national minority until the 1990s, the challenges facing them have been treated not as 'minority protection' issues but as 'social protection' issues.

Methodological implications

This brief historical review shows that Roma vulnerability is linked to non–acceptance and lack of respect from society for their cultural specifics – but only in part. Roma were victims of forced assimilation under the Hapsburgs and state socialism not just because they were Roma, but also because assimilation served the imperial or ideological interests of ruling elites. Roma were victims of ethnic cleansing not because they were Roma, but because they were different, and these differences did not serve the designs of local warlords and paramilitary leaders. Roma vulnerability today is a reflection not just of the above mentioned, but also of displacement, and weak education and skill backgrounds that leave them uncompetitive on many labour markets.

Roma vulnerability today is a reflection also of displacement, and weak education and skill backgrounds that leave them uncompetitive on many labour markets

This complexity has implications for the sampling and data collection methodology underpinning this study. Any sample needs a clearly defined representative population. The uncertainties associated with defining Roma populations described above preclude random sampling, so a 'pyramid' sampling model was used instead.[14] This model is based

13 OSCE/ODIHR 1999. However different sources cite quite different numbers, which generally oscillate between 120,000 and 150,000 for the time before the Kosovo crisis in 1999. For more detailed information see http://www.ian.org.yu/kosovo-info, where data from June 2005 with tables with different groups' population distribution by municipality and settlements are available.

14 For details see the Methodological Annex.

on the premise that national census data provide adequate pictures of the structure and territorial distribution of the individuals who identify themselves as Roma. This Roma sample was taken as representative of the Roma population living in 'Roma settlements or areas of compact Roma population'. Those settlements and areas were defined as settlements where the share of Roma population equals or is higher than the national share of Roma population in the given country, as reflected in the census data.

Such an approach has its pluses and minuses. The samples based on municipalities with average and above-average shares of Roma population are not fully representative for the entire Roma populations of the countries covered in this survey. They do, however, cover roughly 85 per cent of Roma in each country. On the other hand, this sampling methodology may under-represent those Roma who are dispersed and integrated among other communities, and do not self-identify as Roma because of stigmatization. These individuals together with assimilated Roma fall out of the scope of the research, either because being assimilated they don't meet the criterion of 'being Roma', or because they don't meet the vulnerability criterion. In this way, the data from the Roma sample collected here reflect the views of Roma respondents who are visibly distinguishable by outsiders, and who do not deliberately conceal their distinct identity. This population is not necessarily underprivileged (or falls under the category of 'underclass') but many of its members are clearly vulnerable.

The survey data largely reflects the profile of the 'Roma ethno-class', melding ethnic and social criteria

This combination of ethnic and socio-economic markers suggests that in fact the survey data largely reflects the profile of the 'Roma ethno-class', melding ethnic and social criteria. The term "ethno-class" is not new in social anthropology; different studies apply the term *ethno-class* to different groups. For example in Sub-Saharan Africa, Hutus and Tutsis in the Congo and Black Moors in Mauritania are referred to as 'ethno-classes'. In Namibia and Zimbabwe, *Europeans* are also defined as an ethno-class. A similar approach is applied by Graham Smith and Andrew Wilson in regards to Russians and Russo-phones in Estonia (Smith and Wilson, 1997). At least in Africa, ethno-classes are not synonymous with underclass status. Applying the concept to Europe, the 'Minorities at risk' project (which deals with national and ethnic minorities) explicitly treats Roma as an ethno-class in the Balkans as well as in Slovakia (MAR, 2005). Serbian sociologists and experts on Roma issues also use the 'ethno-class' concept in a 2002 survey conducted in Southern and Eastern Serbia.[15]

A particular combination of ethnic, socio-economic, behavioural and outsider identification markers makes the concept of ethno-class particularly applicable to Roma. An "ethno–class" in this context is broader than an 'underclass'. The 'ethno-class' paradigm also captures Roma attitudes vis-à-vis their own community and other communities, the *Gadjé*. And it reconciles group identity with the desire to escape group identification – a strategy often adopted by better-off Roma individuals.

Being an ethno-class may be a common destiny for ethnic groups without nation-states of their own. This paradigm could be applied not only to Roma, but also to other ethnic groups that: (1) self-identify as members of an ethno-class and as socially disadvantaged, excluded, with a suppressed traditional culture; and (2) are perceived by the surrounding communities as an ethno-class as well.

Outlining the determinants of the vulnerability risks Roma are facing is one of the report's major objectives. This should be done in order to distinguish vulnerability risks that are attributable to group identity from those that are group-neutral. Since addressing these risks requires different policies, the analysis is expected to contribute to the design of better targeted and more adequate vulnerability reduction policies.

15 Forty-three per cent of 2,137 survey respondents classified Roma as an ethno-class. See Dordevic 2004.

CHAPTER 1.2

Poverty

Summary

Poverty is the first (and most common) aspect of vulnerability. In this chapter the incidence and depth of poverty and the extent of inequality among Roma across the region is assessed and contrasted with that of the majority, and the major determinants of this poverty are highlighted. Half of all Roma surveyed are found to live in poverty, and more than one in five live in extreme poverty, compared with one in seven and one in 25 of the respective majority populations. In addition, Roma fall into deeper poverty, and fall short of the amount needed to escape poverty by $1.60 a day, compared to the average of $1.20 a day needed to escape poverty for poor majority respondents.

As a consequence of such poverty, Roma have lower average expenditures than majority respondents, and devote a higher proportion of total expenditures to food purchases and a lower proportion to education. Moreover, poor Roma are highly indebted; their average outstanding utility bills amount to more than 12 times their total monthly expenditures.

A number of factors have been shown to affect this poverty. Poverty rates are 60 per cent lower among Roma living in capital cities, due to the higher education and employment opportunities available there. The number of children in a household increases poverty, but Roma households appear to cope with their higher average number of children through the inclusion of children into the labour force. Both education and skilled employment help to reduce the incidence of poverty amongst both Roma and other survey respondents. However, the increases in household welfare associated with education or skilled employment are less noticeable in the case of Roma than majority households, suggesting the existence of barriers preventing Roma from obtaining incomes commensurate with their level of education.

Half of all Roma surveyed are found to live in poverty, and more than one in five live in extreme poverty

Poverty status

Poverty rates

Assessing poverty rates requires categorizing individuals or households as poor or non-poor on the basis of reported welfare levels. Welfare can be assessed in various ways, such as the measurement of consumption or incomes. Here household consumption, measured in expenditure terms, will be used as a proxy for welfare in assessing poverty rates. Such a measure is considered a better indicator of welfare than income, as it permits a direct assessment of the ability of that household to meet its basic needs while avoiding the often erratic and/or non-monetized nature of incomes (Coudouel, Hentschel, and Wodon, 2002). For the purpose of regional comparability, a threshold of PPP $4.30 in daily equivalized expenditures was used as the absolute poverty line, and where appropriate PPP $2.15 is used as a threshold for 'extreme' poverty.[16]

The increases in household welfare associated with education or skilled employment are less noticeable in the case of Roma than majority households

As shown in Table 1-1, the data paint a worrying picture of poverty among Roma in the region: 44 per cent of Roma households are living in poverty.[17] In con-

[16] The poverty and extreme poverty thresholds (PPP $4.30 and PPP $2.15 per day expenditures) are based on thresholds used by the World Bank, 2005a. However an equivalized, rather than per-capita measure of expenditures is taken here. Equivalized expenditures refers to the OECD equivalence scale, which takes into account economies of scale when calculating expenditures per capita. This adjustment is based on the assumption that certain household expenditures are independent of the number of household members. OECD equivalence scales assign the coefficient 1 to the first household member, 0.5 to the second household member, and 0.3 to a child when calculating per-capita household income. Throughout the report, equivalized expenditures are used.

[17] Calculated using the PPP $4.30 equivalized expenditures per day poverty threshold. Total expenditures are based on responses to the question: "How much did your household spend last month in total"?

Table 1-1

Distribution of households and household members by poverty status (%)

	Share of households*		Share of household members**	
	Non-poor	Poor	Non-poor	Poor
Majority	89	11	86	14
Roma	56	44	50	50
Total	74	26	67	33

* Share of households with equivalized expenditures below the poverty threshold

** Share of individuals living in households with equivalized expenditures below the poverty threshold. Unless otherwise stated, this poverty rate is used throughout the report

FIGURE 1 – 1

Poverty rates for Roma

Percentage of Roma living in households with daily equivalized expenditures below PPP $2.15 or PPP $4.30 (with total poverty rates shown above bars)

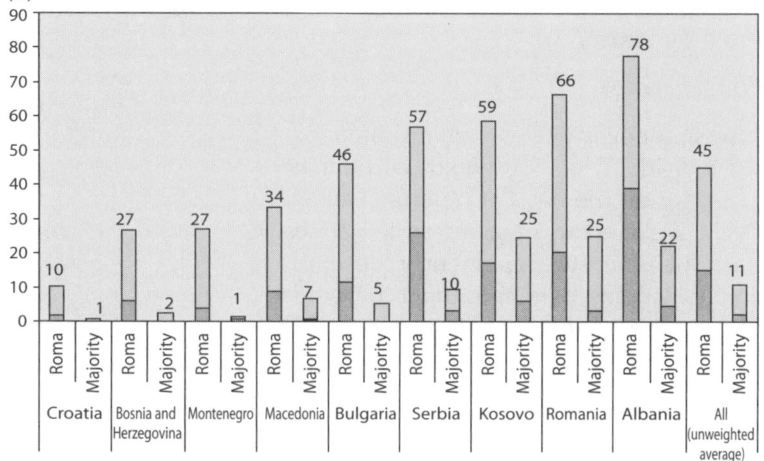

FIGURE 1 – 2

Poverty rates for Roma

Percentage of Roma living in households with daily equivalized income below PPP $2.15 or PPP $4.30 (with total poverty rates shown above bars)

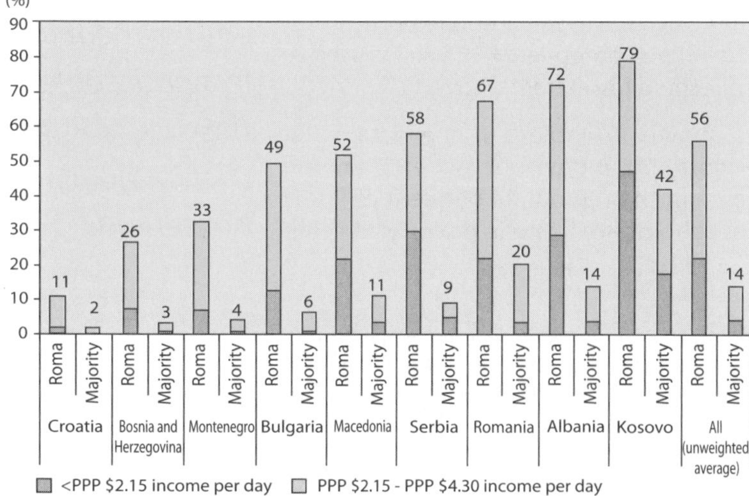

trast, just 11 per cent of majority households in close proximity to Roma live in poverty. Given the relatively large size of poor Roma households, the share of Roma *individuals* living in poverty is even higher.[18]

As can be seen in Figure 1-1, Roma have far higher poverty rates than majority in all the countries under study. Poverty rates among Roma in Albania are particularly high (78 per cent), especially in relation to the majority (22 per cent). However, other countries, such as Serbia, in which poverty rates, on the whole, are substantially lower, also show large gaps between the two groups.

The percentage of Roma facing *extreme* poverty – below PPP $2.15 expenditures per day – is far higher than for the majority (15 per cent, compared to just 2 per cent respectively). Extreme poverty among Roma is particularly high in Albania (39 per cent), Serbia (26 per cent) and Romania (20 per cent).

What do these poverty rates tell us? If we multiply the poverty rate for Roma in each country by the conservative estimates of Roma populations in the countries in question (the minimum values in Liégeois, 2006), this suggests that at least 1,900,000 people (57 per cent of Roma in the region according to Liégeois's estimates) live under the threshold of PPP $4.30 expenditures per day. As shown in Figure 1-2, the pattern of lower expenditures among Roma in the region, shown in Figure 1-1, mirrors their lower incomes.[19] Roma households across the region reported average monthly incomes of 165

[18] The average household size is 2.7 and 3.3 for non-poor majority and Roma households, and 3.6 and 3.9 for poor majority and Roma households respectively.

[19] Total incomes are based on the sum of responses to the question "What sum was made by each of these kinds of incomes in the past month (including wages, benefits, remittances, informal earnings, etc.)"?

euros compared to 336 euros among majority households. The application of the Organization for Economic Cooperation and Development (OECD) equivalence scales to the data in order to estimate income per household member reveals even more pronounced differences. Average individual Roma income is only 41 per cent of average individual income for majority respondents.

Poverty rates based on income are slightly higher than those based on expenditures, which presumably reflects the use of coping strategies by poor as well as the understating of incomes. This is particularly the case in Kosovo where expenditure-based poverty rates for Roma and majority (59 and 25 per cent respectively) are far lower than income-based poverty rates (79 and 42 per cent respectively).

Poverty depth

There are also differences between and within groups in terms of poverty depth. While poor Roma on average live on PPP $1.60 a day less than the poverty line, poor majority households fall short of escaping poverty by PPP $1.20 a day. Dividing the data into five quintiles based on equivalized household expenditures (see Figure 1-3),[20] a clear trend emerges. While more than 50 per cent of majority households fall into the highest three quintiles, the reverse is true for over 50 per cent of Roma households, whose expenditures fall within the two lowest quintiles (see Figure 1-3).

Inequalities

Differences within Roma and majority communities may be no less important than differences between them. The survey data also reveal deeper intra-group inequalities among Roma than majority households. The Gini coefficient of inequality based on expenditures for Roma households (0.44) is slightly higher than for majority households (0.40).[21] Although the extent of inequality among Roma varies across the region – with Gini coefficients ranging from 0.31 in Bulgaria to 0.47 in Serbia – Roma households have higher inequality levels than majority

Box 4: **National MDG targets, vulnerable groups and Roma poverty**

United Nations country teams in all the countries studied here produced national reports on the Millennium Development Goals, adapting the global targets to national realities. Monitoring progress towards these goals and targets not just in terms of national averages but also for particular groups would further increase the policy relevance of the MDGs. The survey data on which this report is based provide the opportunity for such monitoring, particularly in terms of reducing income poverty (MDG 1).

The MDG report for **Croatia** calls for halving relative poverty between 2001 and 2015. This would mean a reduction in the share of people at risk of poverty in Croatia from 18.2 per cent in 2002 to 9.1 per cent in 2015. If progress from the 2004 poverty risk level of 16.7 per cent towards this target is to be linear, annual reductions in this level of 0.7 percentage points would be required. Were poverty risk among Roma households in Croatia to be reduced at this pace, the Roma population would reach the 9.1 per cent target only in 2094.* If the national target for 2015 is also to be achieved for Roma, the pace at which relative poverty in this group is reduced would have to be eight times higher than the pace at which poverty risk would fall for the country as a whole.**

The MDG report for **Romania** called for halving (to 5.5 per cent) the incidence of severe poverty, expressed as the share of people living in households in which incomes are insufficient to purchase the minimum food basket, by 2009. Applying the methodology and taking Romania's 2003 estimate of 8.6 per cent as a baseline, the Roma households surveyed would reach the national target only in 2055. The pace of poverty reduction among Roma households would need to be 10 times greater than national averages if the national target is to be achieved for the Roma by 2009.

* The annual change needed at the national level is expressed as the difference between its current target values, divided by the difference between the target year (usually 2015) and the baseline year. The year in which the target value will be achieved was estimated by multiplying the current value from the survey by the annual change for each respective sample group. The same methodology is applied in all the boxes addressing the issue of national MDG targets and the vulnerable groups in this report.
** The necessary pace of change represents the annual change needed for the sample group to achieve the national target in the target year, divided by the annual change needed for the country as a whole to achieve the national target by the target year. The same approach is applied to other targets in this report.

FIGURE 1 – 3

Distribution of expenditures by group
Percentage of Roma and majority household members falling within each equivalized expenditure quintile

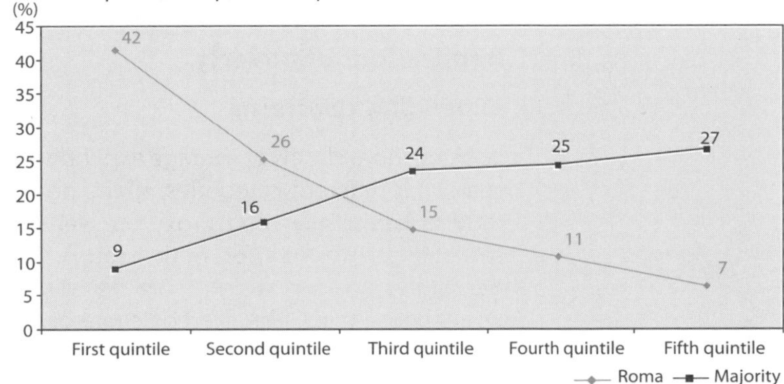

[20] Households were arranged according to equivalized household expenditures, with the first 20 per cent of households (those at the bottom of the expenditure distribution) falling into the first and the second 20 per cent into the second quintile and so on. Hence the first quintile constitutes the poorest one fifth of the sample; the fifth quintile constitutes the most affluent 20 per cent.

[21] A Gini coefficient of 1 means total inequality and a Gini coefficient of 0 means total equality.

Table 1-2

Average equivalized household incomes (in euros) – total for each group and broken down by poverty status

	Total	Poor		Non-poor	
	Income	Income	% of the total	Income	% of the total
Majority	164	49	30%	177	108%
Roma	67	32	48%	95	142%

households (which range from 0.26 in Montenegro to 0.41 in Albania) in all countries in the region. Albania is the exception: the Gini coefficient reported there is higher for majority (0.41) than for Roma households (0.39).[22]

Inequalities in incomes mirror those in expenditures. Average household incomes for non-poor Roma are 42 per cent higher than the average for all Roma (Table 1-2). This difference is just 8 per cent for the majority. Since the average value of incomes for all Roma households is very low, the distance between income of poor Roma and the average income for all Roma is not very large. Since the focus is on household income to measure poverty and inequality between groups, intra-household poverty and inequality cannot be observed, since this approach assumes equal distribution of household income to each household member. However, looking at individual incomes for each household member, one can observe differences in levels between men and women, with women earning invariably less than men. (This is further discussed in the employment chapter 1.4.) The existence of intra-household income inequalities between Roma men and women suggest that Roma women are more vulnerable to risks of dependency and poverty.

Given the larger numbers of children in Roma households, low shares of expenditures on health and education underscore the Roma communities' vulnerability

Implications of poverty

Expenditure patterns

Looking more closely at average expenditure shares for different categories, spending on food (a commonly used proxy for welfare) certainly stands out for both groups. Expenditures on food weigh more heavily on Roma households. The average share of expenditures on food, beverages and tobacco for Roma in the region is 67 per cent, ranging from 90 per cent in Albania to 54 per cent in Croatia. In contrast, majority households in the region spend on average just 52 per cent of their total household expenditures on food. (Table A1 in the Annex provides national-level data and comparisons.)[23]

Roma households devote the smallest proportion of their household expenditures to education (only 3 per cent). All three groups spend similarly low shares on health care, while majority households devote the highest share of expenditures to consumer durables. However, given the larger numbers of children in Roma households, those low shares of expenditures on health and education underscore the Roma communities' vulnerability.

Although 22 per cent of majority households responded that they had purchased a consumer durable item in the past 12 months, just 10 per cent of Roma households reported having made such a purchase. However, those Roma and majority households that could afford to purchase durables show remarkable similarity in their consumer behaviour with 34 and 27 per cent purchasing large household appliances (such as a refrigerator, oven or washing machine), and 27 and 23 per cent purchasing a TV or CD/DVD player, respectively. The only major difference in consumer behaviour between the groups is the lower share of Roma households that purchased a computer (3 per cent) compared to the majority (8 per cent). The survey data therefore indicate that once income differences are corrected, consumer profiles (and related living patterns) are amazingly similar. (Data on durable purchases by households for each group are shown in Table A2 in the Annex.)

The profile of absolute expenditures on major items shows interesting disparities

[22] Gini coefficients for Roma and majority households in all countries in the region are shown in Table A4 in the Annex.

[23] Here and elsewhere in the report, the regional averages for the three groups surveyed are given by the unweighted averages, unless otherwise stated.

between groups. As Table 1-3 shows, Roma expenditures on food are only 88 per cent of majority households expenditures, which suggests that Roma households consume smaller amounts of (as well as cheaper) food. Expenditures on clothes are just 60 per cent of majority household levels. The biggest discrepancy occurs in the area of education, entertainment and housing (respectively 29, 44 and 56 per cent of majority household levels).

Table 1-3
Differences in average household monthly expenditures (in euros) by group

	Majority	Roma	Roma (% of majority expenditures)
Food	301.6	264.1	87.6
Durables*	100.7	91.2	90.6
Clothes	92.3	55	59.6
Housing & utilities	112	62.9	56.2
Alcohol & tobacco	47.6	50.6	106.3
Medicine	39.4	40.6	103.0
Transport	50.8	28.2	55.5
Household goods	36.7	35.5	96.7
Education*	23.9	6.9	28.9
Health care*	11.6	8.7	75.0
Entertainment	31.7	13.8	43.5
Total	848.3	657.5	77.5

* Derived from reported annual household expenditures

Household indebtedness

Poor households have high shares of outstanding payments, particularly for electricity.[24] Poor Roma households are, however, in a more critical situation than the majority households concerning outstanding payments for water, electricity and housing-related payments. Even among those Roma households considered as non-poor in terms of expenditures, total outstanding electricity payments constitute 132 per cent of their household monthly expenditures. Amongst poor Roma the situation is far worse. In combination with the outstanding payments for water and housing, total indebtedness of Roma households often assumes unmanageable proportions. Unsettled utility debts of poor Roma households (Figure 1-4) reach 1,230 per cent of their total monthly household expenditures and 393 per cent of non-poor households. The magnitudes often make prospects for breaking this circle of outstanding payments unrealistic. The severity of the problem is also confirmed by the low share of equalized expenditures on housing and utilities Roma households have – 56 per cent of majority households' expenditures on utilities and housing. Part of the explanation of this shortfall is due to the lower standard of housing Roma use. But the costs of utilities do not differ substantially hence the logical conclusion could be "Roma spend less on housing and utilities because they cannot afford paying regularly utility bills" – despite the threat of being cut off from the electricity or other utilities supply.

The length of delay in settling utility bills can also be a measure of hardship. On average, poor Roma households do not pay their bills for water supply for 20 months and bills for electricity for 19 months. Poor majority households also face much higher shares of outstanding payments for water supply and electricity than the non-poor households. Figure 1-4 outlines the level of indebtedness of households as a share of average (un-weighted) total monthly expenditures. Worth noticing is also the relative similarity between non-poor Roma and poor majority households whose outstanding payments for utilities as a share of their total household expenditures are similar. (A detailed picture of

FIGURE 1 – 4

Outstanding debt

Total outstanding household bills as a percentage of monthly household expenditures

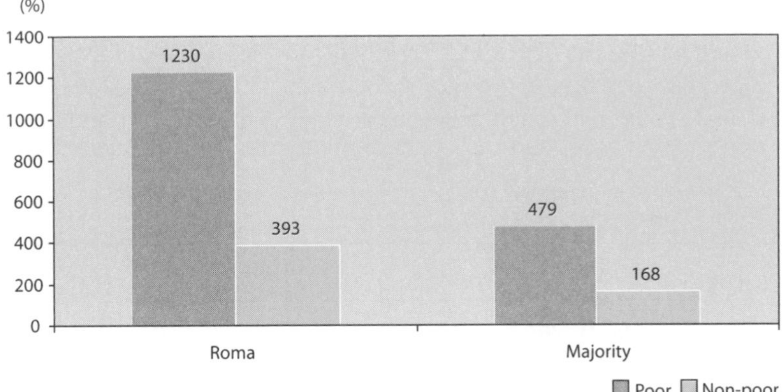

24 Respondents were asked whether they have outstanding payments for electricity, housing and utilities. If they did, they were asked to assess roughly the amounts due for each category.

Box 5: Capacity as the key to inclusion – the case of Dolni Tsibar

Dolni Tsibar is a village located in Bulgaria's Valchidram district, Montana municipality. Roma comprise 1,674 of its 1,720 inhabitants (along with 41 Bulgarians and 5 Turks). All key managerial positions and responsibilities in Dolni Tsibar are therefore occupied and discharged by Roma. The mayor, two financial experts and various specialists, the director and six teachers in the kindergarten, the deputy director of the school and 13 teachers, the town's only policeman and social worker – all are Roma.

As such, Dolni Tsibar is among the few communities in Southeast Europe where Roma manage local government and the numbers of Roma with higher education are sufficient to provide the local administration with qualified Roma staff. Thirty-one Roma have a university degree and work as teachers in the elementary as well as in the primary school. Others are economists, engineers, a doctor's assistant, etc. Currently nine young Roma are enrolled in university courses in law, pedagogy, engineering, economics and social sciences. This was possible by the minority scholarship projects supported by the Swiss charity SOLON and administered by IMIR, a local NGO and research centre.

This does not mean that Dolni Tsibar is a 'Roma paradise': the local unemployment rate, for example, reaches 60 per cent. But it does show that Roma are willing and able to manage their own affairs, with favourable results in terms of social inclusion. It also shows that the presence of a critical mass of educated professionals is a precondition for such self-management. When such a critical mass is present, a virtuous circle of inclusion can be kicked off with positive role models, higher aspirations for younger generations, stronger negotiating positions vis-à-vis other governmental agencies, etc. For example, the municipality is currently negotiating a joint project with the Ministry of Labour and Social Policy to employ 42 people to work in the vegetable gardens and another 50 people to work on the dikes on the Danube river.

The Dolni Tsibar example shows that investing in Roma education and skills development can be a winning strategy in the long run, and that donor-targeted support can be critically important and effective.

Box based on an interview conducted with Kamen Dimitrov, Mayor of Dolni Tsibar, 2006.

FIGURE 1 – 5

Location and poverty

Poverty rates by location (capital, rural, urban) for Roma and the majority

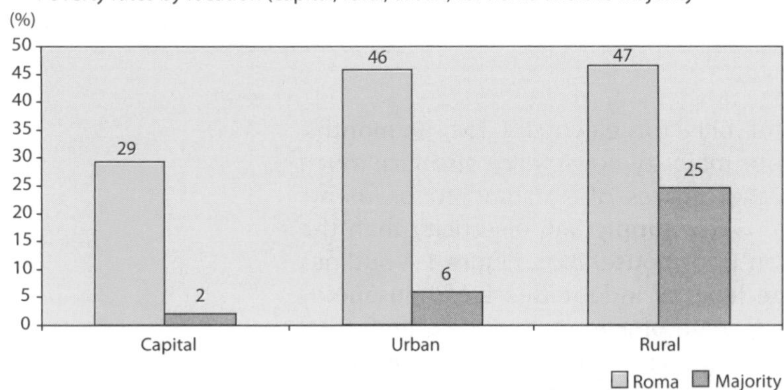

households having debts and the average amount per category (electricity, water and housing) and quintile expenditures can be seen in Table A3 in the Annex.)

While the ratio of outstanding payments to total expenditures is higher for poor households, both groups rely on debt. The share of households having outstanding payments for water, electricity and rent is of almost equal size over the five quintiles. Higher average amounts owed for these items are even found among the richest quintile households (water and rent for Roma and rent for the majority). In addition, the share of households with debts is higher in urban areas than in rural areas. This difference is most predominant for outstanding payments in housing and water, less so for electricity. Looking at the use of electricity in the household, it can be observed that 39 and 37 per cent of Roma households that are in arrears for electricity have a refrigerator and an oven, compared to only 17 and 16 per cent of majority households, which could be a possible explanation for the outstanding payments. Forty and thirty-five per cent of Roma households in arrears use electricity for cooking and heating, compared with much lower shares of majority households (19 and 16 per cent respectively).

Correlates of poverty

In addition to outlining the status and implications of Roma poverty, the key causal factors contributing to this poverty should be identified. The first step in the process is identifying the main factors correlated with high poverty levels, before looking for causal impact.

Locational effects

The location of a household in an urban (rather than a rural) area has been shown to have a significant positive relationship with equivalized household expenditures (Revenga, Ringold and Tracy, 2002). Dividing households into Capital (capital city), Urban (other urban areas), and Rural (rural localities), locational effects on welfare can be clearly seen from the data (see Figure 1-5).

The data in Figure 1-5 show that, for both Roma and majority households, poverty rates are lowest in capital cities and highest in rural areas. However, while for majority households residence in urban areas is associated with far lower incidence of poverty (6 per cent) than those in rural areas (25 per cent), Roma households living in non-capital urban and rural areas have similar poverty rates (46 and 47 per cent respectively).[25]

[25] No allowance has been made to account for the possible higher cost of living in urban areas, which might understate poverty in urban areas.

It appears that capital cities (where poverty rates among Roma households are 'only' 29 per cent) are the only location that has a substantial affect on Roma welfare. Since just 13 per cent of Roma (compared to 18 per cent of majority) households reside in capital cities, these differences could be a quite significant factor behind higher Roma poverty rates. This result reflects the common pattern across the region where capital cities are 'islands of prosperity' and smaller towns are economies in decline. The fact that Roma fare so badly in non-capital urban areas reflects this decline – with few jobs and limited employment opportunities, Roma are perhaps the last in the queue.

FIGURE 1 – 6

Household size and poverty

Poverty rates by number of children for Roma and the majority

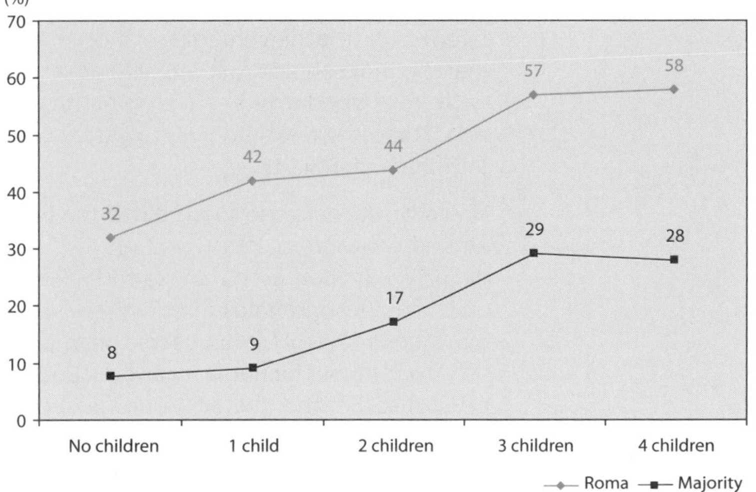

Number of children

The number of children[26] in a household has been shown to have a strong negative relationship with equivalized expenditures in some countries in the region (Revenga, Ringold and Tracy, 2002). The data in Figure 1-6 show this relationship clearly and suggest the importance of family planning for poverty reduction among both Roma and majority households. As Roma households have on average more children than majority households (1.7 versus 0.7), the number of children could be a contributing factor to the higher incidence of poverty among Roma households. But what Figure 1-6 also shows is that the number of children in a family affects poverty rates almost equally for Roma and majority households. A substantial increase in poverty rates for majority compared to Roma households is observed only when the number of children increases from "four children" to "more than four" – a family pattern observed in very few cases for majority households.

Although Roma households seem to receive marginally greater average child benefit payments per child (11.4 euros per month) than do majority households (9.7 euros per month), this difference is unlikely to account for these different trends. It is more likely that Roma have developed coping strategies to deal with larger families in conditions of poverty. A number of such strategies, for example spending less on education and clothes (as shown in Table 1-3) or younger participation in income generation may serve to decrease prospects for Roma children and perpetuate poverty among this group. This is supported by the fact that 6 per cent of children in poor Roma households are engaged in some form of work (compared with none of the children from majority households).

Education

The survey data suggest that the benefits of education for Roma who seek to escape poverty are significant. As shown in Figure 1-7, Roma and majority households that are headed by individuals with no formal education have a 40 and 69 per cent chance of living out of poverty, respectively. But

FIGURE 1 – 7

Education and escaping poverty

Share of non-poor Roma and majority households by the level of education of household heads of working age (over 16 years) of age

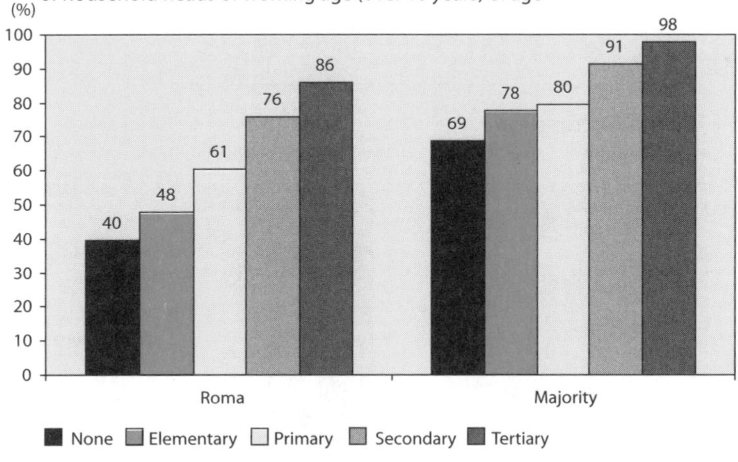

26 A child here is taken as being 15 years or younger.

households whose heads have attained tertiary education have just a 14 and 2 per cent poverty risk, respectively. In addition, as shown in Chapter 1.3, there are major differences in the percentages of Roma and majority households that are able to attain each level of education. This points to the importance of education as a possible determinant of poverty.

However, the data also suggest that the benefits of educational attainment, in terms of poverty reduction, are not the same for Roma and majority households. First, with the same educational level of the household head, poverty risk is higher for Roma for all educational categories. Second, the difference is declining as educational level increases. Poverty rates of households headed by persons with no or elementary education are respectively 29 and 30 per cent higher among Roma than among majority households. This difference falls to 19 per cent for household heads with primary education and to 15 per cent with secondary.

It is not employment per se that matters, but rather the kind of employment – particularly jobs yielding higher incomes that require more skills

Employment

The relationship between Roma employment and poverty reduction is very complex. The survey data show that employment differences between poor and non-poor households as perceived by respondents are not substantial: 50 per cent of poor Roma household members stated that they are not working, compared to 43 per cent of non-poor Roma households. This would suggest that for Roma, employment is not a sufficient (or sustainable) way to escape poverty. The data instead suggest that it is not employment *per se* that matters, but rather the kind of employment – particularly jobs yielding higher incomes that require more skills.

FIGURE 1 – 8

Type of occupation
Share of Roma and majority (over 16 years of age) employed in each occupation

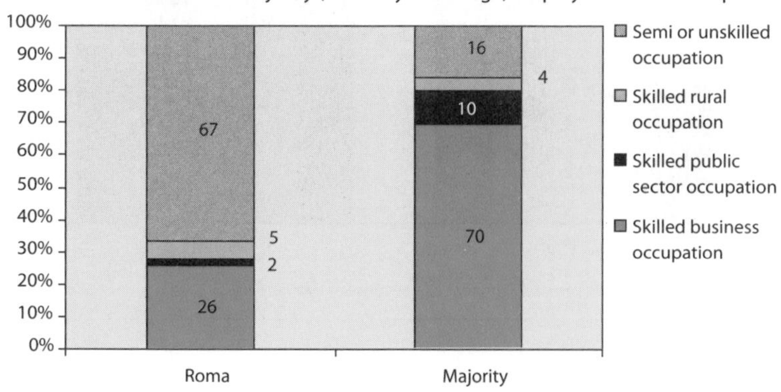

Given the link between education and professional skills on the one hand and the large numbers of poorly educated Roma workers on the other, one would expect to find heavy Roma representation in unskilled occupations. The data summarized in Figure 1-8 support this view. Regardless of poverty status among those who reported being employed in the last 12 months, as many as 67 per cent of Roma reported working in unskilled or semi-skilled jobs, compared to 16 per cent of majority respondents.

The survey data show that Roma are mainly employed in unskilled occupations (see Figure 1-8). They also show that the incidence of Roma employment in skilled occupations increases with each level of education. And they suggest that high unemployment rates among Roma are largely due to weak demand for unskilled labour. But the picture is much more complex.

The data shown in Figure 1-9 suggest that poverty rates fall significantly if the household head is involved in skilled employment. The poverty rate is more than twice lower for majority households where the household head has a skilled compared to unskilled job (respectively 6 and 14 per cent). In the case of Roma the difference is only 30 per cent (a 50 per cent poverty rate in households with an unskilled head and a 38 per cent poverty rate for households with a skilled head). As with education, the returns to investing in acquiring labour market skills are markedly lower for Roma than for majority households. The data also show that the correlation between 'being employed in a skilled occupation' and 'living in a non-poor household' is stronger for majority than for Roma households. This could result from a concentration of skilled Roma workers in low-wage positions that do not generate enough income to escape poverty.

Determinants of poverty

The *Correlates of poverty* section illustrated that factors other than group status (Roma versus majority household) are correlated with poverty. This raises questions about the extent to which higher poverty rates can be explained by these factors, as opposed to other factors associated with being Roma – such as discrimination and cultural factors. In addition, because the factors identified here – locational effects, number of children, education level, employment status – may be closely interrelated, we must ask whether these factors have independent effects on poverty levels and, if so, how important these effects are.

To clarify this issue, the natural log of equivalized (PPP) household expenditures was regressed against each factor identified in this chapter.[27] The results of the analyses – shown in full in Table A6 in the Annex – show that 53 per cent of the variance in log equivalized expenditures can be explained by variations in six factors: group-status (Roma or non-Roma), country of residence, locational effects, number of children in the household, and education and skill levels of household heads. As would be expected, being a Roma, living in a rural area or outside of the country was used as a baseline for the regression,[28] and increases in the number of children in the household all had negative affects on household expenditures. Similarly, in line with the analysis reported here, location in capital cities and the presence of a well-educated household head or one in skilled employment, all had positive effects on household expenditures.

When the effects of locality, number of children, and household head education and skill levels were controlled, being from a Roma household was shown to substantially reduce expenditures. For Roma households located in urban areas with an average number of children and a household head with poor education and employed as an unskilled labourer, the average monthly expenditures across the region would be PPP $129, just 66 per cent of similar monthly expenditures for majority households (PPP $195). This suggests that factors other than education and skill level – such as unequal opportunities – are at least partially responsible for Roma poverty.

FIGURE 1 – 9

Employment and poverty

Poverty rates for Roma and majority households with skilled or unskilled heads

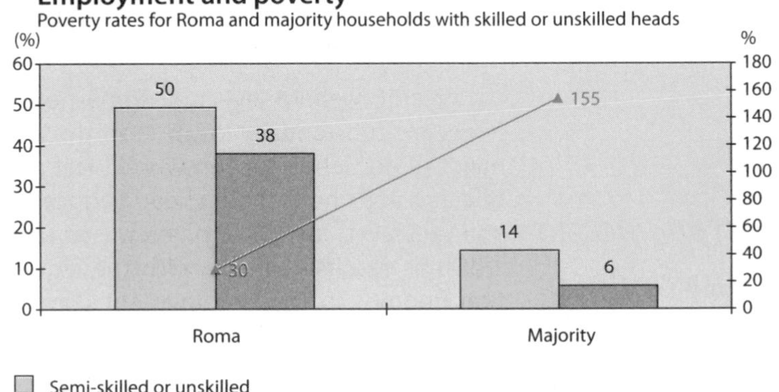

Factors other than education and skill level – such as unequal opportunities – are at least partially responsible for Roma poverty

There is some cause for optimism. The results indicate that improving the education and skill level of Roma households can substantially improve household welfare. Averaging across the region, Roma households headed by well-educated skilled workers can be expected to have PPP $134 per month higher expenditures than Roma households without these education and skill levels. However, as highlighted in the *Correlates of* poverty section, education and employment levels may have a smaller impact on welfare for Roma households than for majority households. This hypothesis is confirmed by separate multivariate regressions for Roma and majority households[29] across the region (shown in full in Table A8 in the Annex). These regressions showed that, for an urban majority household with an average number of children, average household expenditures can be expected to rise by PPP $103 if the household head is educated, and by PPP $230 if the household

27 This model uses the ordinary least square (OLS) method. The following variables were included in the analysis: Roma (1 = Roma, 0 = Majority), country of residence (coded with individual country variables using Croatia – the country with the lowest poverty rates in the region – as a baseline), locality (coded using separate dummy variables for 'Capital' and 'Rural' localities and using an urban locality as a baseline), the number of children in a household (ordinal variable with five categories: 1, 2, 3, 4, or ≥5), education of the household head (1 = well educated, 0 = poorly educated), skill-level of the household heads' employment (1 = skilled, 0 = unskilled). Simple summary statistics and frequencies for all variables in the analysis are included in table A5 in the Annex. The pooling of majority and Roma samples was deemed permissible on the basis of a Chow test (see Chow, 1960) performed on the residual sums of squares of separate regressions conducted separately for the majority and Roma samples (F=-0.37). Details of these analyses follow in the text.

28 With the exception of Bosnia and Herzegovina, where the relationship was not significant.

29 These regressions use ordinary least squares (OLS) method. With the exception of the group-membership variable, all other variables are the same as in the previous model. Simple summary statistics and frequencies for all variables are included in Table A7 in the Annex.

head is educated and has skilled employment. By contrast, the analogous increases in Roma household expenditures are just PPP $59 and PPP $128.[30]

As a result, welfare levels of Roma households are substantially lower than those of majority households, even when locational effects, and household head education and skill levels are held constant (see table 1-4). The results coincide with the simulation findings in the employment chapter: while higher education levels do improve employment prospects for Roma, this improvement is much less for Roma than for majority households. These findings point to weak incentives for Roma to improve their educational status. They also suggest that, in addition to measures to improve the quality of Roma education, reducing barriers to employment and eliminating discrimination in the workplace[31] are needed. It is only through such measures that Roma will receive the opportunity to generate the same income through employment as similarly educated and skilled members of majority communities.

In addition to measures to improve the quality of Roma education, reducing barriers to employment and eliminating discrimination in the workplace are needed

Table 1-4

Opportunity gaps throughout the region

Predicted expenditures for Roma and majority households (in PPP$) if they had similar household characteristics*

Country	Roma	Majority
Albania	130	269
Bulgaria	404	729
Bosnia and Herzegovina[32]	242	361
Croatia (control)	404	729
Kosovo	219	308
Macedonia	257	419
Montenegro	277	421
Serbia	196	294
Romania	153	345
All (unweighted average)	254	431

* - The table shows estimates of the household expenditures Roma and majority households would have had if they had similar average number of children, similarly well-educated household heads with similarly skilled employment and living in urban areas

Conclusions from Chapter 1.2

Data analyzed in this chapter reveal a worrying picture of poverty among Roma of the region, with 44 per cent of Roma households living in poverty. In contrast, just 11 per cent of majority households living in close proximity to Roma live in poverty. Roma poverty is also 'deeper' – the shortfall from the poverty line of average Roma households in poverty is bigger than the shortfall of majority households, making it more difficult to get out of poverty.

Expenditure patterns show the poverty status of Roma households, with high shares of expenditures on food. But they also outline the contours of the poverty cycle Roma are caught in: the smallest shares of their household budgets devoted to education make it more difficult for young Roma to escape poverty.

Indebtedness goes hand-in-hand with poverty, especially in the case of Roma, particularly the poor households. Households accumulate unpaid bills for electricity, water supply and housing. Even among those Roma considered non-poor in terms of expenditures, their total outstanding payments reach unmanageable levels (and the situation is much worse for the poor households). Writing off debts in such cases is the 'easy' solution but given the fact that majority households also face debts, the outcome is increased ethnic tensions and further exclusion of Roma.

Despite their high poverty levels, Roma are not homogeneous in this regard. Data reveal high levels of income inequality among Roma – higher than those of majority communities. While this might suggest the presence of intra-group exploitation, it also reflects the diversity of the 'Roma universe' and its internal distinctions.

The survey data underscore the benefits of education, which serves as the gateway to

30 The analysis also revealed that when factors such as education and skill-level of employment are held constant, the influence of being located in a national capital on Roma household expenditures essentially disappears. Some 51 per cent of Roma living in national capitals are well educated and 46 per cent have skilled employment, compared with just 37 and 34 per cent respectively of Roma living outside capitals.

31 Qualitative studies such as UNDP/Ernst&Young (2005b) on positive business practices to improve integration of Roma into the workforce, and the World Bank's (2005c) qualitative survey aimed at assessing negative attitudes towards Roma among the majority, can be useful in formulating policies aimed at redressing such discrimination.

32 The Bosnia and Herzegovina dummy variable failed to reach significance, indicating that expenditures for Bosnia and Herzegovina do not differ significantly from those in the control country (Croatia).

skilled employment and higher incomes. However, the linkages between education and employment are less clear for Roma than for majority households. The incidence of poverty is higher among Roma households than majority households even when the effects of family size, locational effects, and the education and employment levels of household heads are held constant. This reflects the fact that, among Roma households, education and employment skill levels have a smaller impact on income than among majority households. The implication is that discrimination prevents Roma from obtaining incomes consummate with their levels of education or employment. Efforts to redress the high incidence of Roma poverty should therefore focus on identifying and addressing the attitudes of majority communities (particularly employers) towards Roma. Studies such as the World Bank (2005c) qualitative survey of attitudes towards Roma can assist in initiating appropriate measures to address discrimination.

Discrimination prevents Roma from obtaining incomes consummate with their levels of education or employment

The national action plans of the six countries participating in the Decade of Roma Inclusion—Bulgaria, Croatia, Macedonia, Montenegro, Romania and Serbia—tackle poverty reduction through sectoral measures targeting education, employment, health and housing. While education is certainly a priority for all governments, countries like Bulgaria also focus specifically on improving equal opportunities and reducing discrimination in the labour market, which as outlined in the analysis above is a precondition in order for Roma to reap the gains of education. As poverty is a multidimensional phenomenon, targeting these thematic areas that are major determinants of poverty is a logical approach, and hence our structure follows this in the subsequent chapters.

CHAPTER 1.3

Education

Summary

Better access to quality education is widely seen as a precondition for increasing employment and therefore income potential of vulnerable groups, including Roma. In addition, the completion of a full course of primary schooling is one of the Millennium Development Goals. This chapter describes the status of Roma education, contrasts it with that of majority communities, and highlights the major determinants of this lower education status. It was found that two out of three Roma (compared with one in seven in majority communities) do not complete primary school, and two out of five (compared to 1 in 20 in majority communities) do not attend primary school. Keeping Roma in school was shown to be a central problem: Roma children spend, on average, less than half the time of children from majority households in the educational system. As a result, one in four of Roma surveyed are illiterate.

Roma women are shown to be particularly vulnerable. Three quarters of Roma women do not complete primary education (compared with one in five women from majority communities) and almost a third are illiterate (compared with 1 in 20 women from majority communities). Roma youth are also vulnerable, with less than a third of Roma 11-14 year-olds attaining even an elementary education. The lack of positive role models – in the form of a well-educated household head – has been shown to have a major impact on the level of education of Roma, and creates a self-reinforcing cycle of declining education.

Poverty and associated factors such as the health risks associated with poor-quality housing have been identified as possible causal factors for the lower educational status of Roma, highlighting the need for efforts to improve Roma welfare. However, other factors such as the segregation of Roma into Roma-only schools and attitudinal factors associated with the lower returns to education in terms of employment and incomes among Roma may also play a role. These finding underscore the importance of efforts to integrate Roma into school attended by children from majority communities, and to provide Roma with employment opportunities commensurate with their level of education.

Keeping Roma in school is a central problem: Roma children spend, on average, less than half the time of children from majority households in the educational system

Education status

Attainment rates

The survey data indicate a strong correlation between Roma status and educational attainment. As the data shown in Figure 1-10 suggest, 38 per cent of Roma children do not complete elementary school, compared to only 4 per cent for children from majority households. Far smaller proportions of Roma with elementary education stay on at school to complete either primary or secondary education: only 33 per cent of Roma household respondents had attained primary or above education, compared to 86 per cent of respondents from majority communities.

FIGURE 1 – 10

Educational attainment gap

Percentage of Roma and the majority who are no longer in school but have attained at least elementary, primary, secondary or tertiary education

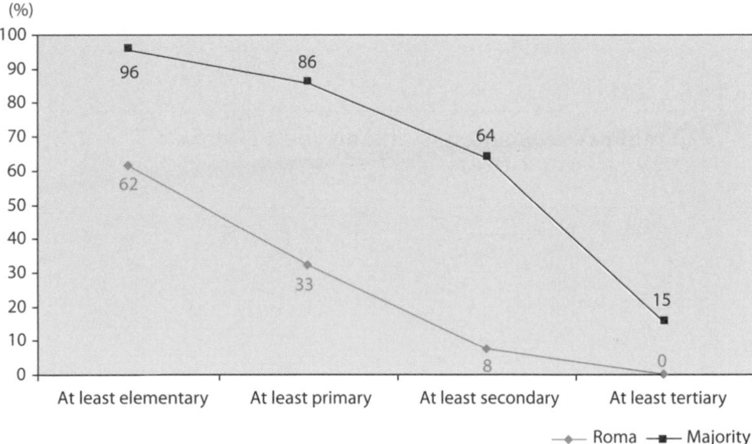

Furthermore, just 8 per cent of Roma respondents reported having completed secondary education or above, compared to 64 per cent of majority respondents. Less than half a per cent of the Roma sample completed college or university (74 out of 15,026 respondents). These figures underscore the importance of targeting Roma elementary and primary education. Policies to reduce Roma educational vulnerability very much depend on correctly identifying the determinants of lower participation at the elementary and primary levels.

Enrolment rates

The data suggest that measures to improve educational attainment for Roma should focus on dealing with the causes of low enrolment rates among Roma. Elementary-, primary-, and secondary- and tertiary-level enrolment rates – estimated by calculating the percentage of household members of elementary- (7-11 years), primary- (12-15 years), secondary- (16-19 years), or tertiary- (greater than 20 years) school age that claim to be enrolled in education – are shown in Figure 1-11. The similarity between this graph and Figure 1-10 suggests a strong relationship between enrolment and attainment. The data reveal a disturbing picture of poor Roma enrolment, with enrolment rates of just 57 per cent among Roma of primary school age. This poses serious problems for the ability of countries in the region to meet their commitments under MDG 2 concerning universal primary school education.[33] Among 7-15 year-olds, 32 per cent of all Roma do not attend school, compared to just 4 per cent of the majority. Roma also appear to have much higher drop-out rates, with the proportion progressing to the next stage of education falling rapidly.

FIGURE 1 – 11

Enrolment gap

Percentage of Roma and the majority attending school, college or university

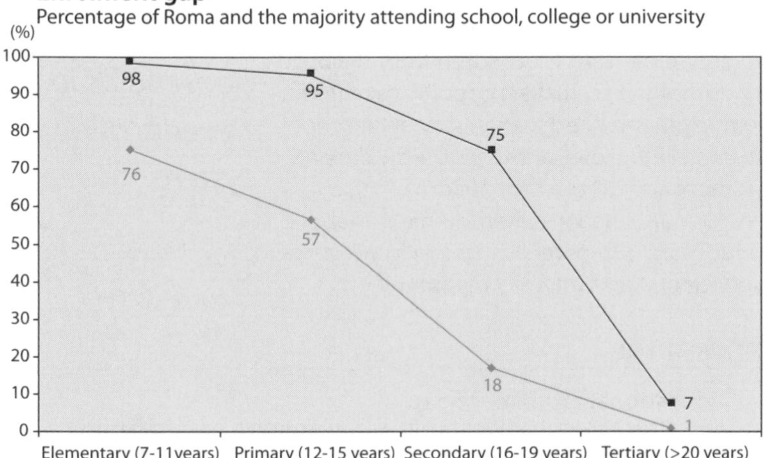

FIGURE 1 – 12

Expanding enrolment gap among young Roma

Percentage of Roma and the majority 7-15 years of age attending school

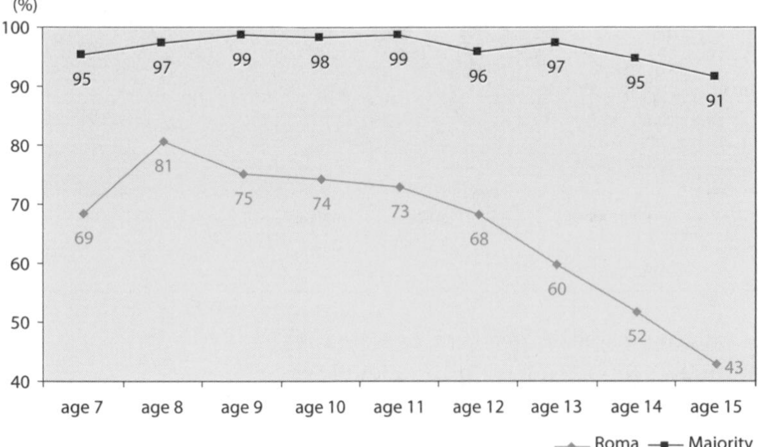

In addition, the data in Figure 1-11 indicate that declining enrolments among Roma begin in elementary and primary school. Examining enrolments at elementary and primary-school levels reveals sharp declines in Roma enrolments through each age cohort, declining to just 43 per cent among 15-year-olds. By contrast, little or no declines in enrolment rates from children from majority families are noted in this age range (see Figure 1-12). This drastic gap in enrolment for Roma is one of the main reasons for low educational achievements and future disadvantages in the labour market.

By secondary school age, large gaps emerge between Roma and majority children in terms of school enrolments. Secondary school enrolment rates for both groups can be compared with reported national averages in some of the countries covered by the survey.[34] Figure 1-13 shows the individual countries' net enrolment rates in secondary education – and enrolment rates for both groups in the survey. The figure shows that, although secondary enrolment rates for children from majority households are comparable to national averages, Roma enrolment rates fall far below these levels.

Years spent in education provide another way of looking at educational opportunities and how they are utilized. On average, Roma respondents report spending less than 4.5 years in education, compared to around 10 years for majority respondents.

---

[33] UN (2005) Millennium Development Goals. http://www.un.org/millenniumgoals/index.html.

[34] Excluding Bosnia, Serbia and Montenegro and Kosovo for which national secondary enrolment rates are not available for these years.

As shown by the data in Figure 1-14, almost a quarter of Roma do not attend school at all, while over a third spends less than four years in education. By contrast, 85 per cent of majority respondents spend more than five years in education. These data highlight the problems of low Roma enrolments and early drop-outs as possible determinants of their lower educational attainment. They also show how MDG 2—which calls for universal primary school completion—remains elusive for vulnerable groups in the countries of Southeast Europe.

The Decade of Roma Inclusion's national action plans for improving Roma education focus particularly on increasing the enrolment and attainment rates for Roma in all levels of education. Particular measures are to be introduced already at the pre-school level to prepare Roma children to continue their education. Emphasis is also placed on parents and teacher education, to ensure parental appreciation of the importance of education to their children's future, and to reduce discrimination by teachers and parents from other communities.

Roma enrolment rates and years spent in education are at best rough proxies for the human capital acquired via education systems. The enrolment rates listed are gross, which include repeaters, thus it is overstating enrolment rates. Likewise, the 'years spent in education' indicator does not necessarily reflect 'years of learning', not to mention 'human capital acquired via educational attainment'. The poor quality of some of the schools that Roma attend adds further reasons for concern. These considerations may make the real picture for Roma children even more alarming than what is presented in the data. This calls for introducing more reliable quality outcome indicators for educational achievements, particularly within the context of the Decade of Roma Inclusion national action plans.

Poor education and illiteracy

Lower levels of education are expressed most drastically in illiteracy. As the data in Table 1-5 show, while literacy rates among majority respondents are close to national literacy rates for adults (over 15 years of age) in the region,[35] the literacy rate for Roma respondents (73 per cent) is far below these levels and lower even than the reported national averages for Kenya (74 per cent),[36] a country considered to be of low human development.

Box 6: National MDG targets, vulnerable groups and primary education for Roma

Enrolment in primary education is a major concern of MDG 2, and most of the national MDG reports for the Southeast European countries set targets in this regard.

In the MDG report, **Serbia** called for raising the net enrolment ratio in primary education to nearly 100 per cent by 2015. At the national level, the country does not have a long way to go, as this rate was 97.9 per cent in 2002. Applying the same methodology as in Box 4 suggests that the Roma households surveyed would reach the national target only in 2165. Attaining the national target by 2015 would require that the growth in Roma enrolment ratios be almost 15 times higher than the national average.

The **Kosovo** MDG report calls for raising the net enrolment rate in primary education to 100 per cent by 2015, from a 2004 rate of 95.4 per cent. When applying linear progress from this level towards the 100 per cent target and the pace needed to achieve this target (annual increases of 0.42 percentage points), the Roma households surveyed would reach the national target only in 2092. If a 100 per cent primary education enrolment ratio is to be achieved by 2015 for the Roma, the growth in the Roma enrolment rate would need to be eight times higher than for the country as a whole.

FIGURE 1 – 13

Enrolment rates by country

Secondary-school enrolment rates for Roma, the majority, and the country as a whole (in percent)

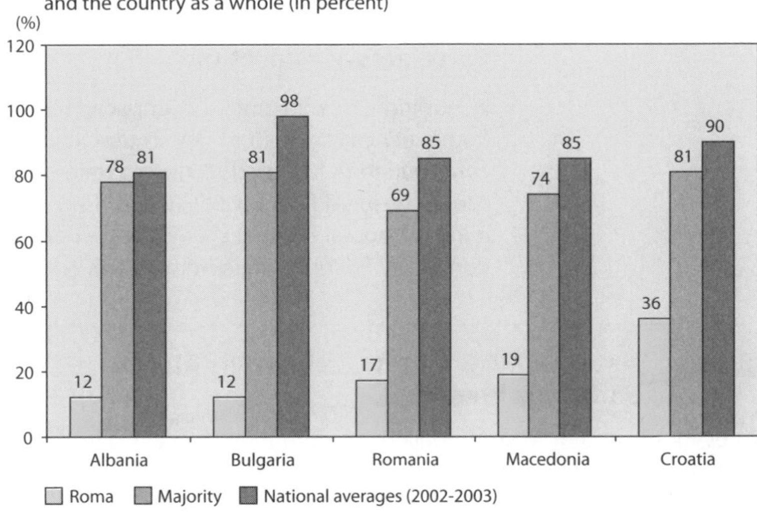

[35] Adult literacy rates in 2003 were 98.7, 94.6, 98.2, 96.1, 97.3 and 96.4 per cent for Albania, Bosnia and Herzegovina, Bulgaria, Croatia, Macedonia, and Serbia and Montenegro respectively (UNESCO Institute for Statistics, 2005: http://www.uis.unesco.org/).

[36] UNESCO Institute for Statistics (2005): http://www.uis.unesco.org/.

FIGURE 1 – 14

Time spent in school

Percentage of Roma and majority household members by years spent in education

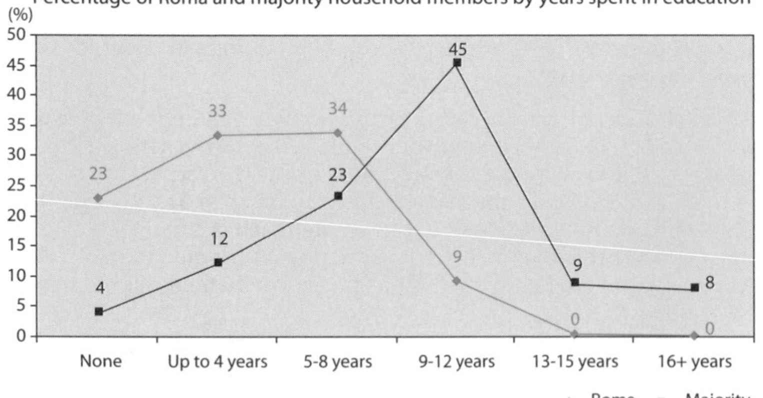

Table 1-5:

Literacy rates for Roma and majority respondents

(Responses to the question "Does the household member read and write?" for household members six years of age or above)

	Roma	Majority
Yes	73.2%	96.4%
No	26.8%	3.6%

Correlates of education

In addition to outlining the implications of Roma education status, key causal factors contributing to lower educational attainment should be identified, for policy and programming purposes. The first step is the identification of key factors correlated with this education status, before examining the independent causal impact of each factor on poverty.

Gender

The survey reveals that women – and Roma women in particular – have weaker education backgrounds than men. As shown in Figure 1-15 there are substantial differences between attainment rates for men and women for both groups and at all levels of education. Moreover the gap between men and women in terms of educational attainment expands across each level of education.

The size of the pro-male attainment gap[37] shows that Roma women are relatively more disadvantaged than women from majority households. These data also show that the expanding `gender gap´ in educational attainment rates expands more rapidly for Roma women, and point to the need for specific measures targeting this sub-group. At least part of the gap in attainment between Roma men and women can be understood in terms of lower enrolments among the latter. This is particularly the case at the primary level where enrolments among Roma girls between 7 and 15 years is just 52 per cent – compared to 61-per cent enrolments among men. The gap in enrolment in education among Roma boys and girls can be attributed to traditional factors, such as early marriages, inadequate appreciation of the importance of female education, household demands (housework, childrearing, etc.). Box 8 outlines how the traditional model of socialization of Roma girls may indirectly influence educational opportunities.

In addition to a lack of educational opportunities, Roma girls also suffer from lower completion rates. The gap between male and female enrolments at each level of education is substantially lower than the gap between male and female attainments. One explanation for this difference may be that girls in Roma households have to devote more time to household work or childcare, compared to boys in these same households. Indeed, among the elementary-, primary-, and secondary-school-age survey respondents (5-19 years) who were not currently enrolled in school or studying and who reported their working status, 63 per cent of Roma women (as opposed to 8 per cent of Roma men) reported housework to be their primary work.

Box 7: National MDG targets, vulnerable groups and Roma literacy

Literacy is a major area of concern for Roma and other vulnerable groups. Improvements in literacy rates are included in almost all of the national MDG reports from Southeast Europe, within Goal 2.

The MDG report for **Macedonia** calls for full literacy by 2015. At the national level, this means only a small improvement (0.28 percentage points annually), as the literacy rate was 96.4 per cent in 2002. However, Roma households in Macedonia would reach the national target only in 2062. Growth in literacy rates would have to be five times higher if 100 per cent Roma literacy were to be attained by 2015.

Montenegro's National MDG report called for the achievement of virtually complete literacy (99 per cent) by 2015, from 96.3 per cent in 2005. At the national level, this means only small annual improvements (0.37 percentage points). At this pace, Roma households surveyed would not reach 99 per cent literacy until 2115. Growth in Roma literacy rates would need to be 10 times higher if the target is to be achieved for Roma by 2015.

[37] The pro-male attainment gap is the difference between male and female attainment rates divided by the attainment rate of men and multiplied by 100.

The impact of such factors reveals itself most noticeably through high illiteracy among women: 32 per cent of Roma women are illiterate, compared to 22 per cent of Roma men. This pro-male literacy gap is far less substantial in the case of majority communities, in which male and female illiteracy rates are low and broadly comparable – 2 and 5 per cent respectively. The education gap between men and women also affects employment opportunities available for men and women (see Employment Chapter 1.4).

While most of the Decade of Roma Inclusion national action plans contain measures to help parents support their children's education, the gender dimensions of Roma education are not explicitly addressed. The need to ensure equal opportunities in education for both girls and boys is largely missing in the action plans, as are education indicators disaggregated by sex.

FIGURE 1 – 15

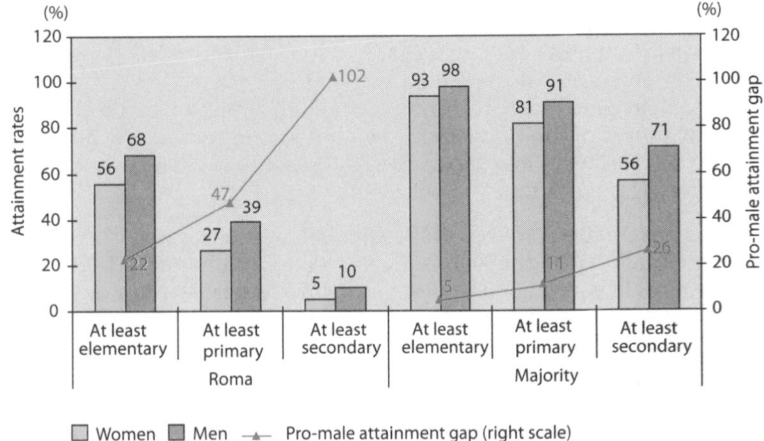

Age and transition

Educational attainment patterns across age groups surveyed can be used as a proxy for educational attainment across time. Looking only at those household members who have reported having finished education,[38] the data show a strong relationship between age and attainment. As shown in Figure 1-16, respondents in the 25-49 year age range were found to be the most likely, while those over 50 or under 19 were found to be the least likely of all age groups to have attained basic education. This is probably due to the high levels of elementary and primary education enforced under the communist governments throughout the post-war period until the late-1980s or early-1990s. In the case of Roma, the percentage of those with elementary education or above falls from 76 per cent for the age group 30-39 to 56 per cent for the age group 15-18, and just 31 per cent for the age group 11-14. Although still large, this drop has been far less sizable among majority communities, with attainment rates of 99 per cent among 25-39 year-olds falling to 76 per cent among 11-14 year-olds.

The fact that recent declines in education (implied by lower educational attainment among under 25-year-olds) are more pronounced among Roma than among majority households indicates that systems of compulsory education, having eroded during transition, have not benefited from sufficient attention to Roma inclusion. Pre-transition systems of education and socialization for vulnerable groups (and primarily Roma) may have been less democratic, but they at least produced some results in terms of educational achievements. Since 1990, those systems have faced progressive quality declines and have not been replaced by new and

Household poverty could be a principal determinant of lower education among Roma

FIGURE 1 – 16

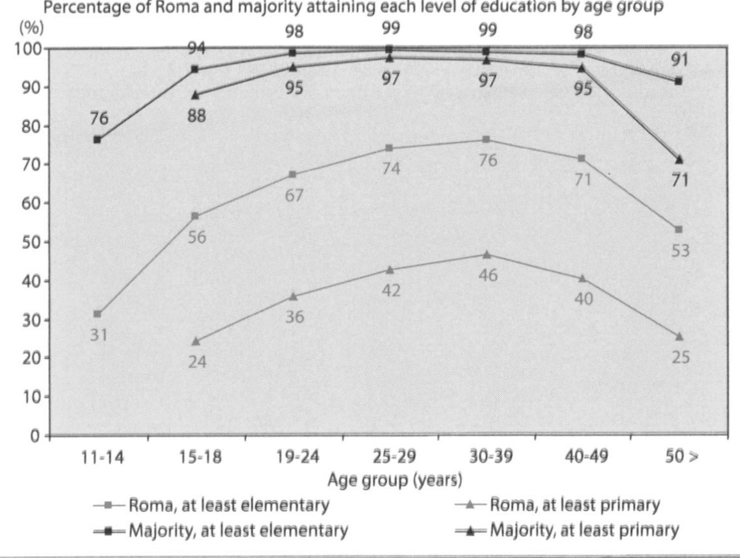

[38] By taking only those who have completed education it is possible to exclude those who may continue to obtain higher levels of attainment and thus avoid underestimating the education level of those in younger age groups.

Box 8: Early childbirth and female socialization among the Roma

Qualitative research reveals tensions between the educational aspirations and limited opportunities of Roma girls due to traditional gender roles in Roma communities. In a recent survey on the status of Roma women in Romania conducted by OSI in 2005 (Surdu and Surdu, 2006), female Roma said they favoured higher levels of education for boys rather than girls, because boys are traditionally seen as the future breadwinners of their families. They also agreed that a girl's success in life depends very much on a successful marriage. Hence education becomes less important for young girls.

These observations reflect the traditional gender roles and models of socialization that characterize many Roma communities. There are three roles in which a female Roma can find herself (Pamporov, 2003, 2004):

- The lowest level: "chshay"/"shey" (a girl);
- The middle level: "djuvli" (a wife without child);
- The highest level: "romni" – a wife with child.

According to tradition, a young woman in the first role is subordinate to all other family members. In the second, she is subordinate to her husband and his parents and some elder relatives. In the third role, she gains the authority to impose her will, at least in her own household.

In other words, a Roma woman acquires maximal authority within the household only by marrying and giving birth. These social patterns create additional incentives for Roma women to give birth early. It also suggests that only through encouraging Roma girls to join the social mainstream can these patterns be altered.

improved ones linked to market demands. This has further contributed to the divide between Roma and majority communities in terms of employment, income and wealth.

FIGURE 1 – 17

Poverty-induced educational attainment gap

Percentage of poor or non-poor Roma and majority household members who finished at least elementary, primary or secondary school, as well as the percentage difference between the two (the 'poverty-induced attainment gap')

		Poor (<PPP $4.30) (%)	Non-poor (>PPP $4.30) (%)	Poverty-induced attainment gap (%)
Roma	At least elementary	53	63	19
Roma	At least primary	19	31	61
Roma	At least secondary	4	8	97
Majority	At least elementary	75	85	13
Majority	At least primary	59	79	33
Majority	At least secondary	31	67	117

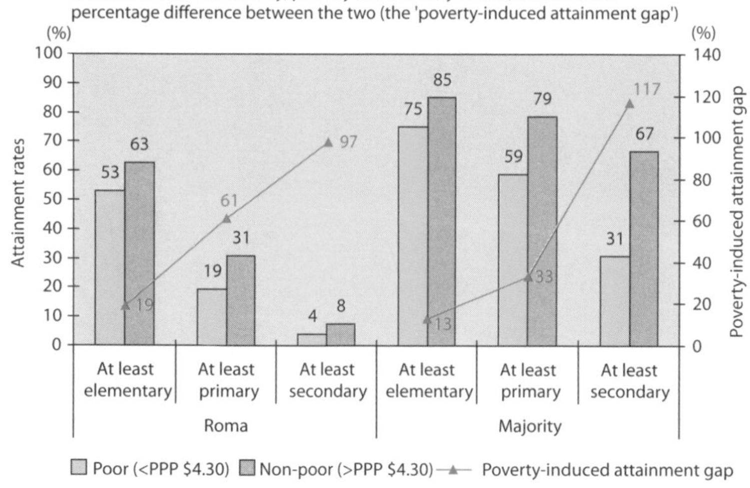

Education and poverty

The discussion in chapter 1.2 shows that poor education is a major determinant of poverty. But questions about reverse causality – the extent to which living in poverty determines poor education (thereby closing the vicious circle of social exclusion) – are also important. Although nominally free, public education is becoming increasingly expensive for households in the region, raising questions about access to education for vulnerable groups. This is because some expenditures on education (books, meals at school) have progressively shifted from the state to household budgets. Other indirect costs of education (like public transportation and children's clothes) that had been subsidized under socialism are no longer supported at the same rate (if at all).

Differences in incomes available to defray educational expenses result in differences in educational attainment. As shown in Figure 1-17, even when the feedback effects of education on poverty are controlled for by examining only those still in education (and therefore not yet in the labour market), the data reveal a strong relationship between poverty[39] and poor educational attainment. Large and expanding percentage differences in the proportion of poor and non-poor who attain various education levels can be observed. Percentage differences between the proportion of poor and non-poor attaining each level of education – the poverty-induced attainment gap – are largest at the secondary level, indicating that the costs of education (or non-employment) are most prohibitive at this level of education.

As the poor are disproportionately concentrated in the Roma sample (50 per cent of Roma respondents are classified as poor, compared to 14 per cent of majority respondents), it is clear that household poverty could be a principal determinant of lower education among Roma. This conclusion is reinforced by the finding that the poverty-induced attainment gap is larger for Roma than for majority households, at least at the elementary and primary levels. The relatively smaller poverty-induced attainment gap at the secondary level in the case of Roma students may be due to the small numbers of Roma that attain this level of education.

[39] In this discussion individuals with daily equivalized expenditures below PPP $4.30 are considered to be living in poverty.

The issue appears to be one of access to education and educational opportunities. As shown in Figure 1-18, poor households report considerably lower enrolment rates than non-poor households, particularly for Roma. Moreover, the gap between poor and non-poor enrolments – illustrated in Figure 1-18 – expands through each level of education, particularly for Roma. These trends underscore problems of limited incentives and opportunities for keeping children from poor (particularly poor Roma) families in school. Poverty disproportionately affects Roma enrolment levels: 52 per cent of Roma children (7-18 years) from poor families do not attend school at all, compared to 34 per cent from non-poor families. Although still sizable, this gap is less pronounced for majority families, with 6 per cent and 16 per cent of non-poor and poor children respectively not in school. The similarity between Figures 1-17 and 1-18 suggests a close relationship between the poverty-induced attainment and enrolment gaps.

Links between poverty and low enrolment, particularly in the case of Roma, are apparent in other respects as well. When questioned about the main reason for school non-attendance, 51 per cent of Roma and 41 per cent of majority respondents cited costs as the major factor. Only 14 per cent of Roma responded that they thought their level of education was sufficient – compared to 23 per cent of majority respondents.

Expenditures on education vary substantially across Roma and majority households. As shown in Table 1-6, average Roma household annual expenditures on education (83 euros) amount to less than a third of those of majority households. With such differences in household incomes and expenditures, meeting urgent needs related to survival (e.g., expenditures on food and other basic needs) would seem to be a priority.

The impact of poverty on education is also apparent in literacy rates. Only 73 per cent of Roma can read and write – but only 66 per cent of poor Roma. For majority respondents, the gap in literacy rates is less pronounced – 96 for total and 92 for the poor. Since these results reflect self-assessments (responses to the question "Can the household member read and write?") rather than in-depth examinations of functional literacy, levels of educational vulnerability may be much higher than what is suggested by these figures.

FIGURE 1 – 18

Poverty-induced educational enrolment gap

Percentage of poor and non-poor Roma and majority household members of elementary, primary or secondary school age still enrolled in school, as well as the percentage difference between the two (the 'poverty-induced enrolment gap')

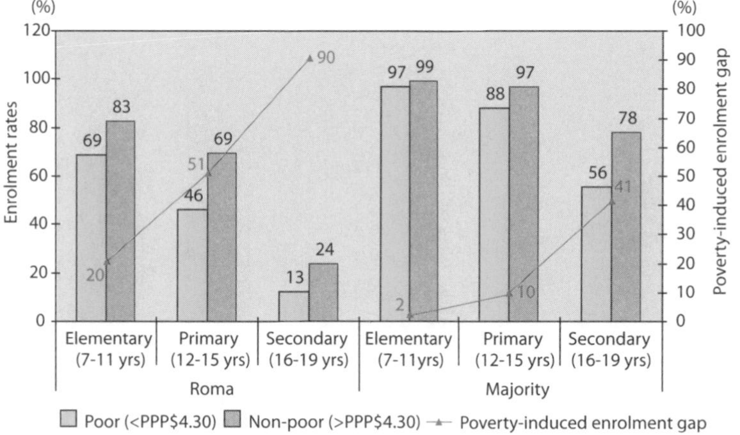

FIGURE 1 – 19

Reasons for leaving school

Percentage of Roma and the majority giving each reason for dropping out of school

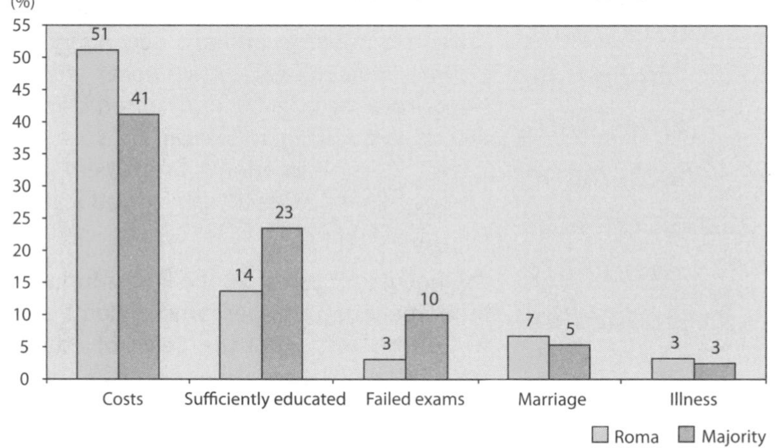

Table 1-6

Average Roma and majority household annual expenditures on education and the number and share of households in each expenditure range*

Household spending on education:	Roma	Majority
Average amount (euros)	83.1	287.3
Up to 50	620 (45.4%)	270 (16.5%)
51-100	286 (20.9%)	269 (16.4%)
101-150	134 (9.8%)	172 (10.5%)
151+	327(23.9%)	928 (56.6%)

* The shares in brackets indicate the percentage of households with respective average amounts of expenditures. They were calculated excluding households that refused to answer or claimed not to know.

FIGURE 1 – 20

Illness-induced educational attainment gap

Percentage of Roma and majority household members with or without chronic illnesses attaining each level of education, as well as the percentage difference between the two (the 'illness-induced attainment gap')

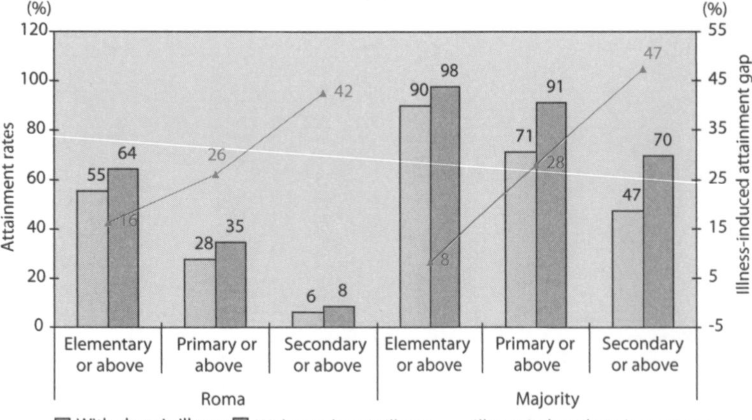

Roma in households with a well-educated head have almost three times higher attainment rates in primary-level education than those in households with poorly educated heads

Education and health

The data indicate that educational attainment is adversely affected by illness, with lower elementary, primary, secondary, or tertiary educational attainment among household members who reported chronic illness. In addition, a link can be seen between lower educational attainment and chronic illness at each level of education (see Figure 1-20).

As shown in Figure 1-20 the illness-induced attainment gap is largest among Roma only for 'elementary or above' level of education. This may be due to poor consumption (which has a particularly negative impact on smaller children), low health expenditure and the poorer housing conditions of this group, which increases their risk of contracting disease. Indeed, 21 per cent of Roma households reported exposure to sanitation-related diseases to be the single biggest overall threat facing their families. Among Roma, poor access to health care may also be a contributing factor, with 14 per cent of Roma households reporting access to health care to be the single biggest threat facing their families. For those with other levels of education, health status does not seem to have a larger impact on Roma educational attainment than it does on that of majority households.

Diffusion effects

The data indicate a strong relationship in education levels for household heads and other household members. As Figure 1-21 shows, whether the household head is 'poorly educated' (with elementary or below education) or 'well educated' (with primary or above level of education) correlates strongly with educational attainment levels for household members. This correlation stands up even when other factors such as poverty are held constant.[40] This reflects both the demonstration or 'role-model' effects of household heads vis-à-vis younger members of the household, and the tendency for household heads to have partners of a similar education status. The 'diffusion-induced group attainment gaps' (the percentage difference between educational attainment rates in households with well- and poorly educated heads) indicate that the relationship between the education level of household heads and household members is stronger for Roma than for majority households.

In fact, Roma in households with a well-educated head have almost three times higher attainment rates in primary-level education than those in households with poorly educated heads. The relationship is even stronger for secondary education. This points to lower relative inter-generational mobility among Roma, and highlights the lack of a positive role model as a possible determinant of lower educational attainment among this group.[41] The situation for Roma is made even more alarming by the fact that only 35 per cent of Roma live in households with heads who have primary-or-above level of education, compared to 78 per cent of majority respondents.

Determinants of education

Key factors responsible for Roma education status

The data shown in the *Correlates of education* section indicate that not only are Roma more prone to lower education, but also that, within Roma households certain individuals – e.g. women, the young,

40 $R_{head's\ education} = 0.38$, $p<0.01$.

41 The role-model effect stipulated here is however limited in interpretation, since the education of the household head is correlated with the education of all members of the household (including the head's spouse) rather than solely with the head's children.

the poor, the chronically ill and members of households without well-educated heads – are all particularly vulnerable to low education status. Assessing the impact of gender, youth, poverty, health and role models on educational attainment is needed to determine programming and policy priorities.

To clarify this issue, the individual impact of such factors on the likelihood that Roma household members attain the next level of education were assessed using logistic regression analyses.[42] The results – shown in full in Table A10 in the Annex – show an inverse-U relationship between age and educational attainment suggested in the *Correlates of education* section. They also highlight the educational vulnerability of Roma women. Chronic illness also had an effect on attainment but only at lower levels of education and had no effect on the odds of achieving secondary rather than primary education.

Living below the absolute poverty line and the presence or absence of a well-educated household head can be seen as major factors affecting the level of education of Roma. Roma in households with a well-educated household head are 1.7 times more likely to obtain primary (as opposed to elementary) education than those with a poorly educated head, while Roma living in poor households are just two thirds as likely as those in non-poor households to attain primary education. This indicates the importance of breaking the mutually reinforcing cycle of absolute poverty, dependency and poor educational attainment among Roma, and the need to identify and highlight positive Roma role models (i.e. academic success stories where society accepted their right to equal access to quality education) in the community. Gender also has a major effect on education levels and Roma men are one-and-a-half-times more likely than women to attain primary (rather than elementary) education, suggesting that highlighting female role models should be a priority.

FIGURE 1 – 21

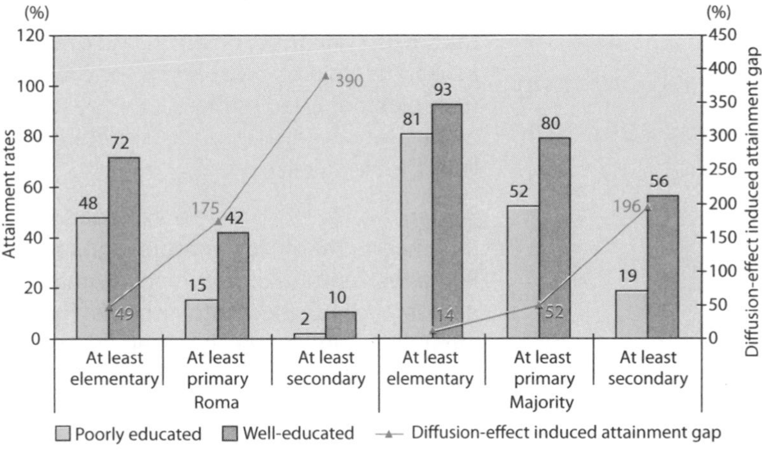

Living below the absolute poverty line and the presence or absence of a well-educated household head can be seen as major factors affecting the level of education of Roma

Segregation and attitudes

In the *Correlates of education* section it has been shown that, in addition to group status (Roma or majority), such factors as gender, age, poverty, illness and the education level of the household head are correlated with education status. This raises questions about the extent to which educational attainment can be understood in terms of these factors, as opposed to factors associated with being Roma, such as segregation and discrimination.

To answer these questions, the individual impact of such factors as gender, age, poverty, illness and education level was assessed using a pooled dataset of Roma and majority data and a dummy variable coding Roma. The results – shown in full in Table

42 Logistic regression analyses have been used increasingly in education research (Peng et al, 2002) and have been used in similar analyses such as the examination of the impact of ethnicity on enrolments (see Hannum, 2002). Two separate analyses were performed in order to assess the impact of each factor on the likelihood of progressing from elementary to primary or primary to secondary education. Due to the limited number of Roma with secondary or tertiary education, the impact of the various factors on the likelihood of progressing from secondary to tertiary education was not estimated. The following explanatory variables were included in the analysis: Gender (1=Male, 0=Female), age and age-squared, Poverty (1=Poor, 0=Non-poor), and Role-model (1=well educated, 0=poorly educated). The proportion of Roma with elementary versus primary or primary versus secondary level education or coded positively for each explanatory variable are shown in Table A9 (in the Annex) along with the mean and standard deviation of the age and age-squared values of the samples.

Segregation is one possible explanation for the unaccountably lower education among Roma

A12 in the Annex – reveal a worrying picture for Roma.[43] Even when the effects of their younger age, higher poverty rates, higher incidence of illness, and relative absence of positive role models are controlled, Roma are just one third, one fifth and one fifth as likely as majority respondents to progress from elementary to primary, primary to secondary, or secondary to tertiary education levels, respectively.

Segregation is one possible explanation for the unaccountably lower education among Roma. In Central Europe, many Roma children are channelled into schools for the mentally disabled, which generally provide inferior-quality education. The survey data indicate that this phenomenon is less widespread in Southeast Europe. Only 48 Roma children (2 per cent of the Roma children attending school) were reported to attend such schools (compared to almost none of the majority). However, the incidence of enrolment at schools for the disabled is likely to be underreported (for reasons described below). Even more important are the reasons why. Of those 48 reported cases of children attending schools for the disabled, less than a quarter (11 persons) had any disability (physical or mental). More than half of the children were attending such schools for reasons unrelated to mental or physical disability (either the family could not afford taking care of the child or such a school was perceived to provide secure food and shelter or because "the school programme there is easier and the child will cope with it"). Even if the real share of Roma children attending schools for disabled is most probably higher than those 2 per cent, the structure of the reasons why outlines the magnitude of the problem and calls for particular attention to the issue.

Although increases in the level of education can bring major improvements in prospects for both skilled employment and employment in general, this is less the case among Roma than majority households

Discrimination in education can also take the form of segregated schooling. Despite constituting less than an estimated 5 per cent of all those enrolled in education,[44] 20 per cent of Roma enrolled in schools are attending classes in which most of the children are Roma and 31 per cent were reported to attend 'mixed classes' with roughly equal representation of different ethnic groups. For children from majority households, 86 per cent attend schools dominated by their ethnic group and 10 per cent attend mixed classes.

These percentages, however, only give a general idea of the problem. To gain a clearer picture, one must examine whether the over-representation of Roma children in certain schools is an outcome of deliberate policies (segregation), or whether it reflects the demographic makeup of some villages with a small non-Roma population. This is a question that can be answered only on a case-by-case basis. Ultimately, what matters is the knowledge children acquire and less so the ethnic make-up of schools.

As the data presented in Chapter 1.4 indicate, although increases in the level of education can bring major improvements in prospects for both skilled employment and employment in general, this is less the case among Roma than majority households. This suggests strong disincentives for Roma to remain in education. Moreover, as the discussion in the Employment Chapter shows, gains from education both in terms of decreasing unemployment and the increasing probability of skilled employment are noticeable only once secondary education has been completed. This pattern suggests a possible self-reinforcing cycle of lower education and unskilled employment for Roma. As schooling at the elementary and primary levels appears to have very little impact on the prospects of finding skilled employment, incentives for Roma to complete these levels of education are likely to be weak. Since most have dropped out before completing their secondary education, very few Roma are able to find skilled employment. By contrast, for members of major-

[43] Separate logistic regression analyses were performed to determine the impact of various factors on the likelihood of progressing from elementary to primary, primary to secondary, or secondary to tertiary education. Group membership was addressed using the dummy explanatory variable Roma (1=Roma, 0=Majority). The other explanatory variables were the same as those used in the Roma-only analysis. The proportion of household members with primary versus elementary, secondary versus primary, or tertiary versus secondary education or coded positively for each explanatory variable are shown in Table A11 (in the Annex) along with the mean and standard deviation of the age and age-squared values of the samples.

[44] Calculated from estimates of numbers of Roma and non-Roma in schools, derived by multiplying estimates of Roma and non-Roma populations in the region 3.3 million and 50.2 million (Liégeois, 2006; Population Reference Bureau, 2005) – by the respective percentages of Roma and non-Roma who claimed to be enrolled in education (around 21 and 26 per cent).

ity communities, completion of elementary and primary education is more-or-less automatic. The prospect of skilled employment can therefore serve as a stronger incentive to complete secondary education.

Conclusions from Chapter 1.3

The worryingly low education levels among Roma – less than one third attain primary education – underscore the importance of efforts to highlight and redress the reasons behind this.

Less than one fifth of Roma of primary school age actually attend school; Roma children spend, on average, half the time of majority children in school (4.5 compared with 10 years respectively). These issues have important gender dimensions as well. Roma women are relatively more disadvantaged than women in majority communities, and the gap between men and women in education is more pronounced for Roma. As such, the data highlight Roma women as particularly vulnerable to lower educational attainment and indicate the need for specific policies and projects targeting Roma girls at school. Initiatives to improve education within the Decade of Roma Inclusion are often missing this gender element. The newly established Roma Education Fund that provides grants for educational programmes, specifically those initiated within the Decade of Roma Inclusion, should prioritize programmes with a clear gender focus.

To make matters worse, Roma educational vulnerability seems to be intensifying: younger Roma report lower educational achievements than older ones. The strong correlation between the education status of the household head and other members of Roma households highlights the need for urgent action, to prevent a further downward spiral in Roma education status.

Poverty is central to this issue. Although nominally free, education is becoming increasingly expensive in the region, as growing numbers of education-related expenditures are being transferred to households. Being caught in poverty, many Roma households cannot find the funds to cover these costs, further reducing educational opportunities for Roma children.

The analysis strongly suggests, therefore, the implementation of policies aimed at encouraging Roma children and their mothers, especially girls and young women and early childhood mothers, to stay in school. Stronger financial incentives to keep children in school, combined with disincentives for tolerating non-attendance, seem critically important in this respect. Practical measures in this regard can include better targeting of social benefits to Roma parents with school-aged children, linking parental receipt of social benefits to verified school attendance by their children, as well as better funding of public education in general, particularly at the elementary- and primary-school levels.

The analysis also indicates that problems of Roma educational performance are linked to factors such as segregation and attitudes. The disproportionately high presence of Roma in 'Roma-only' or substandard 'mixed' schools reinforces the low education status of Roma and often limits the quality of education available to them. On the other hand, the barriers to employment for Roma highlighted in Chapter 1.4 create strong disincentives for Roma to stay in education. Since most well-educated Roma are from integrated families, efforts should be made to integrate Roma into 'majority' schooling and provide them with the same kind of employment opportunities available to other communities.

The data highlight Roma women as particularly vulnerable to lower educational attainment and indicate the need for specific policies and projects targeting Roma girls at school

Box 9: **Closing the educational gap: The Roma Education Fund**

The idea of forming the Roma Education Fund took shape in July 2003, at the high-level 'Roma in an Expanding Europe: Challenges for the Future' conference held in Budapest. At a donor conference in Paris on 2-3 December 2004, eight bilateral donor countries, private foundations and multilateral agencies, pledged a total of $ 42,390,000 to support the Roma Education Fund as part of the Decade of Roma Inclusion (2005-2015). The Fund was formally established in January 2005; it has been functioning since June 2005, with offices in Budapest and Paris.

According to its website (www.romaeducationfund.org), the Roma Education Fund's main goal is to help close the educational gap between Roma and non-Roma. Supporting measures to desegregate educational systems is a major emphasis. One of the Fund's main functions is grant-making with both private and public education sectors as beneficiaries, primarily in the region of the Roma Decade countries, but also other countries belonging to the Council of Europe. The Fund's main focus is on grants aimed at systematic reform and educational improvements for Roma.

As of October 2005, the Roma Education Fund had approved 12 projects. Three projects approved in Bulgaria are being implemented by Roma NGOs. One project focuses on six Bulgarian municipalities where desegregation action plans are in progress, and on disseminating the positive experiences from already functioning desegregation projects. In the second project, local Roma activists introduce non-Roma administrators and other actors to Roma language, culture and history, while at the same time working towards the end of school segregation in their region. The third project aims to create a scholarship fund for Bulgarian Roma students not eligible for other sources of funding. Accompanying it is a number of other skills-training and knowledge-sharing activities. In Hungary, the Ministry of Education has joined forces with Bulgarian and pan-European Roma foundations to disseminate know-how on securing funds for Roma education. In Kosovo, the Roma Education Fund will finance a project implemented by a Catholic charity that will provide educational support to Roma children and teenagers from refugee camps, including interethnic activities. The Macedonian Ministry of Education and the local branch of the Open Society Institute will implement the largest project, providing scholarships and mentoring support to 500 Roma secondary school students. Activities in Macedonia financed by the Fund include projects to organize an awareness-raising campaign for journalists and policy makers, enlarge the existing Roma Educational Network, and improve the quality of Roma education. A Romanian NGO will train 50 Roma teachers, 10 of whom will be further trained as trainers. In Montenegro, five NGO-school partnerships will be established to promote Roma inclusion. In Serbia, the National Council of Roma and the Ministry of Education will give small grants to institutions applying for Roma preschool education projects. Also, the National Council of Roma, the Ministry of Education and other institutions will develop projects in 20 schools assisting young adult Roma who have not completed their basic education.

The Roma Education Fund represents an important institution in terms of improving Roma access to quality education. Its strong emphasis on initiatives that yield practical and tangible results is an important characteristic that is worthy of emulation by similar programmes. Some recommendations for its further development are as follows:

- In addition to its emphasis on desegregation and access to education issues, the Roma Education Fund should encourage projects to address the overrepresentation of Roma in special schools for children with disabilities;
- Special attention should be paid to projects supporting the further education of teenage Roma who might otherwise drop out (the survey data suggest that most young Roma leave school at age 14-15);
- In addition to supporting enrolment, the Roma Education Fund should support projects that monitor and evaluate the long-term sustainability of Roma education efforts (e.g., monitoring the number of Roma students who actually graduate from universities);
- The Fund could emphasize assistance for Roma at universities, particularly non-traditional students, in order to help create a critical mass of Roma intellectuals and experts;
- The Fund should consider encouraging applications from specific fields, in order to accelerate the development of Roma specialists in under-represented thematic areas; and
- The Fund should place a stronger emphasis on introducing human rights-based approaches to education, as well as ensuring the appropriate gender equality and non-discrimination components in all the projects they support.

CHAPTER 1.4

Employment

Summary

Inadequate employment opportunities, reflecting both weak labour market competitiveness and the effects of discrimination, are widely perceived as major causes of the poverty and exclusion experienced by Roma. Employment is a principal source of the income needed to escape poverty. However, given the difficulties in the definition of unemployment examined further in this chapter, it is not by chance that the Lisbon Targets of the EU's European Employment Strategy make reference to raising employment (as opposed to reducing unemployment) rates.[45] This chapter goes beyond the cliché that unemployment and low-skilled employment are bad, and examines the links between employment and unemployment on the one hand and Roma vulnerability on the other. It investigates the determinants of labour market outcomes for vulnerable groups, and makes suggestions about the better design and implementation of targeted policies in this area.

A number of general conclusions emerge from the survey data concerning Roma labour market characteristics in Southeast Europe. Measured unemployment rates in the region are significantly higher for Roma than for majority communities—in some countries, twice as high. 'Subjective' unemployment rates among Roma, based on respondents' perceptions of whether they were unemployed, are higher still. Since for many Roma the lack of a regular job is synonymous with unemployment, high subjective unemployment rates may indicate a combination of greater involvement in the informal sector and a greater willingness to accept the stigma of declaring oneself unemployed.

Roma employment is concentrated in the trade, agricultural, construction and public utilities sectors; representation in white-collar professions, and in the police or security services, is generally quite weak. Low-skilled work predominates and is associated with low incomes, poor job quality, and weak social and employment protection. Differences in unemployment and the type of employment influence the sources and level of Roma income. Workers from majority communities derive a much higher share of their income from wages. But for Roma, unemployment and child benefits, as well as informal employment income, play a large role in household income.

Self-employment is less common among Roma than among workers from majority communities, with most Roma-owned businesses engaged in trade. Limited access to bank finance is a serious constraint; prospective borrowers are often hampered by their lack of credit history and collateral (which are major problems for the poor in general, not just Roma.) When Roma borrowers do get bank loans, the average loan size is about 25 per cent of what is obtained by borrowers from majority communities, Roma borrowers typically apply for credit for artisanship, trade and agriculture, as well as for personal expenditures and social obligations, including weddings.

Age is less of a factor in Roma unemployment, in that differences in unemployment rates between youth and adults at the prime of their careers are smaller than in majority communities. Unfortunately, this largely results from the poor labour market opportunities available to prime-aged Roma adults. Gender also matters: women have higher unemployment rates than men in majority as well as Roma communities. The employment rate targets set in the Lisbon Agreement (of 70 per cent overall and 60 per cent for women) are often met in majority communities in these countries, but not for Roma. Employment rates for Roma women in some countries are below 20 per cent.

Inadequate employment opportunities are widely perceived as major causes of the poverty and exclusion experienced by Roma

Low-skilled work predominates and is associated with low incomes, poor job quality, and weak social protection

[45] The employment rate is defined as employment divided by the working-age population. Thus while it is similar to the unemployment rate in terms of the phenomena it is representing, it is defined with respect to the population and not the labour force and as such it also incorporates the extent of labour force participation.

Differences in unemployment rates for Roma and majority communities are much lower in rural areas than in towns and cities

Location is an important determinant of unemployment: differences in unemployment rates for Roma and majority communities are much lower in rural areas than in towns and cities. While this may result from weaker labour demand for all workers, it may also reflect the willingness of Roma to undertake low-paying jobs in agriculture, in which workers from other communities are reluctant to engage. Seasonality also matters, since Roma take agricultural jobs during the fall (harvest) and spring (planting) seasons. The greater prevalence of traditional gender roles (work at home vs. labour market) amongst Roma in the countryside keeps women out of the (formal) labour force, thereby reducing rural unemployment rates for Roma women. The collocation of Roma and majority households in mixed neighbourhoods also affects unemployment: Roma unemployment rates are higher in segregated than in mixed communities.

Employment-related benefits of education for Roma are lower than for workers from majority communities, with unemployment rates much higher for Roma with higher education. Roma workers face significant difficulties in finding skilled employment, regardless of their education. On the other hand, once in a job, the returns to education in terms of wages, are the same for workers from both Roma and majority communities.

FIGURE 1 – 22

Unemployment rates

Percentage of Roma and the majority between 15 and 55 years of age who are unemployed

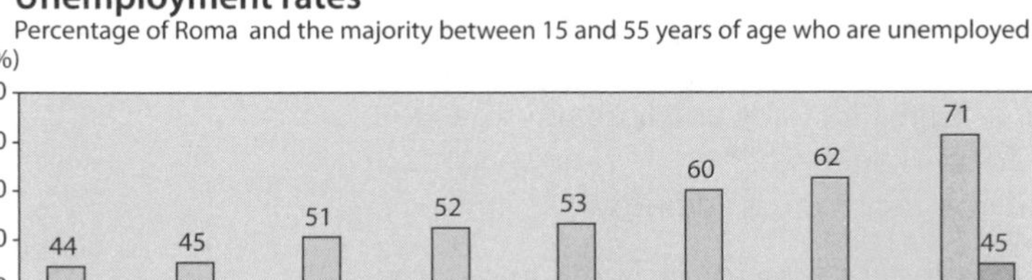

Employment status

Unemployment rates in Southeast Europe

How should unemployment and unemployment rates be measured? The survey approached this question by asking about the socio-economic status of each household member (unemployed, employed, student, retired and so on). This subjective self-assessment was then complemented by more objective criteria associated with labour force survey methodologies. Each household member was asked whether she or he had earned any income in the previous month, and if so, how. This helped make possible the exclusion of self-declared 'unemployed' who had in fact worked in the previous month.

According to the internationally accepted International Labour Organization (ILO) definition, in order to be considered unemployed, a person must be:

a) without work;

b) willing and able to work; and

c) actively seeking work.

The survey data described here reflect a broader definition of unemployment, in which discouraged workers are treated as unemployed.[46] The survey data indicate that unemployment rates (so defined) are far higher among Roma than in majority households (see Figure 1-22).[47] In some cases, such as in Bulgaria and Croatia, Roma face unemployment rates which are more than twice as high as their similarly placed colleagues in majority communities.[48]

46 The appropriateness of using the active job search criterion in defining the unemployed has often been questioned. For example, for Hungary, Micklewright and Nagy (2002) have found that, amongst those without employment, those who did not seek work but wished to work (and who are invariably excluded from the unemployed under the standard strict ILO criteria), took less time to find jobs than those who actively sought work through registration at employment offices (invariably included in the unemployed according to strict ILO criteria).

47 Unemployment rates were based on both the willingness and ability to work. The unemployed includes all those whose principal working status were defined as 'not working' as opposed to, for example, 'studying', 'doing housework' or 'working' AND who did not have any earned income in the last month. Clearly here the question arises as to the extent to which the 'not working' category capture willingness and ability, however, it was felt preferable to use this in preference to the alternative (self-definition) of unemployment.

48 It should be emphasized again that the majority population used as a basis of comparison here refers to majority communities living in close geographic proximity to the Roma sites selected for the survey, as opposed to the overall average for the majority in the country as a whole. In this way, the idea is to compare groups that, apart from their status identification, face similar conditions.

Subjective perceptions of Roma respondents invariably produce higher estimates of unemployment rates than the perceptions of respondents from majority households (see Figure 1-23).[49] For majority respondents, by contrast, subjective unemployment perceptions were higher than reported unemployment rates in only Bosnia and Herzegovina, Macedonia, Serbia and Kosovo. Even in these areas, differences between subjective perceptions and unemployment rates are smaller for majority communities than for Roma. Differences between subjective perceptions of unemployment and reported unemployment rates (as defined here, with discouraged workers counted as unemployed) would seem to reflect two distinct phenomena: some people define themselves as unemployed even though they have recently worked (perhaps to maintain eligibility for unemployment benefits); while others do not define themselves as unemployed but would be so classified according to the criteria used here. Since, for many, unemployment is associated with the absence of a regular job, those involved in informal or irregular employment may define themselves as unemployed, even though they may be engaged in some sort of work.

The data support the view that Roma tend to be involved to a greater extent in informal employment, while declaring themselves to be unemployed. On the other hand, many Roma respondents may associate the state of unemployment with the receipt of unemployment benefits. Respondents who are not working, who would work if work were available, and who are not collecting unemployment benefits, may not see themselves as unemployed per se. Moreover, the stigma associated with the self-declaration of unemployment may further depress subjective declarations of unemployment. The benefits and stigmatisation effect may be more common for majority respondents. The relationship between subjective perceptions of employment and unemployment rates is therefore difficult to determine a priori.

Figure 1-23 suggests that the use of subjective rates tends to overestimate the difference between Roma unemployment rates and those of the majority populations. But even without the overestimation, the difference is substantial especially when one recalls that they are living in a similar socio-economic environment, thus facing the same conditions.

FIGURE 1 – 23

Subjective perception of unemployment
Percentage of Roma and majority labour force participants who reported being unemployed

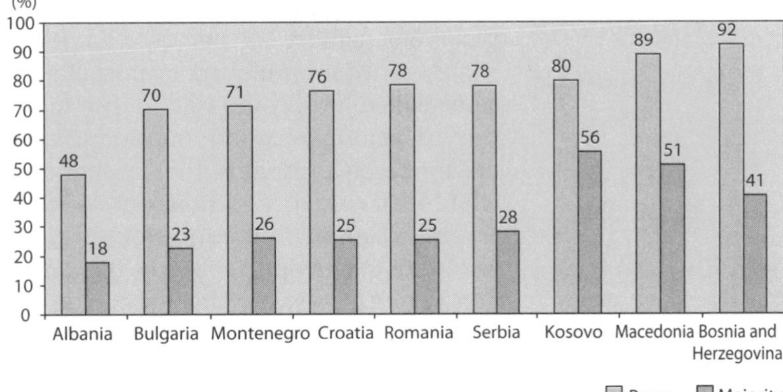

Roma unemployment rates are higher in segregated than in mixed communities

Differences in types of employment and sources of income

The data in Figure 1-24 show that Roma employment tends to be heavily concentrated in the trade, agricultural, construction, and public utility sectors, with the

FIGURE 1 – 24

Employment by sector
Percentage of Roma and the majority employed in each sector

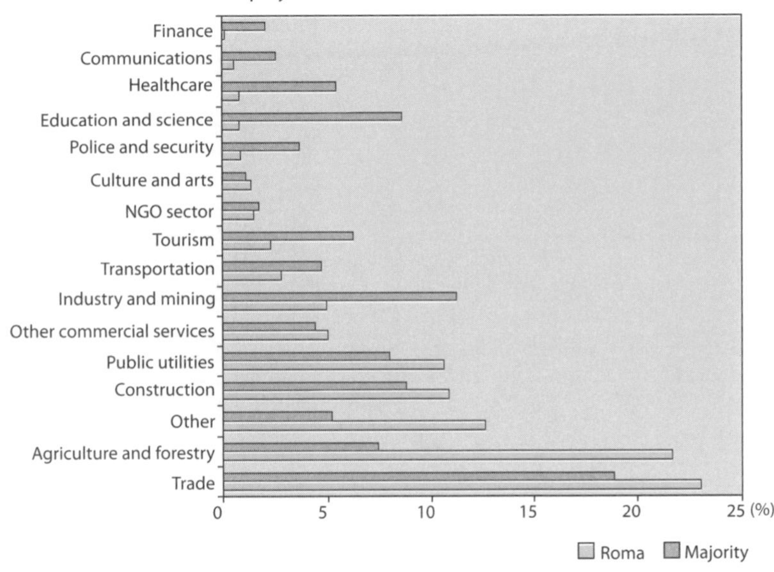

49 Subjective perceptions of unemployment are based solely on respondents' self-assessment of their working status.

Roma involvement in informal-sector employment is on average four or more times more common than the involvement of majority households in such activities

latter most probably including the bulk of public-works job-creation projects. These are sectors dominated by manual labour and low-skilled employment. Roma are mainly concentrated in low-skilled employment: almost 67 per cent of Roma surveyed were employed in unskilled or semi-skilled jobs, compared to just 16 per cent of majority respondents. Roma workers are barely present in such higher-skill, white-collar sectors as financial services, communications, and education; they are also very underrepresented in the police and security services. This reflects a pattern of mutual mistrust – both of majority communities towards Roma, and of Roma vis-à-vis those institutions.

As shown in Figure 1-25, large proportions of both Roma and majority households seem to derive income from informal-sector activities. As a whole, involvement in the informal sector is particularly high in Southeast Europe.[50] These activities are often associated with low incomes, poor job quality, and weak social protection (ILO, 2002). Examining informal-sector employment (understood as activities for which income was not reported for tax and social security purposes) across the region shows that Roma involvement in such activities is higher in each country in the region, and is on average four or more times more common than the involvement of majority households in such activities.

FIGURE 1 – 25

The informal sector

Percentage of workers employed in the informal sector by country

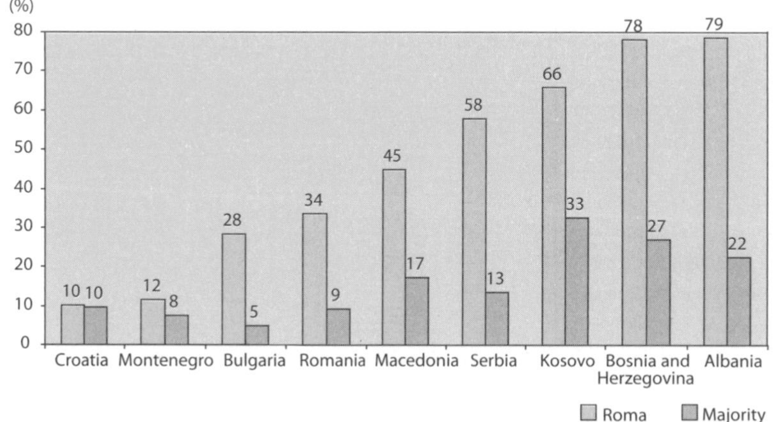

Differences in unemployment rates and types of employment affect both the level and the sources of the income gained by Roma and majority households. Table 1-7 shows that income sources for Roma and majority households differ substantively: wages constitute 73 per cent of majority household incomes, but just 54 per cent of Roma household incomes. Not surprisingly, given the higher levels of Roma unemployment, unemployment, poverty and local social assistance benefits constitute on average 11 per cent of Roma household incomes, but just 2 per cent of majority household incomes. As shown in Table 1-7, Roma households also derive a larger proportion of their income from pawning or petty trade and informal means (such as begging or gambling) than do majority households. (These activities are ways in which Roma household incomes may be supplemented to offset lower employment opportunities.) These data point to labour market gaps between Roma and majority communities, both in terms of finding employment and in terms of the quality of work for those that do have jobs.

Important gender gaps appear here as well. Roma women earn only 58 per cent of Roma men's average monthly income, compared to 69 per cent for women (vis-à-vis men) in majority communities. A variety of factors may account for this difference. Women may have lower education levels (as discussed in Chapter 1.3); they are also more involved in child care, housework and other domestic activities that are not reflected in monitored income.

The data in Table 1-7 suggest that the share of income derived from agriculture (a common survival strategy for vulnerable groups) is lower for Roma than for majority households. One explanation could be inappropriate skills or weak adaptation to modern agricultural processes among Roma communities. Another could be limited access to land – only 13 per cent of Roma (compared to 32 per cent of majority) households reported having access to agricultural land.

Self-employment and access to credit

Because of their abilities to adapt to changing market demands, generate employ-

[50] Estimates in Schneider (2004) suggest that in 2002-03 the informal sector as a percentage of GDP in Southeast Europe was as follows: 35 per cent in Albania, 37 per cent in Bosnia and Herzegovina, 38 per cent in Bulgaria, 35 per cent in Croatia, 36 per cent in Macedonia, 37 per cent in Romania and 39 per cent in Serbia and Montenegro. As productivity in the informal sector tends to be low, the percentage of total employment accounted for by the informal sector can reasonably be assumed to be higher than the estimates of the informal sector output as a percentage of overall GDP.

ment, diversify economic activity, and contribute to exports and trade, small- and medium-sized enterprises (SMEs) can play a critical role in economic development. The promotion of SMEs has been a principal aim of the Central European Initiative, in which the eight countries of this survey (Albania, Bosnia and Herzegovina, Bulgaria, Croatia, Macedonia, Romania, Serbia and Montenegro) are all members (along with 12 other European states).[51]

Unfortunately, Roma communities have been largely left out of such activities. According to the survey data, in 16 per cent of majority households attempts were made to start a business, compared to 10 per cent for Roma households. Of these, 79 per cent of majority-community businesses were registered, compared to 41 per cent of Roma businesses. Most businesses were in the trade sector, (48 per cent of majority and 67 per cent of Roma businesses). However, while the second most important sector for majority-community entrepreneurs, tourism and restaurants, accounted for 10-15 per cent of these businesses, Roma entrepreneurs reported no significant 'secondary' sector. Given the local nature of those services, Roma self-employment opportunities may be largely dependent on local purchasing power—which, since many Roma communities are located in poor regions—is often well below national averages. Prejudices and ethnic divisions may fragment local markets and further reduce local purchasing power.[52]

Inadequate access to capital in general, and bank credit in particular, is typically a serious barrier to self-employment and entrepreneurial activities for vulnerable groups. The poor (over-represented among Roma) often have no access to formal financial institutions because of the high costs of time, money, and bureaucracy, collateral requirements, and institutional disinterest in administering microcredits for the poor. Roma do have access to informal money lenders, but they charge ruinously high interest rates and are often linked to organized crime. Inadequate legal protection of vulnerable groups' formal and informal property rights is a major development issue and an unused opportunity, both in general and for the Roma. The absence of clear property titles limits the poor's ability to collateralize their assets and thereby gain access to formal financial institutions (de Soto, 2003). Legal reforms to redress these problems can have a large impact in terms of poverty reduction, often opening the door for more intensive involvement of the private sector (UNDP, 2004).

Table 1-7

Average household income from all sources
(absolute value in euros and as a share of total household monthly income)

	Roma (3,427)		Majority (3,464)	
Source of Income	euro	Share (%)	euro	Share (%)
Wages & earnings	91	54	251	73
Unemployment, poverty and local assistance benefits	18	11	3	2
Child support	12	7	3	2
Gifts and remittances	11	7	14	5
Pawning or resale	9	6	1	0
Pensions	12	7	31	13
Informal means (gambling, begging)	4	2	1	0
NGOs and charitable giving	2	2	0	0
Agriculture	2	1	8	2
Stipends and scholarships	1	0	1	0
Lending and interest	1	1	2	1
Total average household income	168	100	336	100

Microfinance has grown rapidly with the transition in Central and Eastern Europe, helping households to absorb structural shocks and increase self-employment (Forster et al., 2003). The microfinance sector has developed somewhat 'in parallel' with formal financial institutions, working largely at the community level and involving NGOs rather than banks per se. For many commercial banks, microlending is unattractive: small loans are more expensive to administer (on a per unit basis); vulnerable groups have difficulties in providing collateral; small businesses often do not follow strict accounting rules, making it difficult for bankers to assess their creditworthiness; and many small entrepreneurs lack the experience (and

The poor (over-represented among Roma) often have no access to formal financial institutions

51 As outlined in the 'CEI Declaration on SMEs at the Dawn of the 21st Century' (UNECE, 2001).
52 This is particularly likely in post-conflict regions, where boycotts of former adversaries' businesses are frequent.

sometimes the ability) needed to write the business plans that are required for bank loans. As a result, both banks and micro-entrepreneurs often choose to avoid each other. Microlending remains largely outside the scope of banks, which prefer less risky forms of lending. Vulnerable groups such as Roma rarely qualify as low-risk clients. The sad result is that the rapid deepening of financial systems in many Southeast European countries has yet to provide significant benefits to those small businesses most in need of access to finance.

Lack of collateral, lack of credit history and lack of skills are more pronounced for the Roma than for other respondents

While the survey data suggest that Roma and majority community entrepreneurs do use credit, they also show that the three major barriers to bank credit – lack of collateral, lack of credit history and lack of skills – are more pronounced for the Roma than for other respondents. Whereas 26 per cent of the majority households surveyed said they had used some type of credit, only 15 per cent of Roma households made this claim.

The data in Figure 1-26 show that Roma households rely more on informal borrowing from friends and family and informal money-lenders than the other groups surveyed. They are also the least involved in credit cooperatives or credit unions, which further limits their access to microfinance services. These data also suggest that NGO-provided micro credit programmes should be transformed into credit cooperatives as a way to bring microfinance practices closer to prudent microfinance banking requirements. Diversifying loan portfolios and extending the scope of services provided are among the instruments that can be used for decreasing the risk associated with lending for vulnerable groups, thereby bringing about sustainable increases in Roma access to finance.

FIGURE 1 – 26

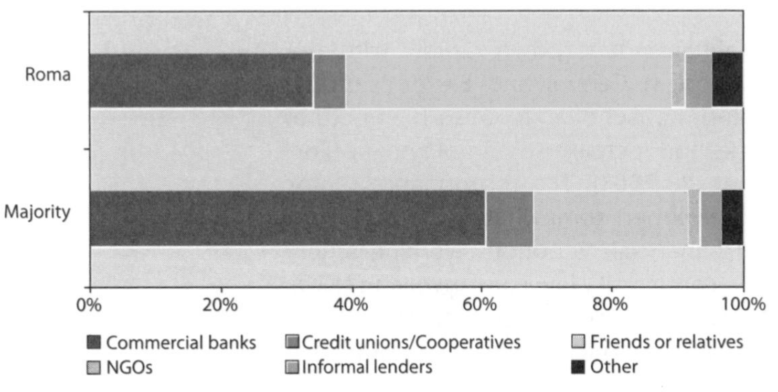

Examples from projects implemented in the region support the argument that Roma tend to fall out of the scope of formalized channels of business support. Although overrepresented among the unemployed, Roma are usually underrepresented as formal borrowers, even in projects explicitly designed to provide vulnerable groups and the unemployed with access to micro-credit. This raises questions about the extent to which small-business projects can address such issues as Roma unemployment. Examples from other countries also provide evidence that Roma borrow less than other groups.

What is special about Roma in this respect? Perhaps the answer is that Roma belong to 'first world' societies but live in pockets of poverty that have 'third world' characteristics. In less developed countries, a small loan can have a much larger impact on poverty reduction. But most Roma live in Europe, where a loan of even a thousand dollars is too small to provide working capital, even for a micro-enterprise (Ivanov and Tursaliev, 2006). Unclear prospects for the cash income generation needed for loan repayment and dependence on a single economic activity are additional important reasons why microlending is not considered for vulnerable groups (CGAP, 2002). On the other hand, the smaller volumes of formal borrowing by Roma entrepreneurs can not be explained solely by higher poverty rates. As shown in Figure 1-27, while reductions in poverty result in increased borrowing from formal financial institutions by both groups, the relationship between increasing expenditures and formal borrowing is less pronounced for Roma. This indicates that other factors – an unwillingness by banks to lend to those without formal addresses, high illiteracy rates among Roma that limit their ability to fill out loan applications, discrimination on the basis of ethnicity, and a distrust among Roma of formal institutions such as banks – may play a significant role in limiting Roma access to credit.

The survey data indicate that the average loan size for Roma is 707 euros, compared to 2,729 euros for majority community borrowers. This disparity is both a cause and an outcome of limited business opportunities for Roma. Barriers to entry due to low competitiveness and discrimination mean that

Roma entrepreneurs face difficulties generating the revenues needed to pay back loans. Moreover, Roma entrepreneurs typically seek credit for activities in the crafts, trade or agricultural sectors. Because these activities are often seasonal or small scale, they are therefore rarely liquid enough to generate the cash flow needed for regular loan payments.

The data in Figure 1-28 also show that the small sums borrowed by Roma are primarily for personal (often for unexpected health-related expenditures) and family matters, such as weddings. Business-oriented borrowing is a relatively small share of the total, and thus cannot generate the revenues needed for repayment. Borrowing to finance durable goods purchases may also be problematic in this regard, although some of these goods (e.g., mobile phones, cars) may boost labour market competitiveness and productivity. These small amounts of borrowing overall, combined with the preponderance of borrowing for non-business purposes, means that borrowing by Roma entrepreneurs for commercial purposes is very small. The average Roma household reported borrowing just 1,961 euros for business development, compared to 5,012 euros for majority households. Also, when the effects of borrowers' income (estimated through the equivalized daily expenditures (PPP$)) on the size of the loan are held constant, the correlation between Roma group status and the size of loans remains negative ($r_{RomaLoan.\ Expenditures} = -0.12$, $p \leq 0.01$). This suggests that the small volume of Roma borrowing (relative to majority households) cannot be fully explained by lower income levels; and that other factors – such as the lack of a registered address, illiteracy, distrust of formal financial institutions, and possibly discrimination – also play a role.

In sum, the data confirm that Roma are in a disadvantaged position on (and often excluded from) credit markets, particularly formal ones. When combined with the absence of robustly successful Roma microlending projects, they suggest that microlending should not be seen as a 'stand alone' tool or as a starting point for poverty alleviation. Such projects are most likely to be successful if applied in a concerted manner with training and traditional business support activities, including assistance in marketing and professional skills development (Csongor et al., 2003). Some business skills and practices should be in place before turning to microfinance, in order to put already existing development potential to good use. Among other things, this means that the most vulnerable and marginalized are not the best target groups for such projects. Such individuals should instead be aided through other activities with a strong community-development focus.

FIGURE 1 – 27

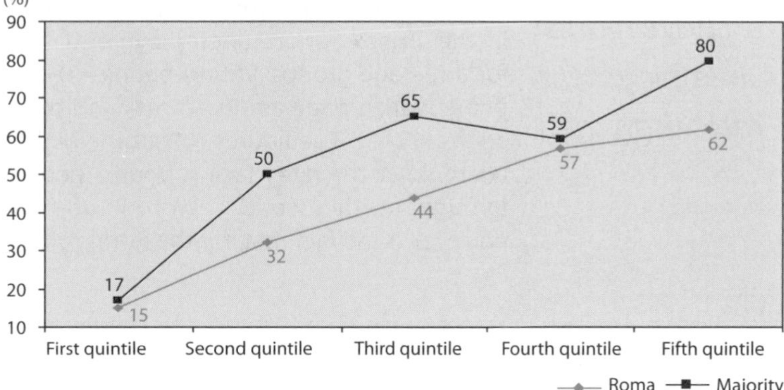

Microlending should not be seen as a 'stand-alone' tool or as a starting point for poverty alleviation

The Decade of Roma Inclusion national action plans focus particularly on self-employment and entrepreneurship. Measures include providing business and skill trainings, establishing agricultural cooperatives, and promoting Roma handcrafts. While the need to go beyond traditional Roma products and focus on current market demands is widely recognized, aligning these measures with the logic of market demands and sustainability may prove to be quite a challenge.

FIGURE 1 – 28

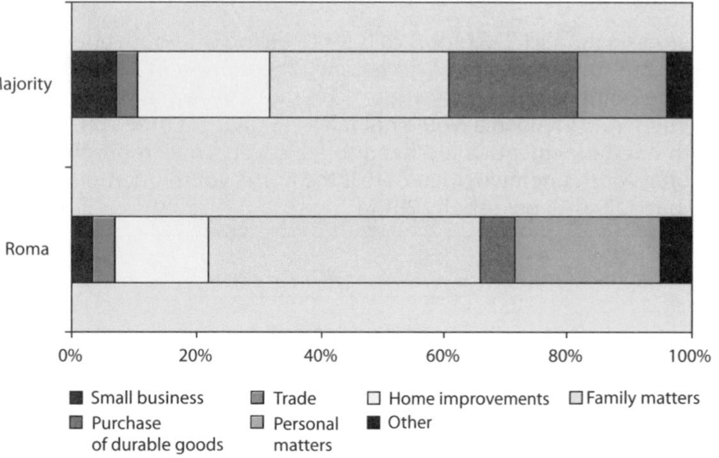

For both Roma and the majority, women have higher unemployment rates than men

Correlates of employment

Age

The MDGs identify youth unemployment as a special cause for concern. Figures A2- A4 in the Annex report unemployment rates for three age groups: young people (15-24), prime working-age adults (25-44) and older adults (45-59). The figures reflect the higher unemployment rates facing young people throughout the world.[53] Worthy of note however, is the fact that, for the Roma, differences between youth and adult unemployment rates are much smaller than for majority households. While youth unemployment rates among majority communities are more than twice (2.2) those of prime working-age adults, young Roma workers face unemployment rates that are less than one-and-a-half times those of adults. The main reason for this is clearly the poor labour market conditions facing prime working-age Roma adults. In contrast to the experiences of majority communities, Roma labour market prospects do not improve significantly with age.

FIGURE 1 – 29

Employment rates by age

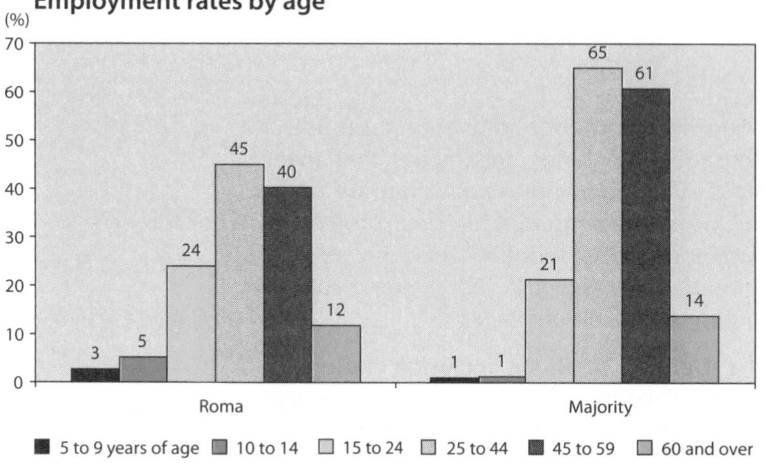

Figure 1-29 shows differences in employment rates for Roma and majority communities in different age groups across the region.

The data in Figure 1-29 show that employment rates for Roma youth (up to and including 24 years of age) are higher than for those from majority communities. This is no doubt attributable to the much higher educational enrolment levels of youth from the latter communities. The converse is true for those over this age. The data in Figure 1-29 also point to higher incidence of child labour among the Roma: some 2 per cent of Roma children under 15 years of age are working. Most of these are involved in occasional jobs and do not attend school.

Box 10: National MDG targets, vulnerable groups and Roma youth unemployment

Reducing unemployment rates for 15-24 year-olds is of particular importance for countries in Southeast Europe. They are generally captured in the national MDG reports under MDG 1 (poverty eradication).

In **Bosnia and Herzegovina**, the national MDG report calls for reducing the unemployment rate for 15-24 year-olds from 34.8 per cent in 2001 to 12 per cent by 2015. Linear progress towards this target implies an annual decrease of 1.63 percentage points. Moving at this pace, Roma households surveyed would reach the 12 per cent target in 2039. If the 12 per cent target were to be reached by 2015 for Roma, the Roma youth unemployment rate would have to fall three times faster than the national rate.

Albania's national MDG report calls for reducing the youth unemployment rates to 15 per cent by 2015, from 22.8 per cent in 2002 (0.6 percentage points annually). Moving at this rate, the Roma youth unemployment rate in Albania would not fall to 15 per cent until 2082. Roma youth unemployment would need to fall seven times more than the national youth unemployment rate if the Roma youth unemployment rate is to fall to 15 per cent by 2015.

Gender

Figure 1-30 and Figure 1-31 report unemployment rates for men and women. Throughout the region and for both Roma and the majority, women have higher unemployment rates than men. This in part reflects the broad definition of unemployment: persons who would normally be defined as being outside the labour market because they are not actively seeking work are here included amongst the unemployed. Since women (like young people) generally have lower labour force participation rates than men (particularly prime working-age men), a broad definition of unemployment will naturally produce higher unemployment rates for women. Women may also be less likely to define their social status in terms of labour market outcomes, and so will be less likely to see themselves as 'unemployed' as such.[54]

[53] O'Higgins (2003, 2004) provides a description and some discussion of youth unemployment in transition countries as a whole. O'Higgins (2001) discusses in more detail why young people face higher unemployment rates than other age groups.

[54] The unemployment rates suggest a more mixed picture, although even these indicate that women generally have higher unemployment rates than men in Southeast Europe. Clearly, the extent to which the lower labour market attachment view holds will vary across countries and age groups.

The data in these figures underscore the double disadvantages facing Roma women. Beyond the consistently higher unemployment rates for women, there does not seem to be a strict pattern in the extent of the relative disadvantage facing Roma women. In Serbia for example, the data indicate that the disadvantages facing women are greater for Roma than for women from majority communities. In nearby Kosovo, the situation is reversed. In Bulgaria and Romania, the relative disadvantage of women is smaller than in other countries, albeit still fairly pronounced.

The survey data show that while labour market trends among majority communities in many Southeast European countries are in line with the Lisbon target employment rates of 70 per cent overall and 60 per cent for women, for the Roma these targets are very distant, particularly for women. In the majority of these countries, employment rates for Roma women are below 20 per cent (and below 50 per cent for men). Figure 1-32 and Figure 1-33 report employment rates for working-age men and women separately by country.

The Decade of Roma Inclusion national action plans focus on two broad areas in promoting employment for Roma: training courses for skills upgrading, and different forms of active labour market policies. However, few of these measures reflect the gender differences apparent in labour market trends. As such, they should be complemented by concrete, gender-sensitive measures. The Lisbon Agenda is another driving force for improving workplace opportunities for Roma, and especially Roma women. Unfortunately, the Decade action plans are often weak in terms of concrete mechanisms for better cooperation with employers, in terms of integrating Roma into the workforce. Encouraging public dialogue on Roma employment, as planned in the Bulgarian national action plan, is particularly important in this respect.

FIGURE 1 – 30

Unemployment rates for Roma by sex

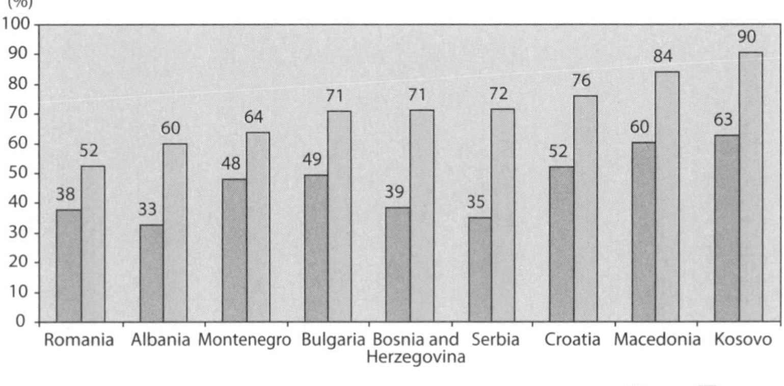

FIGURE 1 – 31

Unemployment rates for the majority by sex

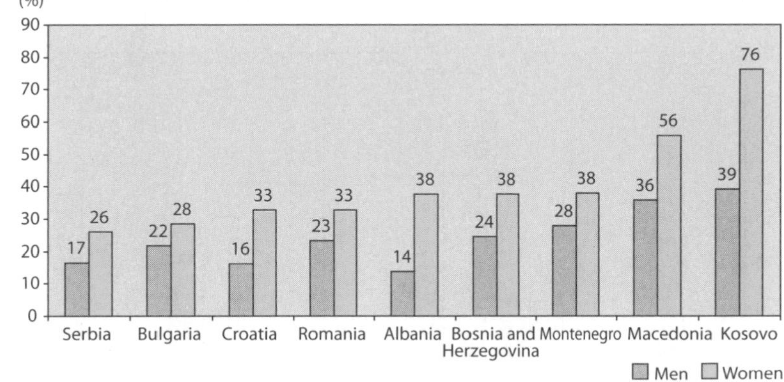

FIGURE 1 – 32

Employment rates for Roma by sex

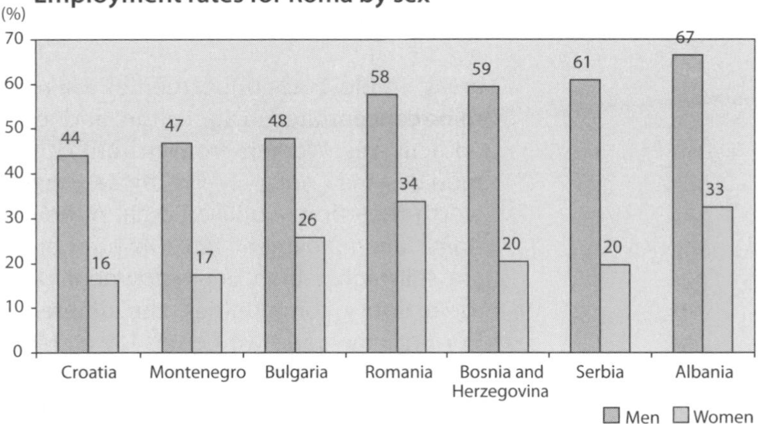

Locational effects

Figure 1-34 reports separate unemployment rates for urban and rural areas (and by ethnicity and sex) for the region as a whole. The results are striking. Whereas unemployment rates for Roma living in urban areas are higher for both men and women, for workers from majority communities the opposite is true. Consequently, differences in unemployment rates between Roma and majority workers are much smaller in rural than in urban areas. The implication is that the lack of rural employment opportunities is spread more evenly, or that Roma take up low-paid jobs in agriculture, which workers from majority communities are reluctant to take up, or both.

These data also indirectly point to labour market stratification by ethnicity. In rural

FIGURE 1 – 33

Employment rates for the majority by sex

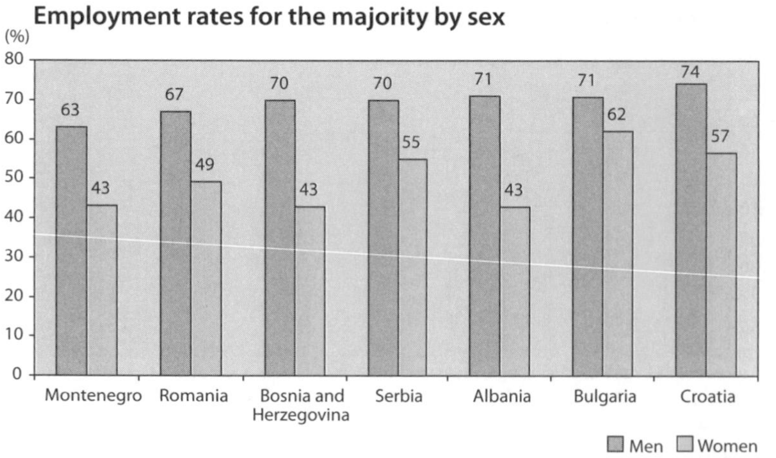

FIGURE 1 – 34

Unemployment rates by sex and location (urban and rural)

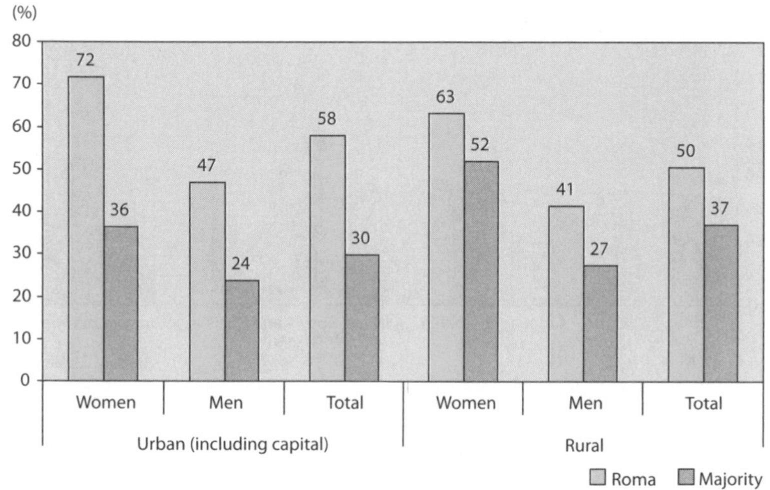

areas, employment opportunities will tend to be concentrated in agriculture and related activities. Workers from majority communities may not perceive those jobs as worth the effort – unlike Roma. Although Roma unemployment rates in rural areas are still higher than unemployment rates for majority communities, the difference (for both men and women) is lower. More attractive urban employment opportunities may therefore be better utilized by workers from majority communities. This 'crowding out' effect may contribute to this urban-rural unemployment gap between workers from Roma and majority communities. Seasonality may also contribute: the field-work of the survey was conducted in September-October 2004, when disproportionately large numbers of Roma workers were engaged in seasonal harvesting activities.

For Roma women, differences between unemployment rates in rural and urban settings are particularly pronounced. In urban areas, the unemployment rate for Roma women is twice that of the majority women surveyed (72 per cent as opposed to 36 per cent), while in rural areas, this difference is much smaller (63 per cent as against 52 per cent). These rates may also reflect the greater prevalence of traditional gender roles (work at home rather than on the labour market) amongst Roma in the countryside.

Unemployment rates can also be influenced by the degree of residential segregation or integration. The survey approached this issue by posing questions about the ethnic mix of the respondents' settlement, village, town, city or immediate neighbourhood. The results did not differ greatly according to the extent of residential segregation. Figure 1-35 reports unemployment rates according to the ethnic mix of the neighbourhood (as defined in terms of the relevance of ethnicity for the respondents' employment prospects).

The survey data suggest that unemployment rates are lower in mixed, well-integrated neighbourhoods. This is true for Roma, but, more surprisingly, also for majority communities. This seems to be a clear argument supporting the hypothesis that if properly addressed, diversity can be a source of development opportunities. Mixed communities with their diversity of lifestyles and patterns may generate broader demand for diverse goods and services, creating broader employment opportunities.[55] In the case of Roma, it supports the view that Roma have traditionally provided important complementary services to rural economies in the region, and continue to do so. If correct, this argument is an additional explanation for the differences between rural and urban unemployment rates for workers from Roma and majority communities.

Education

Weak education backgrounds are often cited as a key contributing factor to the high levels of Roma unemployment. Figure 1-36 reports unemployment rates by education

[55] Further research is needed to develop this argument and find statistically significant correlations between diversity and development opportunities.

levels for workers from Roma and majority communities. Not surprisingly, unemployment rates fall with education levels. What is possibly less obvious, but of great significance here, is the fact that the relative labour market advantage accruing to those with higher levels of education is much less pronounced for workers from Roma communities than from majority communities.

At very low levels of education, the unemployment rates amongst the majority population are actually higher than for Roma. This may reflect the fact that Roma unemployment tends to be long-term. Ineligible for unemployment benefits, they are more involved in informal-sector activities and are therefore not counted as unemployed. Unlike their Roma counterparts, uneducated workers from majority communities may still have access to unemployment benefits, reducing the pressure to seek income generation opportunities in the informal sector. At secondary and especially tertiary levels of education, however, unemployment rates are much higher for Roma than for workers from majority communities. For example, Roma workers with tertiary education report unemployment rates that are double those for workers from majority communities (30 per cent as opposed to 14 per cent).[56] This is consistent with the results of recent research showing that skilled Roma workers seldom get 'mainstream' jobs; it seems that Roma can only enter a certain segment of the labour market – as assistant teachers, for example (Hyde, 2006).

The difficulties skilled Roma workers face in career advancement weaken incentives to pursue higher education and skills development, as is discussed below. This argument is supported by a simulation which found that, if the education level of the Roma sample were to be raised to that of majority respondents, the unweighted average unemployment rates for Roma would fall from 56 per cent to only 52 per cent. This would still leave a gap between the unemployment rates for workers from Roma and majority communities of 19 percentage points.[57] These results suggest that education levels alone are not sufficient to explain the difference in employment opportunities between Roma respondents and respondents from majority communities.

The impact of education on the probability of finding employment was estimated for the entire regional sample using a simple probit model. Table A13 in the Annex reports the results of estimating the effects of education on the probability of finding employment separately for respondents from majority and Roma communities, as well as for men and women.[58] The results support the argument that Roma gain much less in terms of employment opportunities from improving their level of education than do workers from majority communities. Improvement in employment chances associated with increasing one's education level

Unemployment rates are lower in mixed, well-integrated neighbourhoods

FIGURE 1 – 35

Unemployment and ethnicity

Unemployment rates for Roma and the majority by ethnic mix of the neighbourhood

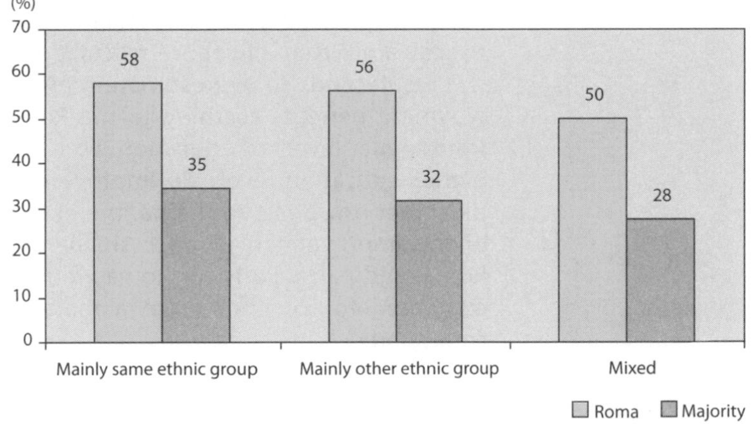

FIGURE 1 – 36

Unemployment and education

Unemployment rates by level of education

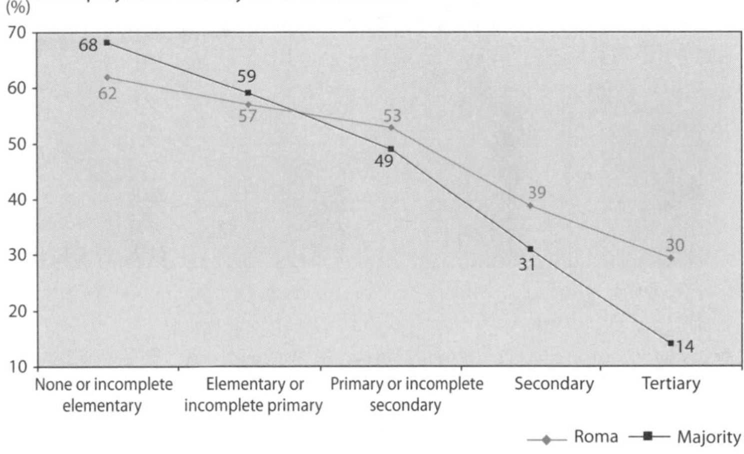

56 The absolute numbers of Roma tertiary graduates is very low, however, so the data should be viewed with caution.

57 The simulation was based on the estimates of the effects of education on employment probabilities reported in Table A13 in the Annex.

58 The probit model also includes country fixed effects, age and age-squared.

The extent to which higher education levels do improve employment prospects is much smaller for Roma, and particularly for Roma women

are larger (and more often statistically significant) for workers from majority communities than for Roma.

In order to understand the implications of these results, Figure 1-37 reports the estimated effect of education in terms of increased chances of finding work arising from staying in school longer[59] for a hypothetical person with no more than incomplete primary education. Thus, for example, a young male from a majority community will increase his employment chances from 56 per cent to 65 per cent by completing primary education, from 65 per cent to 72 per cent by attaining a secondary education, and from 72 per cent to 85 per cent by attending tertiary education. The corresponding figures for a male Roma are 53 per cent to 55 per cent, 55 per cent to 67 per cent and 67 per cent to 78 per cent. Since no account is taken of statistical significance in these calculations, this result tends to overestimate the employment benefits accruing to the Roma from higher levels of education. So while higher education levels do improve employment prospects for Roma, the extent of this improvement is much smaller for Roma, and particularly for Roma women, compared to someone from a majority community.

FIGURE 1 – 37

Education and the probability of employment
Expected probabilities of employment for Roma and majority men and women with each level of education

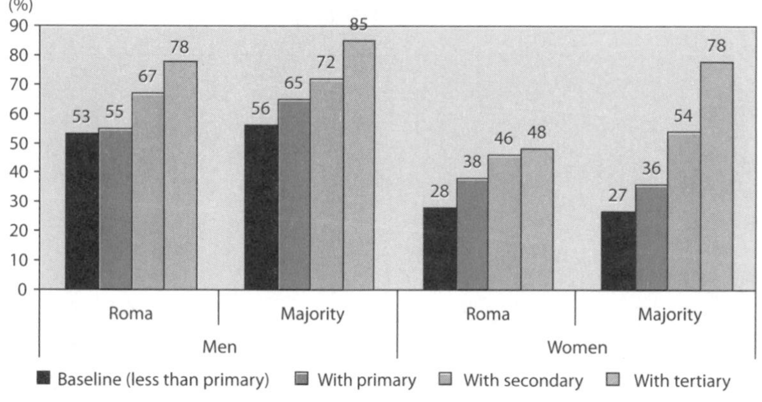

Once employment has been secured, education also has a differential impact on the quality of the employment and income levels. As shown in Figure 1-38, education substantially increases the proportion of both majority community and Roma workers that find skilled employment. However, there are notable differences between the two groups in this respect. Greater proportions of workers from majority communities are involved in skilled labour irrespective of their level of education. While attaining elementary education substantially increases the proportion of workers from majority communities involved in skilled employment, it has no effect on the proportion of Roma that obtain skilled employment. Roma workers' employment prospects increase substantially only after secondary level education is attained. Such factors as a lack of information among Roma of employment opportunities, or a lack of physical access to suitable positions due to the concentration of Roma in segregated areas, solidarity among majority communities, and discrimination against Roma workers could account for these differences.

Barriers to employment are also reflected in the fact that education for Roma does not lead to wages equivalent to those of similarly educated workers from majority communities. Although a returns-to-education estimation[60] shows that, for Roma workers, increases in each level of education (with the exception of tertiary education in the case of women) results in significant wage gains, these are from much lower levels and as such continue to leave large earnings gaps (see Tables A14 and A15 in the Annex). Indeed, in most cases education, even at a tertiary level, does not even bring Roma wages in line with regional averages for unskilled workers from majority communities. For women, the results are particularly worrying. On average, a Roma woman in Albania earns 36 per cent of the average wage of an Albanian female survey respondent.

So while education is an important determinant of labour market success, its importance is less for Roma workers than it

59 On the basis of the estimated coefficients, whether statistically significant or not. The baseline used is the gender- and ethnic-specific regional employment 'rate' for labour market participants (in other words one minus the unemployment rate) with no more than incomplete primary education.

60 A basic Mincerian regression in which the natural log of wages was regressed against age, age-squared and education level. The model was estimated separately for men and women and for each of the groups.

is for workers from majority communities. Furthermore, education does little to compensate for initial labour market disadvantages. Discrimination by employers may account for some of these differences: 9 per cent of Roma respondents reported having (at some point) competed for a job with a person from a majority community who had the same (or fewer skills) but who nonetheless obtained the position. By contrast, just 4 per cent of majority respondents reported having such an experience.[61] Moreover, as shown in Figure 1-39, perceptions of such discrimination become more acutely felt as education levels increase – particularly among Roma. If correct, this perception suggests that at least some employers may believe that Roma should be engaged in low-skilled employment or occupy such `Roma-oriented´ labour market segments as Roma assistant teachers, rather than seeking to perform 'mainstream' jobs (which are needed for non-Roma).

The above-mentioned simulation of education and wages suggests that obtaining appropriate employment generates wage gains for Roma that are similar to or even higher than those of majority respondents (see Table A14 in the Annex). Once they are employed, on more equal terms, Roma can start to make up the lost ground. This underscores the importance of education and anti-discrimination work, but also of vocational training, welfare-to-work, job subsidies, and comprehensive active labour market policies. In combination with anti-discrimination public awareness campaigns (which are gaining momentum in the region), such an approach can launch a virtuous circle of inclusion. As Roma enter the labour market and prove their competitiveness, employers will be more willing to hire them, if only to preclude charges of discrimination.

Getting to this stage is the hard part, underscoring the importance of 'work first' and welfare-to-work principles. Working directly with companies to integrate Roma into the workplace and promoting positive examples can be extremely beneficial in this respect.[62] This business side has not yet been effectively addressed, either in the Decade of Roma Inclusion national action plans

FIGURE 1 – 38

Education and type of employment

Percentage of Roma and the majority (over 16 years of age) with each level of education employed in a skilled profession

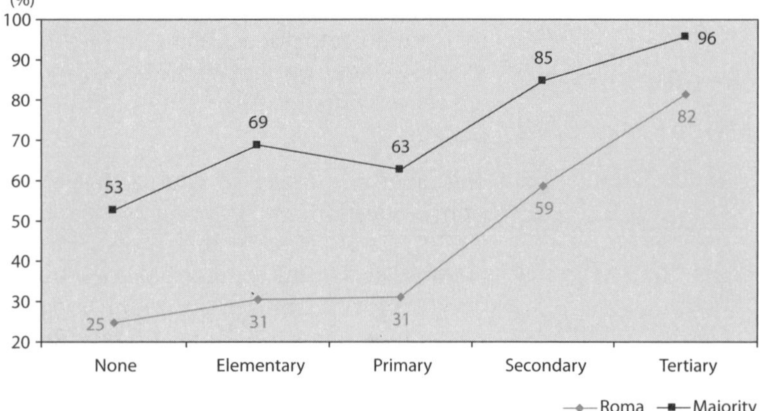

FIGURE 1 – 39

Perceptions of discrimination

Percentage of respondents who said that a position they applied for was given to a less-skilled member of the majority

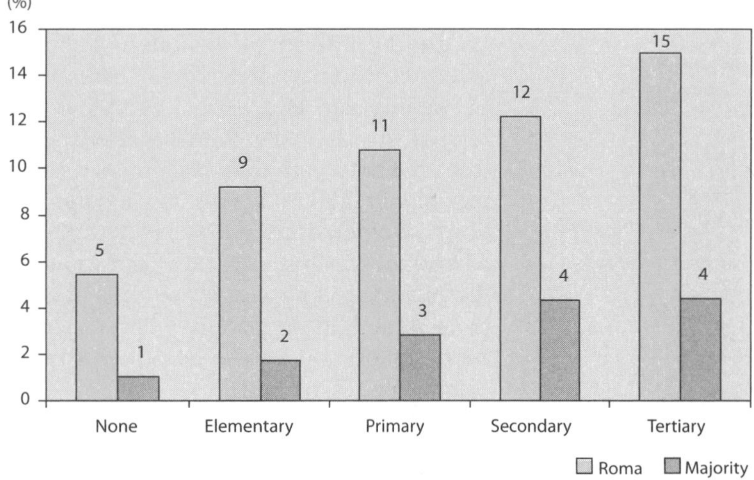

[61] Recent research on discrimination against Roma in the labour market carried out by the ERRC in the period May-September 2005 found that two out of every three working-age Roma are likely to experience employment discrimination. Of those, 49 per cent were directly told by the employer that they will not be employed because they are Roma (Hyde, 2006). The differences in registered levels of labour market discrimination in both surveys may be due to various factors. One is the fact that the ERRC survey was explicitly focused on issues of discrimination (unlike UNDP surveys, which monitor discrimination practices in the broader socio-economic context). The scope of countries is also different (the ERRC survey was carried out in Bulgaria, the Czech Republic, Hungary, Romania and Slovakia).

[62] For a more thorough discussion of these issues see UNDP (2005b) *Employing the Roma: Insights from Business.* UNDP Regional Bureau for Europe and the CIS.

Creating a platform for companies to discuss Roma employment should become a priority if the governments are serious about their commitments to the Decade of Roma Inclusion

or in other policy frameworks. If companies are not willing to provide employment opportunities and on-the-job training, active labour market policy measures in this area will not be sustainable. Creating a platform for companies to discuss Roma employment should become a priority if the governments are serious about their commitments to the Decade.

This does not mean of course that gains from education will completely eliminate the effects of factors that depress incomes for unskilled Roma workers. While education improves earnings in roughly equal percentage terms for Roma and non-Roma workers, these increases are not sufficient to fully compensate for income gaps, particularly for Roma workers with low levels of education.

Conclusions from Chapter 1.4

The data suggest that there are large intra-group differences in unemployment levels. For Roma respondents, differences between youth and adult unemployment rates are much smaller than for respondents from majority communities, while women face higher unemployment rates than men. Roma women face particularly high unemployment rates, reflecting the multiple disadvantages of being born Roma and female. Active labour market policies need to be designed and implemented with these disadvantages in mind.

The survey data suggest some interesting patterns in terms of the spatial distribution of unemployment. Whereas for Roma unemployment rates are higher in urban areas, majority respondents living in rural areas face higher unemployment rates. Differences in unemployment rates between workers from Roma and majority communities are therefore much lower in rural areas than they are in cities and towns. The implication is that the risks of unemployment are spread more evenly across the different communities in rural areas, and that the greater prevalence of traditional gender roles amongst Roma in the countryside may help reduce female unemployment rates in rural areas. Unemployment rates are also lowest in mixed neighbourhoods, which is true for Roma, but, much more surprisingly, also for workers from majority communities.

Weak educational backgrounds definitely contribute to Roma unemployment. However, the labour market advantages accruing to those with higher levels of education are much less pronounced for Roma respondents than for respondents from majority communities. Although weak educational backgrounds contribute to poor Roma labour market outcomes, they are not sufficient to explain the difference in employment opportunities between Roma and majority workers. Other factors, such as discrimination and/or the concentration of Roma in depressed areas with few employment possibilities, appear to be playing a major role in Roma labour market disadvantages. Simply increasing Roma educational status is not enough to improve employment prospects; such measures should be matched by national strategies on employment, anti-discrimination campaigns seeking to overcome existing social prejudices and dialogue with employers, to provide positive examples of Roma professional advancement.

Roma tend to be concentrated in low-skilled, low-quality forms of employment. Here too, it would appear that education is not sufficient by itself to level the playing field. Although the income gains from education are similar in percentage terms for Roma and non-Roma, this is not sufficient to compensate for vastly different starting points. Even where the gains from education appear to be relatively high (such as for university educated Roma men), they are still less than the disadvantages to be made up, which may be related both to discrimination and quality of education (not necessarily associated with the level attained). On the other hand, the data indicate that significant income gains do accrue to education for Roma, in the form of better employment prospects and higher labour incomes.

CHAPTER 1.5

Health and security

Summary

'Vulnerability' is a rather fluid and potentially all-inclusive concept. In the previous chapters, vulnerability was approached sectorally, in terms of poverty, employment, and education. But human security (understood as the absence of, or protection against, such vulnerability) can also be defined to include health status and nutrition security, community relations, access to social services and threat perception.[63]

This chapter analyses the health and nutrition conditions, different threat perceptions and housing situation of Roma and majority communities. Many Roma survey respondents stated that their health status had deteriorated over the past year. Some important gender differences exist in terms of incidence of chronic illnesses, with more women affected by chronic illnesses among both groups. In addition, Roma lack access to a family doctor (general practitioner) and often cannot afford to buy medicines that are prescribed. The lack of proper identity and health documents is a particularly pronounced barrier for Roma, too. Roma are much more likely than majority community respondents to go to bed hungry because they cannot afford food. Particularly Roma children are affected by these nutrition risks. Insufficient vaccination coverage—reflecting inadequate information or inappropriate medical identification—is also a major determinant of vulnerability, particularly for Roma children.

With regard to housing, a large percentage of Roma live in dilapidated houses or shacks with substandard sanitation infrastructure. Roma households are much less likely than majority households to have access to toilets or piped water inside the house or yard. They possess fewer basic household items, such as a bed for each household member, furniture or major household appliances. Lack of access to information and communications technology is also manifested in the Roma situation. Roma households use primarily wood for cooking, while majority households use electricity.

The most common threat reported by both Roma and majority respondents lies in the perceived 'lack of sufficient incomes'. However, there are important differences with regard to other threats. While hunger, poor sanitation, and inadequate housing are reported by large proportions of Roma respondents to be the greatest threats to their households, these do not appear to be major concerns for majority respondents, who are more concerned with issues such as crime and corruption. Roma households also feel strong threats of diseases caused by poor sanitation. When asked who would be the best placed to handle such threats to personal security as low incomes, hunger, and inadequate housing, both groups responded that the extended family—rather than central or local government bodies—is best placed to manage these threats.

Health and nutrition

The lack of proper identity and health documents is a particularly pronounced barrier for Roma to get access to quality health care

Respondents from the two groups reported moderate deterioration in their health status during the past year. The average score on the five-step scale ('5' meaning 'much worse' and '1' meaning 'much better') was 2.9 for majority and 3.0 for Roma respondents. However, this subjective assessment differs across age groups, with younger respondents assessing much better their health status today than older respondents. The most frequent diseases encountered during the last year were colds and influenza (reported by 42 per cent of majority respondents and 44 per cent of Roma respondents). As a result, on average majority respondents lost 14 days of normal activity as a result of illness, while a Roma respondent lost 17 days. Health issues for the Roma may therefore be more serious, and/or access to treatment more difficult.

The survey data on health status show important gender disparities. As Table 1-8

[63] The survey did not ask questions related to violence, though it is confirmed that violence, including inter-personal violence, is a major health threat that particularly affects women.

Table 1-8

Gender aspects of health status

	Majority		Roma	
	Male	Female	Male	Female
Average self-assessment of health improvement/deterioration in the last year, (with '5' representing 'much worse' and '1' meaning 'much better')	2.8	2.9	2.9	3.0
Incidence of chronic illnesses (percentage of those who reported having chronic illness)	17	22	17	22
Average number of days of normal activity lost as a result of illness in the past 12 months	13.9	13.4	16.3	18.0

FIGURE 1 – 40

Share of households that cannot afford prescribed medicine

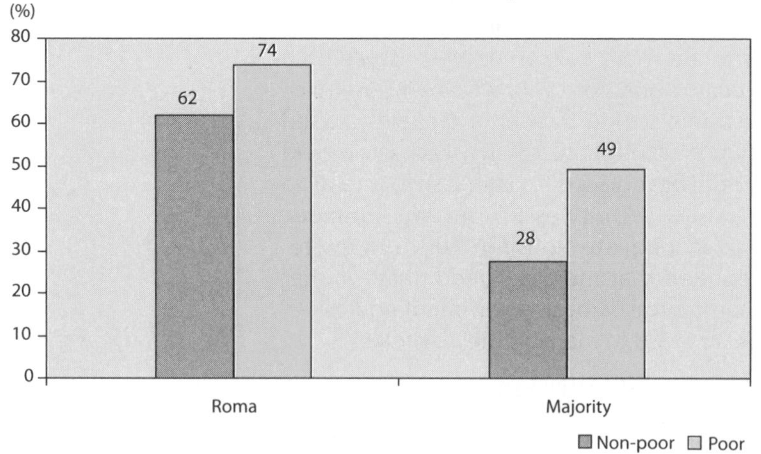

shows, for both groups women report only slightly worse health during the last year than men. Differences in incidence of chronic illnesses are more pronounced, however. What is most surprising, however, is the average number of days of normal activity lost as a result of illness: women from majority communities report fewer days lost than men, despite the fact that women reported less favourable health status. This suggests that women are either more likely to report their illness to be 'chronic', are less likely to let illness affect their everyday activities, or are engaged in everyday activities that are less disrupted by illness.[64] Although most countries plan to carry out specialised health surveys and research within the context of the Decade of Roma Inclusion national action plans, gender-sensitive perspectives on health problems among the Roma seem to be only rarely addressed.

Days lost due to illness correlate with the way the illness was treated. Of those who had been sick, 66 per cent of majority respondents consulted a doctor, while only 57 per cent of Roma respondents did so. The survey data indicate that these differences reflect reduced access to health services:[65] fewer Roma than majority households have a family doctor (52 per cent versus 63 per cent). The Decade national action plans focus particularly on improving access to health services. Different types of assistance is envisaged, ranging from opening health centres in predominantly Roma areas to awareness campaigns among Roma on their health status, and offering trainings for medical personnel. Such holistic approaches are important, as improving access to health services often needs to be accompanied by better understanding of their use by Roma households.

Data suggest that access to health care is not determined by physical remoteness. By contrast, inadequate incomes seem to be a much more important barrier, particularly for Roma. Twenty-nine per cent of majority households reported that in the past 12 months there were periods when they could not afford purchasing prescribed medicines – compared to 66 per cent for Roma! These disparities are even more pronounced in terms of intra-group differences: over 70 per cent of poor Roma households cannot afford to buy prescribed medicines (see Figure 1-40). The differences between poor and non-poor Roma households are much smaller than the intra-group disparity for majority households. Some 62 per cent of non-poor Roma households cannot afford to buy prescription medications, as even most non-poor Roma households have low incomes (although they are above the poverty threshold) as the quintile distribution showed in Chapter 1.2.

Lack of proper identity documents (health insurance cards) is also a problem for Roma

64 Although similar numbers of men and women reported working in the surveyed month, only 15 per cent of Roma and 26 per cent of majority working women respondents (compared to 35 per cent of Roma, and 58 per cent of majority working men respondents) reported being involved in regular work (either part- or full-time).

65 Given the multidimensionality of questions of access to health services (which includes such issues as access to emergency medical care, quality of health care establishments, etc.), 'having a family doctor' (or in some countries – a personal doctor) is used as a proxy indicator.

respondents, 8 per cent of whom reported that they had been denied medical service because of lack of proper documents. Only 3 per cent of majority respondents reported such instances. Registration and documentation issues, as a major problem encountered by the Roma in terms of access to health care, are addressed in most countries' Decade action plans.

The data also indicate that health status is directly related to nutrition, which in turn reflects expenditure and income levels (i.e., poverty). Reported differences in nutrition security are much more pronounced than differences in health status. As was shown in Table 1-3 in Chapter 1.2, Roma household expenditures on food are much lower than in majority households. This is one of the major causes of nutrition vulnerability reflected in Figure 1-41. Twenty-eight per cent of Roma households reported not having enough to eat four or more times during the month preceding the survey (September 2004). Another 18 per cent reported 2-3 such cases during the month. Only 47 per cent of Roma did not face such problems at all, compared to 93 per cent of majority households. Especially children are vulnerable to nutrition risk. In Roma households, 50 per cent of Roma children face nutrition risks more than twice monthly, compared to only 6 per cent of majority children. Regular check-ups of children's health status to prevent nutrition risks should be among the activities implemented throughout the Decade initiative.

Incomplete vaccination coverage is an important determinant of health vulnerability, particularly for children. The survey data indicate that, whereas 4 per cent of majority children up to age 14 are not vaccinated, this figure rises to 15 per cent for Roma children. As with other health indicators, vaccination coverage is correlated with poverty. Only 73 per cent of poor Roma children received basic vaccinations, compared to 80 per cent of non-poor Roma children. In contrast, vaccination rates among children from majority communities are above 90 per cent for both poor and non-poor households. Inadequate information or appropriate medical identification is often responsible for incomplete vaccination coverage (Figure 1-42). To combat these problems, a wide range of information and immunization campaigns are planned within the Decade of Roma Inclusion to increase childhood vaccinations.

Women, and especially pregnant women, face large health risks in Roma communities. In some Central European countries, questions have been raised about disproportionate numbers of Roma women who have undergone reproduction-related medical procedures (in particular abortion and sterilization, but also abuse and discrimination in maternity wards, denial of access to medical records), coupled with allegations that their informed consent for these procedures had not been obtained (CRR and POLP, 2003).[66] In this survey, 159 out of 5,965 (3 per cent) Roma women

Inadequate information or appropriate medical identification is often responsible for incomplete vaccination coverage

FIGURE 1 – 41

Nutrition vulnerability

Percentage of households in which a member went to bed hungry in the past month because he or she could not afford food

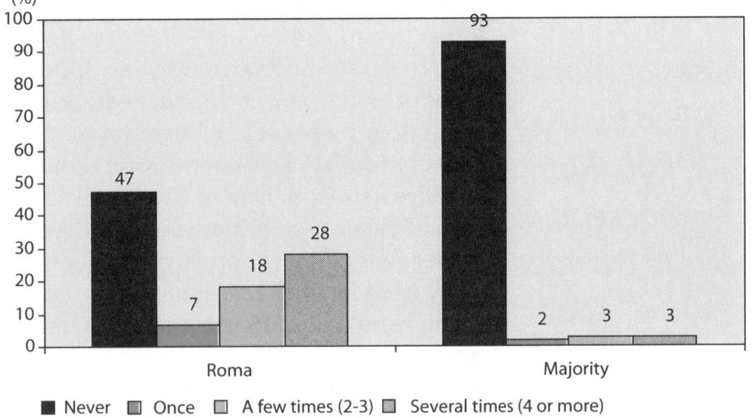

FIGURE 1 – 42

Vaccination coverage of Roma children

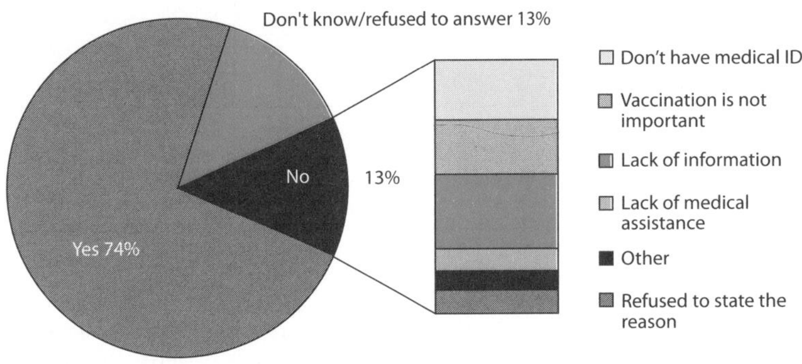

[66] For more information on alleged coercive sterilization of Roma women in Slovakia and the Czech Republic, see *Roma Rights*, No. 3 and 4, 2004, pp. 103-14, available at: http://www.errc.org.

One third of poor Roma households live in dilapidated houses or shacks. Two thirds of poor Roma households live in crowded spaces

confirmed that they had been advised to have an abortion without being informed of possible consequences, compared to 78 such cases (2 per cent) out of 5,164 women from the majority respondents. Looking at the age differences of those women who had been advised to have an abortion without being informed about possible consequences, 29 per cent of Roma and 22 per cent of majority respondents were between 15-29 years, 49 per cent of Roma and 42 per cent of majority were between 30-49 years, 20 per cent of Roma and 36 per cent of majority were over 50 years, and 2 per cent of Roma were below 15 years of age. Over 40 per cent of those Roma women had no or incomplete elementary schooling, or had at best attended some primary school classes, which raises questions about whether better education might have made them less vulnerable to medical malpractice.[67] Here, again, the Decade of Roma Inclusion can provide a platform for a wider information campaign against these practices and to raise awareness among Roma women about their rights.

Housing status

Housing quality, both in terms of dwelling status and available infrastructure, is an important determinant of vulnerability. While just 3 per cent of majority households live in dilapidated houses or shacks, this share reaches 25 per cent for Roma households (Figure 1-43).

FIGURE 1 – 43

Housing quality

Percentage of Roma and the majority living in each type of housing (properties were evaluated by an interviewer)

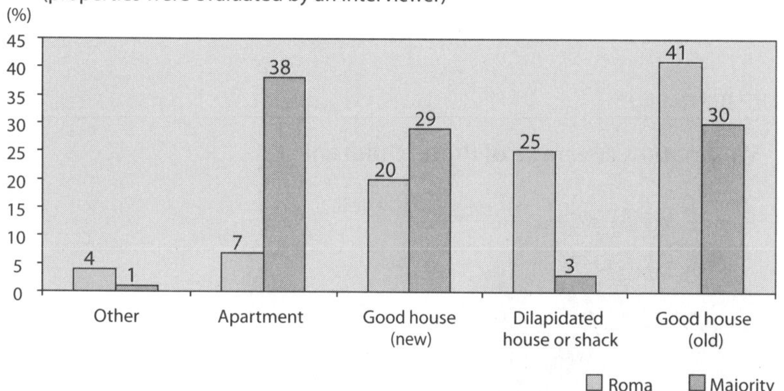

Both groups surveyed reported cleavages in quality of housing between poor and non- poor respondents, with poverty determining to a large extent housing conditions. The percentage of households living in dilapidated houses or slums is not surprisingly higher for poor than for non-poor households. One third of poor Roma households live in dilapidated houses or shacks. Two thirds of poor Roma households live in crowded spaces with less than one square metre per head.[68] This is related to the fact that poor households tend to be larger. Although poor households are definitely worse off, housing conditions for non-poor Roma households are often close to those of poor respondents.

Access to basic infrastructure is an additional useful proxy of household vulnerability, and is included by some Southeast European countries among national sets of MDG indicators.[69] Levels of housing deprivation for Roma households are much higher than for majority households: 61 per cent of Roma households reported the absence of indoor toilets compared to 19 per cent for majority households; similar proportions live without access to a bathroom or sewerage for waste disposal in their homes (Figure 1-44). For poor households, this share rises to 70 per cent for Roma, and 22 per cent for poor majority households.

The proportions of Roma households without access to secure housing (i.e., living in dilapidated houses or shacks), improved water sources (i.e., piped water within the dwelling or garden/yard), or improved sanitation (i.e., toilet or bathroom inside the house), are far higher than the respective proportions of majority households (Figure 1-45). Improving the housing situation is another priority outlined in the Decade of Roma Inclusion's national action plans.

---

67 Due to the small number of observations in this regard, this data should not form the basis for general observations – wider-scale statistical surveys would be needed to adequately measure the existence of this phenomenon.

68 For example, 20 per cent of poor Roma respondents who have three children live in one room; 33 per cent live in two rooms; and only 26 per cent live in three rooms. For those with five children, 33 per cent live in one room, 34 per cent have two rooms, and 16 per cent live in three rooms.

69 See UNDP, *National Millennium Development Goals: A framework for action* (forthcoming June 2006).

In addition to improving the provision and repair of housing and communal service infrastructure, the action plans also focus on legislation to clarify and codify property rights, as well as modernizing urban planning frameworks.

Other deprivation indicators include lack of furniture and other basic household items. Only 47 per cent of Roma have a bed for each household member, compared to 90 per cent for majority households. Only 59 per cent of Roma households have a refrigerator, 53 per cent have an oven, and 31 per cent have a washing machine (see Table A2 in the Annex). Roma households are also worse off in terms of access to information and communications technology, such as Internet connections, computers, fixed line and mobile telephones and radios (Figure 1-46).

Household access to energy (another MDG indicator) provides another example of Roma household's deprivation. Whereas Roma households use primarily wood for cooking, majority households use electricity. However, both groups use primarily wood for heating (see Table 1-9), which is an important non-income poverty indicator.

Threat perceptions

The top five threats reported by Roma and majority respondent facing their households are shown in Figures 1-47 to 1-48. 'Lack of sufficient incomes' was the biggest threat for both groups of households, particularly for large families. For example, 75 per cent of families with five children consider insufficient incomes to be at the highest threat level, while 41 per cent of families with five children reported going to bed hungry more than four times in the last month.

However, there are important differences between groups in terms of threat perception. While hunger, poor sanitation and inadequate housing are seen by many Roma as the greatest threats, these do not appear to be major concerns for majority respondents, who are more concerned with issues such as crime and corruption. Such differences cannot be explained simply by the lower incidence of poverty among majority households compared to Roma, as these differences in threat perception are seen within each equalized expenditure group. It is possible that, for majority

FIGURE 1 – 44

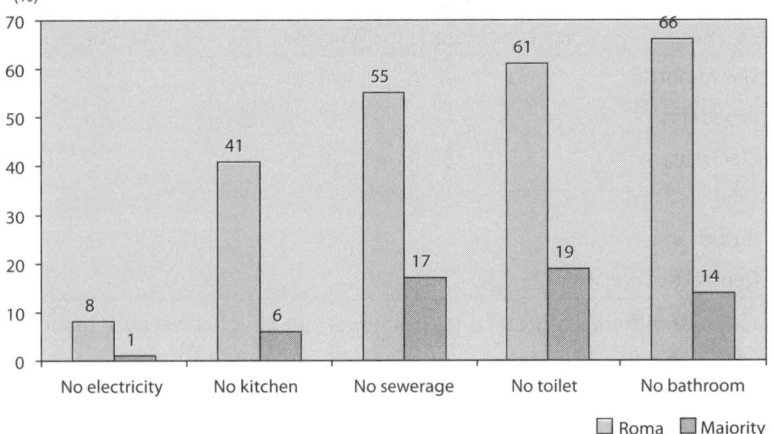

FIGURE 1 – 45

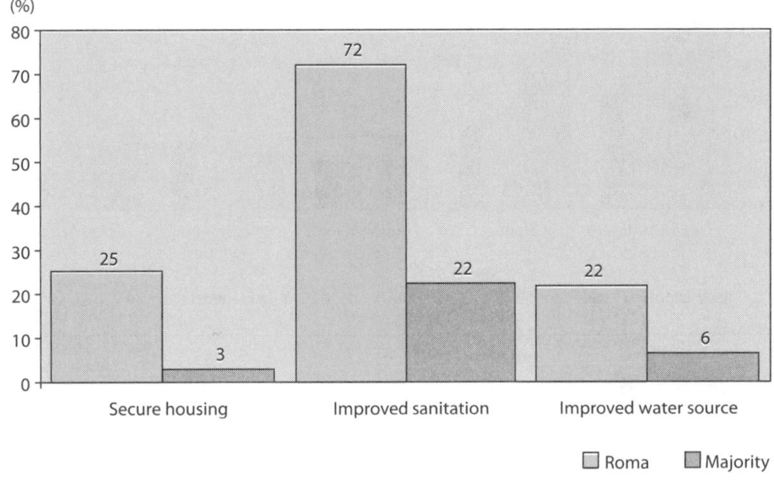

FIGURE 1 – 46

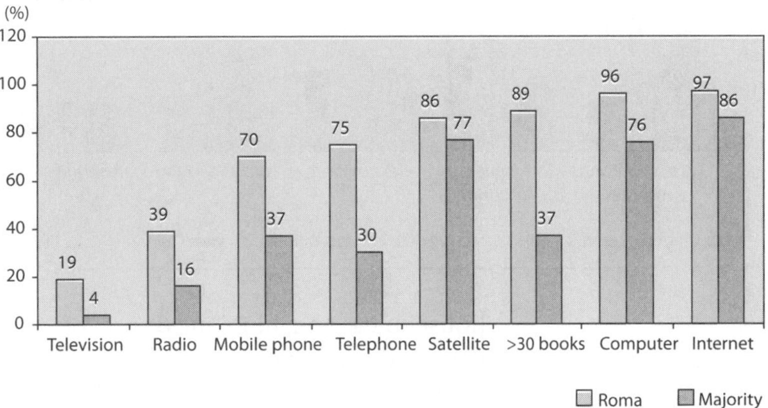

Table 1-9:

Household energy balances
(Share of households using each energy source, in percentage*)

	Cooking		Heating	
Source	Majority	Roma	Majority	Roma
Gas in bottles	35	17	8	2
Piped gas	11	4	8	3
Electricity	58	34	26	15
Coal	3	6	10	15
Wood	33	68	53	83
Central heating			17	1

* The sum for each group does not equal 100 per cent because many households have access to (and use) multiple energy sources.

FIGURE 1 – 47

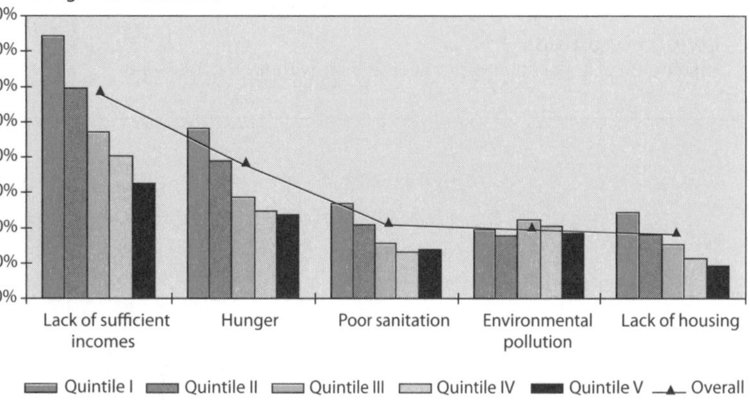

FIGURE 1 – 48

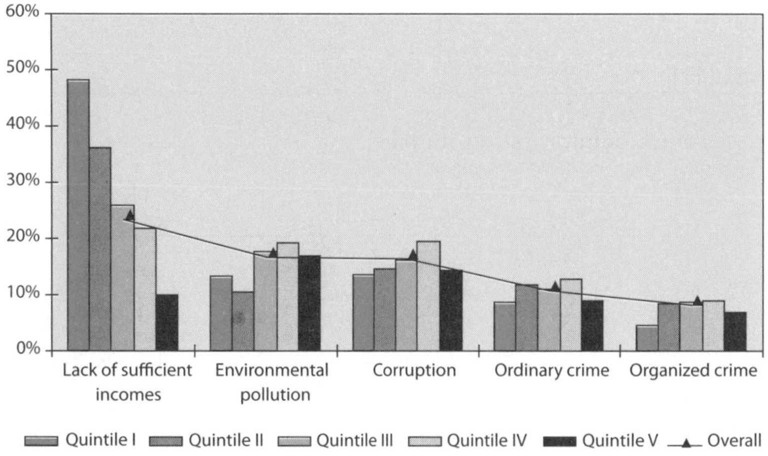

households, the high incidence of perceived threat from 'governance-related' issues like corruption and crime may indicate a higher level of social integration. Or, since they are living in proximity to Roma communities, they may feel more threatened by perceived Roma criminality. For Roma, these data are perhaps evidence of social distance and the separation of Roma and majority communities along ethnic lines: facing marginalization and exclusion, Roma may be less interested in social relations with majority communities, and hence be less exposed to governance-related threats. They might also have more modest expectations vis-à-vis the state, particularly in light of Roma respondents' answers to questions about who is best placed to handle the threats.

As would be expected, among those households with lower expenditures, the 'lack of sufficient incomes' is most commonly seen as the primary threat. A similar relationship is seen between poverty and the numbers of Roma reporting 'hunger', 'poor sanitation', and the 'lack of housing' as the primary threats to their households. However, among both Roma and the majority households, pollution is perceived to be the biggest threat among respondents of middle rather than lower expenditure levels. Similarly, high expenditure majority household members are more likely to report corruption as the major threat to their household than those with lower expenditure levels, possibly because the higher expenditures of these individuals make them more likely to encounter corruption.

Threats associated with sanitation-related diseases are also linked to poverty. As the data in Figure 1-49 show, Roma feel most exposed to this threat. Whereas only 7 per cent of majority respondents believe that diseases caused by poor sanitation represent the most serious threat to their households, 21 per cent of Roma respondents considered this to be the most serious threat.

When asked who is best placed to manage the response to these threats, respondents' answers varied according to the threat in question (see Figure 1-50). Across both groups, for respondents who reported low incomes, hunger or inadequate housing to be the greatest threats to their households, the greatest proportion believed their family would be best placed to manage these threats. Of those who emphasized corruption or poor sanitation as the greatest threats, the highest proportion responded that the police, NGOs, or local government were best placed to tackle them. For those who view pollution as the worst threat to their households, the preferred response agent varied across groups. The highest percentage of Roma suggested local government, while the largest numbers of majority respondents indicated that NGOs would be best placed to respond.[70] The real message here is the similarity in profiles of actors envisaged as capable of dealing with various threats between the two groups. Worth noting is also the importance of 'family-focused' strategies of poverty alleviation among both groups as well as the negligible role given to central government in this regard.

FIGURE 1 – 49

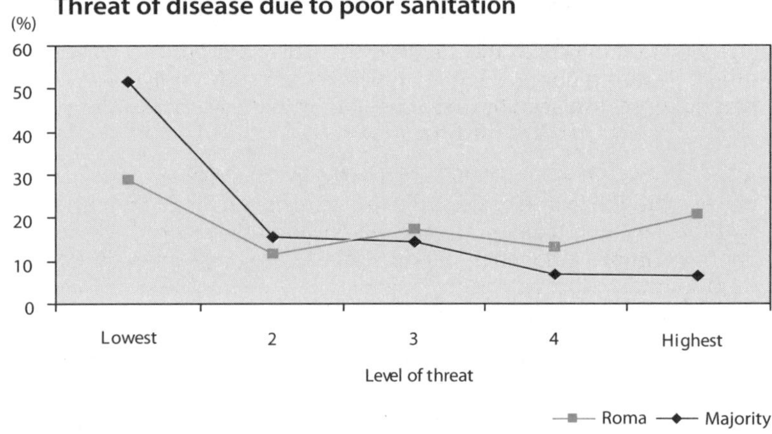

FIGURE 1 – 50

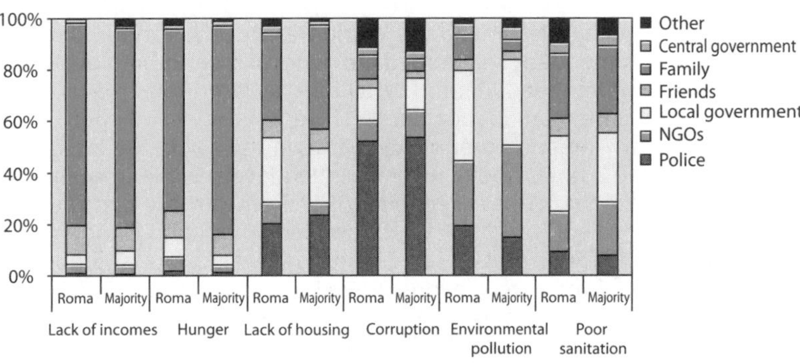

Conclusions from Chapter 1.5

Respondents from both Roma and majority households report moderate deterioration in their health status during the last year, with respondents above 50 years complaining more often than the younger generation of worsened health status. The most frequent afflictions across all groups have been colds and influenza. However, these data should be treated with caution, as they are based on respondents' subjective assessments rather than on professional evaluations. (Medical professionals with field experience treating Roma patients often note that Roma understate the gravity of their health problems.) Compared to majority respondents, a higher percentage of Roma respondents suffer from (i) digestive-system diseases, (ii) respiratory-system infections and dis-

Box 11: National MDG targets, vulnerable groups and Roma households' access to improved sanitation

MDG 7 addresses the need for improvements in water and communal service infrastructure. The share of households with access to improved sanitation facilities can be an indicator of progress in this respect.

The national MDG report for **Montenegro** calls for universal access to improved sanitation by 2015. This constitutes a 0.15 annual increase over the 98.5 per cent baseline rate in 2005. Moving at this pace, Roma would not achieve universal access to improved sanitation until 2457. If Roma in Montenegro are to obtain 100 per cent access to improved sanitation by 2015, the growth in the share of Roma households with access to improved sanitation would need to be over 41 times higher than the pace of its increase for the country as a whole.

The national MDG report in **Serbia** also called for universal access to improved sanitation by 2015. This implies annual improvements in access of 0.78 percentage points, relative to the 88.3 per cent rate reported in 2000. Moving at this pace, Roma would not achieve universal access to improved sanitation until 2068. If Roma in Serbia are to obtain 100 per cent access to improved sanitation by 2015, the growth in the share of Roma households with access to improved sanitation would need to be six times higher than the pace of its increase for the country as a whole.

[70] This may indicate relatively low levels of trust by Roma in NGOs—an observation made also in UNDP, 2002.

Box 12: Displaced Roma in Mitrovica: the double vulnerable caught in no-man's land

The violent conflicts in the 1990s in the Balkans produced waves of ethnic cleansing unprecedented in size since World War II. Roma were among those displaced by these conflicts, with the Kosovska Mitrovica example being perhaps the best known.

After the Kosovo war in 1999, Roma living in the southern part of the city of Mitrovica (south of the Ibar river) were driven out of their homes by Albanians in retaliation for alleged collaboration with the Serbian enemy. Without a nominal "nation-state" to gravitate towards, Roma from southern Mitrovica faced the choice of interminable stays in refugee camps or migrating to other Roma ghettoes.

To avoid a major humanitarian disaster, the UN Mission in Kosovo (UNMIK) that took over administration of the province after the NATO invasion set up three refugee camps in the northern part of Mitrovica, on lands that had been part of the Trepca mining and metallurgical complex. Soon after the Roma moved in, the United Nations realized that the camps had been established on severely contaminated land. While originally envisaged as temporary settlements to house the Roma for a short time before their return to their homes could be guaranteed, these camps remain in place seven years later.

Several reports by UNMIK and the World Health Organization dating to 2000 recommended their immediate removal, but nothing decisive was done. By October 2004, the WHO had declared the area in and around the camps uninhabitable. WHO reports revealed that contamination by lead and other heavy metals in the soil in the Zitkovac camp was 100.5 times above recommended levels, while in the Cesmin Lug camp, the levels exceeded by 359.5 times those considered safe for human health. In 2004, WHO sampled 58 children living in the IDP camps, and found that 34 had blood lead levels above acceptable limits. Twelve of the Roma children were found to have exceptionally high levels; six of these may have fallen within the range described by the United States Agency for Toxic Substances and Disease Registry as constituting a medical emergency (=>70μg/dl). By October 2004, the WHO recommended the immediate removal from the camps of children and pregnant women, calling the case of the Roma 'urgent'.

On 19 October 2005, the Society for Threatened Peoples of Goettingen, Germany, brought Dr. Klaus-Dietrich Runow to Kosovo to test for toxic heavy metals in these camps. Hair samples were collected from 48 children between the ages of 1-15. The readings ranged from 20 to 1200 μg/g; 'normal' readings would be in the range of 3-15. Despite this, the Roma still have not been moved to a safe location. Roma rights groups claim that as many as 31 Roma have been killed by diseases associated with lead poisoning. In February 2006, the European Roma Rights Centre filed a case with the European Court of Human Rights in Strasbourg on behalf of 184 Roma residents of camps against UNMIK as the acting government in Kosovo failing to prevent the humanitarian disaster.

This case illustrates the complexity of the problems displaced Roma are facing. UNMIK officials may or may not have deliberately neglected the health warnings about lead levels in the Mitrovica camps. It is clear, however, that the chronic lack of employment and income generation possibilities for inhabitants of the Mitrovica camps create incentives to engage in illegal lead trading. The Roma community's return to its previous neighbourhood south of the Ibar river, or its relocation to new settlements, would require the endorsement of the Albanian community that drove the Roma out of their Mitrovica homes six years ago, or of communities elsewhere in the event of resettlement. Easy solutions to the Mitrovica problem, and to the challenges facing displaced Roma in other parts of the Balkans, often do not exist.

eases, and (iii) skin infections. Therefore, policies need to be based on estimations from medical professionals – and less so on self-assessment.[71] Specialised research on Roma health status, particularly from a gender perspective, should be carried out, to effectively address the different health needs and problems of Roma men and women. The Decade of Roma Inclusion national action plans contain extensive public awareness raising campaigns, and emphasize improved access to health care and registration documents for Roma, in order to address vaccination and preventive care issues. Further, the countries should regularly monitor children's nutrition risks.

The quality of Roma housing is an especially serious concern. The majority of Roma often lack basic infrastructure, live in extremely small spaces, and are deprived of basic access to sanitation. Housing conditions are correlated with poverty and other deprivation indicators concerning household appliances and energy supply, and show that Roma households are worse off in these areas than majority households. Policies need to focus on changing legislation to clarify and strengthen property rights and land ownership. The provision of social housing as well as the improvement of infrastructure in Roma settlements and access to information about housing opportunities also deserve emphasis.

Both Roma and majority households perceive low incomes as major threats, but believe that the family is best suited to manage this threat. The view that the family (rather than the state) is best able to prevent poverty is accompanied by relatively low trust in government and NGO institutions by Roma households. This suggests that policies concerning employment, education, health and housing issues should have more explicit local and community focus within an area-based development framework actively involving communities in decision-making and implementation.

[71] Danijela Korac-Mandic, MD, Novi Sad Humanitarian Center (NSHC), at the UNDP Serbia Vulnerability Report consultation meeting in Novi Sad, 9 December 2005.

Part II.

Displaced persons

CHAPTER 2.1

Displaced persons in the Balkan context

Refugees and internally displaced persons are among the most tragic victims of the violent dissolution of former Yugoslavia

The 1990s were some of the most dramatic years in the recent history of the Balkans. The countries in the region witnessed the collapse of the Yugoslav Federation, which led to population movements and human suffering unprecedented in the post World War II period. Armed conflicts in Slovenia, Croatia, Bosnia and Herzegovina, and Kosovo, (and the near conflagration in Macedonia in 2001) involved hundreds of thousands of soldiers and produced millions of refugees and internally displaced persons. The conflicts in Bosnia and Herzegovina and Kosovo (and the Macedonian developments of 2001) generated military interventions by the North Atlantic Treaty Organization (NATO), and the Kosovo developments produced a major UN presence.

These events convinced the European Union to deepen and accelerate its integrative processes with the countries of the Western Balkans. The European Commission (EC) extended invitations to begin accession negotiations to Croatia and Macedonia in 2005; the other countries (plus Albania) are covered by the Stabilization and Association Process that was put in place following the Kosovo developments in 1999. All of these countries have declared EU accession to be their overarching foreign policy goal; they would in this respect follow Bulgaria and Romania, whose accession is expected during 2007 or 2008. While integration with the EU imposes many obligations on candidate countries, responsibilities in the area of social inclusion (vis-à-vis the victims of ethnic cleansing and ethnic minorities more broadly) are among the most important.

Where do the displaced come from?

Refugees and internally displaced persons are among the most tragic victims of the violent dissolution of former Yugoslavia. In order to understand the issue of displaced and the challenges they currently face, an overview of the Federation's dissolution is necessary.[72]

Slovenia was the first constituent republic to secede from the Socialist Federal Republic of Yugoslavia (SFRY), after a relatively limited conflict with the Yugoslav army in 1991. The Slovenian parliament's declaration of independence in June 1991 elicited a military response from the Yugoslav People's Army, which was resisted successfully by Slovenian forces. The short duration of hostilities (only 10 days) meant that casualties on both sides were small.

Parallel developments were occurring in neighbouring Croatia, where in March 1991 the so-called Serb Autonomous Region of Krajina announced its secession from Croatia. The Yugoslav People's Army entered Krajina on 28 April 1991 under the pretext of protecting the Serbian majority from Croatian nationalists. This precipitated Croatia's formal declaration of independence in June 1991, led to five years of hostilities in Krajina and Slavonia, mostly between the Croatian army and Serbian paramilitaries. The thousands of Croatians (and others) who fled the Serb-controlled areas of Croatia during 1991-1995 were followed by the displacement of some 200,000 people (mostly Serbs) when the Croatian army in 1995 re-established control over the areas of Krajina and Slavonia that had been taken by Serbian paramilitary forces. Only some 70,600 have since returned (Maksimovic, 2004; Nincic and Vekic, 1995).

In March 1992 the parliament in Bosnia and Herzegovina voted in favour of independence from Yugoslavia. Following the example of Krajina, six municipalities in northeastern Bosnia declared their independence from Bosnia

[72] The dissolution of former Yugoslavia was a complex process involving multiple interests and stakeholders. All those involved had (and often still have) their own rationale for, and interpretation of, what happened, why and where responsibility rests. All this makes a consensual narrative of the recent history extremely difficult. This brief study sketchs the roots of the problems faced by displaced populations, but does not attempt to be comprehensive or to provide more than a general introduction to the issue. No attribution of blame of any sort is intended.

and Herzegovina in early 1992, establishing so-called 'Bosnian Krajina'. This parastate subsequently expanded to 22 municipalities with a population of approximately 1 million with the administrative centre in Banja Luka. After Bosnia and Herzegovina's declaration of independence in April 1992, Bosnian Krajina was transformed into Republika Srpska, which declared its desire to join with Serbia proper (Malcolm, 1994; Woodward 1995). Although JNA, the Yugoslav army, officially never participated in the conflict in Bosnia, some of the units transformed into the army of Bosnian Serbs and led by General Ratko Mladic, invaded Bosnia and Herzegovina and began the siege of Sarajevo that lasted for three-and-a-half years, claiming at least 10,000 lives. The war in Bosnia – perhaps the most dramatic and brutal military operation in Europe since World War II – lasted until the signing of the Dayton Agreement in 1995 (Bougarel, 1996). The agreement put an end to the violence but at a high long-term cost – splitting a previously truly multiethnic territory into three ethnically defined entities, which is a major factor contributing to prolonged displacement (Dimitrijevic and Kovács, 2004).

Radical Albanian and Serbian nationalisms in Kosovo mutually reinforced one another, weakening voices of moderation in both communities

According to the 1991 census, the population of Bosnia and Herzegovina had been 4.4 million. According to 1999 data, the conflicts in Bosnia and Herzegovina produced more than 2.2 million displaced (both IDPs and refugees), as well as some 250,000 casualties and another 350,000 wounded. By December 2002, some 946,000 (43 per cent) of these displaced had returned, both from locations in Bosnia and Herzegovina, from other Yugoslav successor states, and from further abroad. Although refugee returns have continued since then, it seems that close to a million Bosnians retain some form of displaced status.

Kosovo has been the second major source of displaced people in the Balkans. In light of its multiethnic status (with Albanians being the largest single ethnic group), Kosovo in 1968 acquired a regional parliament and constitution, and the Albanian language received official and equal status up to the level of university education. Constitutional reforms introduced in the Socialist Federal Republic of Yugoslavia in 1974 made Kosovo an autonomous region within the Republic of Serbia, recognizing the specificity of the ethnic composition of the area, where the consistent majority of the population was Albanian. After Tito's death in 1980, centrifugal forces began to intensify across Yugoslavia, and Kosovo was no exception. In Kosovo—a territory with great emotional and symbolic meaning in Serbian history—these initially took the form of demands by the Albanian community that Kosovo be declared a constituent republic within Yugoslavia (i.e., enjoying the same status as the Republic of Serbia). These demands fed growth of Serbian nationalism, whose leaders by the late 1980s were increasingly manipulating the historical symbolism of Kosovo for nationalist mobilization.

In 1989, Milosevic cancelled the province's autonomous status within Serbia without the consent of the Federation, and over the course of the 1990s increasingly relied on the security forces to maintain Serbian rule in Kosovo. Albanian political leaders within Kosovo responded by declaring an independent republic. During most of the 1990s, 'independence' in Kosovo meant engagement in parallel political, social, economic and cultural activities by the Albanian community, in opposition to state structures that were generally staffed by Serbs loyal to Belgrade. The civil conflict that took place in neighbouring Albania in 1997 changed this, by providing radical resistance leaders with small arms and other weapons. This helped strengthen the position of the Kosovo Liberation Army (KLA) within the Albanian community, and weakened the position of moderate political leaders associated with President Ibragim Rugova. These trends culminated with the KLA's legitimization by the international community as the leader of the Albanian delegation during the Rambouillet negotiations on Kosovo's future in 1998. Radical Albanian and Serbian nationalisms therefore mutually reinforced one another, weakening voices of moderation in both communities and making prospects for a viable political settlement ever more remote. Armed resistance against Serbian rule further consolidated Milosevic's regime, and provided additional arguments to persecute independence movements in Kosovo. In early 1999, following the failure of the Rambouillet negotiations, Serbian military and para-military forces intensified their operations in the province. The intensified violence proved unacceptable to much of the international community and NATO launched air raids against Serbia. After the start of the air strikes, the Serbs, feeling legitimized by what they perceived as an international aggression, dramatically intensified the persecution of Albanians and hundreds of thousands of Albanians were forced to flee Kosovo by military and security forces loyal to Milosevic, becoming refugees in Macedonia and Albania proper. In the face of a threatened NATO invasion, Milosevic's troops were pulled out of the province and Kosovo became a UN protectorate.

The Milosevic era ended with the presidential elections in Yugoslavia in 2000. This change boosted democratic reforms and allowed the 'European agenda' to take hold across the region: today all the countries of the Western Balkans (including Serbia and Montenegro) aspire to full membership in the European Union; invitations to begin membership negotiations were in fact extended to Croatia and Macedonia in 2005. Preparations for EU accession in turn can play a critical role in building the capacity needed in state and NGO sectors for the more effective social efforts that are needed to reverse the consequences of vulnerability and displacement that were both produced by and preceded the Yugoslav wars of secession.

On the other hand, the withdrawal of Serbian forces from Kosovo led to waves of reverse ethnic cleansing, directed primarily at Serbs, but also at other ethnic groups (e.g., Roma and other non-Albanian minorities) who were perceived as having collaborated with Belgrade. Representatives of the international community have since 1999 attempted to protect ethnic minorities from these waves, within the context of gradually transferring power to local institutions that would respect international and European standards concerning the protection of minority rights. Matters have been further complicated by uncertainties about when and whether this process will culminate in international recognition of Kosovo's statehood, and by the fact that in portions of northeastern Kosovo (where most of the province's remaining Serbian communities are located) local leaders express their loyalty to Belgrade and sometimes refuse to cooperate with UNMIK (Dimitrijevic and Kovács, 2004).

This decade of violence in the Western Balkans displaced millions of people in a region that does not possess the institutional and organizational infrastructure to accommodate such displacement. The conflicts in Croatia and Bosnia and Herzegovina sent some 530,000 refugees to Serbia. During 1999-2000, they were joined by another 200,000 - 250,000 internally displaced persons from Kosovo; 50,000 more fled to Montenegro. Some 70,600 moved back to Croatia (primarily from Serbia and from Bosnia and Herzegovina). In Bosnia and Herzegovina alone some 1 million people are classified as 'returnees' – part of them former internally displaced, part former refugees (Milicevic, 2003).

The current 'mapping of displaced peoples' in the region looks like the following:

- **Bosnia and Herzegovina**: Of the 2.2 million individuals who were displaced by the war during the early 1990s, more than 1 million have since 'returned'. However, most of these displaced persons have not returned to their pre-war communities and residences. Many 'returnees' in Bosnia and Herzegovina therefore continue to feel like IDPs (Bougarel, 1996; Woodward, 1995). While such individuals can legitimately be regarded as victims of displacement and vulnerability, they are not covered by this study.
- **Serbia**: According to recent UNHCR data, currently there are 106,700 registered refugees in Serbia, of which 28,285 are from Bosnia and Herzegovina and 78,415 from Croatia. Most of the others have returned to their place of origins or integrated acquiring Serbian citizenship. Out of those still registered, 6,090 are still living in collective accommodation (3,179 in recognized collective centres, 1,083 in unrecognized collective centres, 1,675 in specialized institutions and 154 in student dormitories). The remaining 207,293 registered IDPs from Kosovo cannot change their status (unless they decide to return to Kosovo), at least until the issue of the Kosovo status is settled. However, these figures may underestimate the true dimensions of displacement, since some displaced persons have not undergone registration because of a lack of documents or other reasons. Unfortunately, most of these individuals (particularly Roma) are likely to be vulnerable. In total, some 700,000 - 800,000 displaced persons came or returned to Serbia during the 1990s, of which some 350,000 were from Croatia, 200,000 from Bosnia and Herzegovina, and 230,000 from Kosovo. Although not all of these can still be considered vulnerable, there are no exact estimates of how many of them changed their status from beneficiaries of (declining) humanitarian relief to beneficiaries of (scarce) social assistance, either in their country of origin (through the return process), or in the country of asylum (by opting for a new citizenship).

The decade of violence in the Western Balkans displaced millions of people in a region that does not possess the institutional and organizational infrastructure to accommodate such displacement

- **Montenegro**: There are 8,329 registered refugees in Montenegro (6,090 from Bosnia and Herzegovina, and 2,239 from Croatia). Of these, 546 live in collective accommodations. Out of the 17,864 IDPs registered in Montenegro, 1,251 live in collective accommodations. Other estimates suggest that the displaced number some 50,000 - 70,000 – mostly from Kosovo, of which by the end of 2004 some 18,000 were Roma (Jaksic, 2002).

Vulnerability of the displaced

The status of displaced persons in the Western Balkans reflects the specifics of nation-building projects in the region

In addition to the physical hardships of displacement *per se*, further difficulties are associated with the status of displaced persons who, in the Western Balkans, reflect the specifics of nation-building projects in the region. The distinction between refugees and IDPs depends on whether the displaced person has crossed an internationally recognized state border.[73] Until the beginning of the 1990s, internally displaced persons were defined negatively: they were people who had fled their homes, but were not refugees, as they remained within their 'home' country (Phuong, 2004). The many changes of borders, statehood, and legal status seen in the Western Balkans during the 1990s – changes which, in all likelihood, have not yet run their course – combined with the displacement of thousands of Roma (some of whom do not have identity documents) underscore the importance of devising a more comprehensive definition of internally displaced persons. An important step was taken in 1992 when the UN Secretary-General proposed a new working definition (UN Doc. E/CN.4/1992, 23, para 7); this definition was revised in 1998. The Guiding Principles on Internal Displacement now define internally displaced persons as: "persons or groups of persons who have been forced or obliged to flee or to leave their homes or places of habitual residence, in particular as a result of or in order to avoid the effects of armed conflict, situations of generalized violence, violations of human rights or natural or human-made disasters, and who have not crossed an internationally recognized state border" (UN Doc. E/CN.4/1998/53/Add.2). Thus, Serbs who have been displaced from Croatia and settled in Serbia have the status of refugees, while Serbs who have been displaced from Kosovo and settled in Serbia do not (but are instead considered IDPs). The IDP category includes also citizens of Bosnia and Herzegovina, who moved to the entity in which their ethnic group is in the majority and which does not correspond to the entity in which their town of origin is located.

The difference is not a matter of semantics: refugees enjoy a specific set of rights under the 1951 Refugee Convention and can avail themselves of protection from the international community, such as UNHCR, UNDP, and UNICEF. IDPs, on the other hand, continue to be protected by the national laws of their State as well as by international human rights and humanitarian law; displacement does not change their status under international law. It is therefore first and foremost their national government which bears the responsibility to protect and assist its IDPs.[74] As national authorities might be unable or unwilling to do so, the international community has a right to offer its services, with various agencies and organizations coordinating their responses through the collaborative approach.[75]

In the Western Balkans, thousands of families have been victims of multiple displacements: during 1992-1996, thousands of Serbian and Roma refugees from Croatia and Bosnia were resettled by the Milosevic government in Kosovo, in order to dilute the numerical preponderance of the Albanian community. Many of these 'settlers' had to flee Kosovo when the NATO bombing ended and Kosovar Albanians returned from their displacement. Because many had to leave Kosovo in haste, they did

---

[73] Compare Article 1 of the 1951 Convention Relating to the Status of Refugees (according to which a refugee is a person who "owing to a well-founded fear of being persecuted [...] is outside the country of his nationality, and is unable to or, owing to such fear, is unwilling to avail himself of the protection of that country...") to UN Doc E/CN.4/1998/53/Add.2, Introduction, paragraph 2,

[74] The mandate of the representative of the Secretary-General on the human rights of internally displaced persons is limited to: (1) engaging in coordinated advocacy in favour of the protection and respect of the human rights of IDPs, (2) continuing and enhancing dialogues with governments as well as non-governmental organizations and other actors, (3) strengthening the international response to internal displacement, and (4) mainstreaming the human rights of IDPs into all relevant parts of the UN system (Commission Resolution 2004/55).

[75] www.reliefweb.int/idd.

not always bring with them identification or other official documents proving their 'refugee' status. Some were therefore reclassified as IDPs and lost some of the protection they had previously enjoyed.[76]

From a vulnerability perspective, the differences between refugees and IDPs seem less important than their similarities. This is why this part of the report deals with issues of 'displaced persons' as a joint group. Only in some specific areas (such as poverty analysis) are refugees and IDPs analyzed separately.

Unlike the challenges facing Roma (analyzed in Part One), displaced persons were not necessarily vulnerable before their displacement. Most had property, homes, work, and at least middle-class social status. Displacement brings a double blow: in addition to becoming refugees or IDPs, the displaced have lost their middle-class status and find themselves among the most excluded, surviving at the bottom of society. Refugees and IDPs can also differ in their attitudes towards displacement, which can influence their survival strategies. While refugees may more easily give up on the belief that they will return to their native places, IDPs are more likely to cling to the hope that someday they will return to their native land, which may push them towards more short-term survival strategies at their site of displacement.

The younger generations of the displaced pose special problems, particularly in terms of being prone to exclusion from education. This raises the spectre of a possible 'Palestinian syndrome' in the Balkans, in which a generation of children is born and raised in collective accommodations, with all the attendant consequences for life opportunities, political attitudes and behaviour. In the case of the displaced in the Balkans, the first children born in collective accommodations are now starting school.[77]

IDPs from Kosovo, most of whom fled after the 1999 campaign, are another special case. As Kosovo has moved towards *de facto* independence, the province's Serb and Roma communities feel unwelcome and insecure. Most Serbs or Roma who have returned generally live in Serb enclaves in hotels that serve as collective accommodations. Although IDPs have the right to work, in practice this right is not exercisable because of unemployment rates that are close to 50 per cent. This makes IDPs unwelcome competitors on the labour market, particularly in smaller towns where inflows of IDPs can significantly affect the number of inhabitants. When household incomes are at stake, 'ethnic solidarity' often falls by the wayside. Many of the displaced who have returned to Kosovo have done so because they received safe jobs in public institutions such as schools, hospitals, universities or local administration. Double salaries—paid once out of the Serbian budget and again (in euros) by UNMIK—have provided additional incentives to return. Since the Serbian government has already obliged many of these returnees to renounce UNMIK subsidies, as part of efforts to strengthen Belgrade's claims over parts of Kosovo populated by Serbs, it remains to be seen whether these returnees will stay in Kosovo in the long term.

Roma IDPs are also a special case. In response to hostility from local communities, displaced Roma often seek shelter with other Roma, living with relatives or friends in some of the poorest parts of the Balkans. The construction of temporary accommodations (*bidonvillas*) next to the dilapidated homes of their hosts is not uncommon. However, because outsiders do not notice these additions to the Roma ghetto (which was 'always there'), they can easily fall outside of the scope of efforts to address the problems of the displaced (Jaksic, 2002). This provisional, generally unregistered residential status compounds the problems of inadequate access to social services that are associated with improper identity documents. These problems are too often faced even by those Roma who are not displaced.

The numbers of returnees (1 million) in Bosnia and Herzegovina suggest that problems of displacement are finding better solutions there. But these 'peaceful' population movements contain many unnatural elements that create serious psychological tensions for those involved. For example, these returns have often

Unlike the challenges facing Roma, displaced persons were not necessarily vulnerable before their displacement

IDPs are more likely to cling to the hope that someday they will return to their native land, which may push them towards more short-term survival strategies at their site of displacement

[76] Women's Commission for Refugee Women and Children (WCRWC), 2001.

[77] UNICEF's Project Officer, Svetlana Marojevic, sums it up well: "Adolescent refugees and IDPs are especially affected by wars and displacement and remain the most neglected group. They need to feel useful and included and to get some qualifications. They are in need of psychosocial support and interventions, educational encouragement, counselling and clubs where they can talk about their animosity and how they can work through it to help in the process of building civil society".

Table 2-1

Displaced persons sample – origin, status and current residence (households)

Internally displaced persons					
		Households currently residing in:			
Coming from:	Status	Bosnia and Herzegovina	Croatia	Serbia	Montenegro
Within the district/country – rural	IDP	31	30	8	
Within the district/country – urban	IDP	41	27	7	
Other entity (for Bosnia and Herzegovina – i.e., Serbian Republic for people in the Federation, and vice-versa)	IDP	267			
Kosovo	IDP			250	83
Total IDPs:	744	339	57	265	83
Refugees					
Bosnia and Herzegovina	Refugee		92	43	61
Croatia	Refugee	39		69	40
Kosovo	Refugee	9	6		
Montenegro	Refugee	3	1		
Serbia	Refugee	1	30		
Macedonia	Refugee			1	
Slovenia	Refugee			1	
Other	Refugee			16	
Refused/ Don't Know/ Missing	Refugee	7	11	8	20
Total refugees:	458	59	140	138	121

The human security and human rights-based approaches can provide the conceptual framework needed to address the multi–dimensional problems of displacement and vulnerability

been facilitated by the informal 'trading' of houses and property among the three ethnic groups (Serbs, Croats, Bosniaks). This property could easily be seen as belonging to the victims of ethnic cleansing (or their heirs); and the organizations engaged in this trade could be seen as trafficking in war booty. For these and other reasons, many 'returnees' in Bosnia and Herzegovina continue to feel like IDPs (Bougarel, 1996; Woodward, 1996).

The Yugoslav wars of secession therefore generated multidimensional problems of displacement and vulnerability, the response to which requires appropriately conceived measures. The human security and human rights-based approaches can provide the conceptual framework needed to address this vulnerability, especially if applied within a consistent regional framework. Since these problems of displacement go beyond national borders, such a regional focus is a precondition for addressing vulnerability. Countries of origin and countries of current residence need to work together to resolve these issues of vulnerability and displacement. Not only does the welfare of their citizens require such an approach: so do their EU accession prospects.

The populations under study in this report

The complexity of these issues cannot be addressed sufficiently in one report. This report focuses on defining the challenges, providing quantitative estimates of the magnitude of the vulnerability problems facing the displaced in Southeast Europe, and galvanising the search for policy solutions.[78] Such a debate is necessary now more than ever, when the final status of Kosovo is being negotiated, and the Union of Serbia and Montenegro (the final successor to Tito's Yugoslavia) heads for *de facto* if not *de jure* dissolution.

---

[78] The existing information and data gaps on displaced populations are widely recognized. As the latest *Internal Displacement* report states, "for most countries, not even the scope of the displacement crisis is known with any level of accuracy, let alone more specific information on IDPs' living conditions and needs" (IDMC, 2006).

The data used in this part of the report derive from the 'displaced persons' component of the 'vulnerable groups' survey.[79] The 'displaced persons' sample was based on official registries and data on displaced populations, based on which the sampling clusters were determined through random sampling. Due to financial constraints, IDPs and refugees were not sampled separately in individual countries. The two sub-groups were instead identified by dividing the merged regional 'displaced' sample on the basis of the country of residence and country of origin.[80] Displaced households whose country of origin matched their country of residence[81] were classified as IDPs; households whose country of origin did not match were classified as refugees (see Table 2-1). However, such a split is probably not advisable at the national level, unless additional research is first conducted. Likewise, this report generally refrains from detailed analyses of the different sub-groups; the focus is instead on vulnerability associated with displacement.

As can be seen from Figure 2-1, most of the households surveyed moved in 1999 (the year of the Kosovo crisis) and between 1992 and 1996 (the years of the war in Croatia and Bosnia and Herzegovina). The largest share of refugees and IDPs listed 'safety/were forced to move' as the main reason for their displacement. However, 19 per cent of IDPs in Croatia moved for economic reasons, while 20 per cent of IDPs living in Serbia, 14 per cent of IDPs living in Bosnia and Herzegovina, and 17 per cent of IDPs living in Montenegro moved for political reasons. In contrast, 9 per cent of refugees living in Croatia, 22 per cent of refugees living in Bosnia and Herzegovina, 23 per cent of refugees living in Serbia, and 10 per cent of refugees living in Montenegro moved for political reasons.

The displaced households sample does have several limitations and therefore leaves room for future research in this area. The sample cannot be divided into the displaced who seek to return to territories for which they were previously displaced by war or conflict versus displaced returnees who are returning to their 'native soil' (i.e., to their former places of residence in territories that are under the control of their titular nationalities) but their houses, jobs, wealth and relational/social capital have been destroyed. Vulnerability may be very different for these different types of 'returnees' and national policies are likely to be much more attuned to the needs of the second group than the first.

FIGURE 2 – 1

Migration and the displaced

Percentage of households that moved in a given year

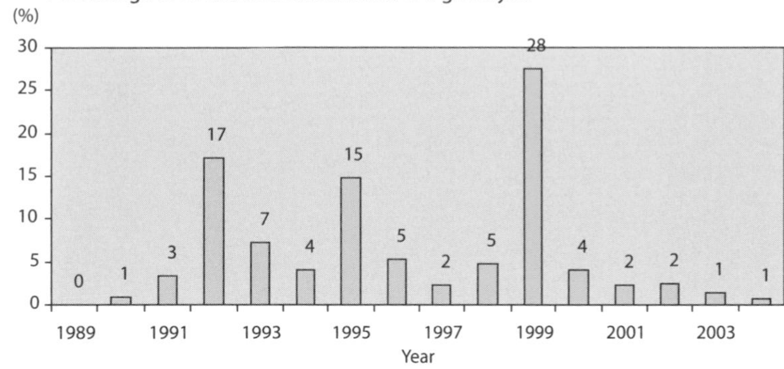

[79] For a detailed description of the methodology and distribution of the sampling clusters, see the Methodological Annex.

[80] Based on answers to the question 'From where did your household move here?', among all those displaced who responded that they did not live in the current location 15 years ago (i.e. in 1989).

[81] With Serbia, Kosovo, and Montenegro treated as a unitary single state.

CHAPTER 2.2

Poverty

Summary

Poverty is the most important and common dimension of vulnerability. This chapter examines both levels of poverty and its correlation with major variables for the displaced. Applying the human security perspective, the chapter outlines the levels of risks individuals and households are facing, and describes the determinants of their vulnerability to poverty. Such household characteristics as education levels, locational effects, gender, or employment status that can make a household particularly vulnerable to poverty are investigated. Household welfare is estimated by household consumption expenditures; these are considered a better indicator of welfare than income as they permit a direct assessment of a household's ability to meet its basic needs while avoiding the often erratic and/or non-monetized nature of incomes (Coudouel, Hentschel, and Wodon, 2001). For purposes of regional comparability, a threshold of PPP $4.30 a day in equivalized expenditures is taken as the absolute poverty line, and where appropriate PPP $2.15 is taken as the threshold for 'extreme' poverty.[82] However expenditures alone do not capture all aspects of welfare: households may be risk averse and prone to saving. As such, in the discussion that follows expenditure data are complemented with the relevant income data where advisable.

The survey data show poverty rates among the displaced to be higher than those of majority respondents, with one in five displaced persons living in poverty (compared with fewer than one in seven for majority respondents). The displaced in Serbia are particularly vulnerable, with two fifths of internally displaced persons living in poverty and more than one in six living in extreme poverty. Displaced households tend to fall into deeper poverty, with poor displaced households falling short of escaping poverty by $1.60 a day compared with the $1.20 required by the poor majority. This poverty affects the expenditure patterns of the displaced, forcing them to spend less on food and such consumer durables as refrigerators and ovens.

A number of factors are shown to affect this poverty. Poverty rates among the displaced are almost double in capital areas. This reflects the smaller number of opportunities in capitals for the displaced who usually end up in refugee centres while in rural areas they benefit more from state support and extended family networks. Although the number of children in a household also appears to be correlated with poverty, this may be due to the fact that the number of children is related to other factor(s), such as the education of the household head. The education and skill-level of employment of the household head has been shown to be the principal factor affecting welfare: displaced households with a well-educated household head in skilled employment can be expected to increase household expenditures by 174 per cent. However, it is also clear that controlling for the effects of location, education and employment, the displaced remain disadvantaged vis-à-vis majority households. This highlights the potential importance of such factors as employment discrimination, which has been documented, for example, in the concluding observations of human rights treaty bodies.[83]

Poverty rates among the displaced are almost double in capital areas

[82] The poverty and extreme poverty thresholds (PPP $4.30 and PPP $2.15 per day expenditures) are based on thresholds used by the World Bank (2005). However, an equivalized, rather than per-capita measure of expenditures is taken here. Equivalized expenditures are based on the OECD equivalence scale, which takes into account economies of scale when calculating expenditures per capita.

[83] See http://www.ohchr.org/english/issues/idp/visits.htm. In its concluding observations, the Human Rights Committee also expresses concerns "about the lack of full protection of the rights of internally displaced persons in Serbia and Montenegro, particularly with regard to access to social services in their places of actual residence, including education facilities for their children, and access to personal documents. It expresses its concern with regard to high levels of unemployment and lack of adequate housing, as well as with regard to the full enjoyment of political rights". (CCPR/CO/81/SEMO).

Table 2-2

Distribution of households and household members by poverty status (%)

	Share of households		Share of household members	
	Non-poor	Poor	Non-poor	Poor
Majority	89	11	86	14
Displaced	84	16	81	19

FIGURE 2 – 2

Poverty rates for the displaced

Percentage of refugees and IDPs living in households with daily equivalized expenditures below PPP $2.15 or PPP $4.30
(with total poverty rates shown above bars)

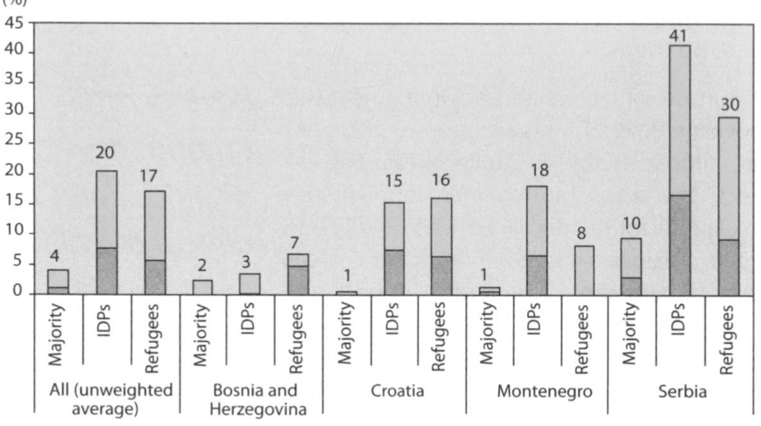

<PPP $2.15 expenditures per day   PPP $2.15 - PPP $4.30 expenditures per day

FIGURE 2 – 3

Poverty rates for the displaced

Percentage of refugees and IDPs living in households with daily equivalized incomes below PPP $2.15 or PPP $4.30 (with total poverty rates shown above bars)

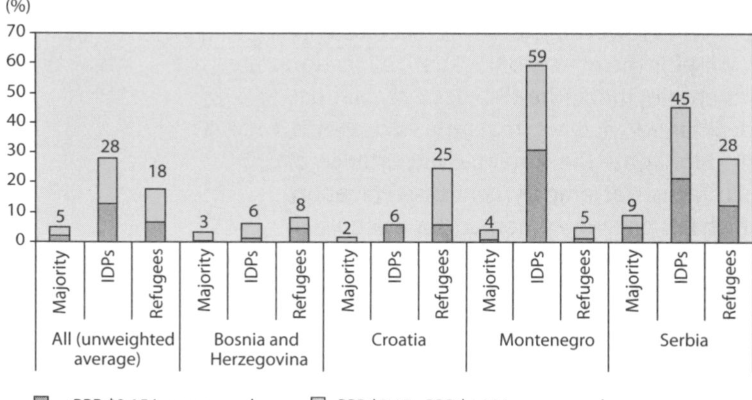

<PPP $2.15 income per day   PPP $2.15 - PPP $4.30 income per day

Poverty status

Poverty rates

As the data in Table 2-2 show, although not nearly as high as that of Roma, poverty rates among displaced households and their members are still substantially higher than those for majority households.[84]

Poverty rates among the displaced vary substantially in the region. Displaced households in Serbia face the highest risk of poverty, followed by those in Montenegro, Croatia, and Bosnia and Herzegovina (see Figure 2-2). However, poverty rates, particularly extreme-poverty rates (individuals in households with expenditures less than PPP $2.15 a day) are dramatically higher for the displaced than for majority households all across the region. In addition, the 311 self-identified Roma in the displaced sample (7 per cent of the sample) are believed to be doubly vulnerable, being both displaced and Roma. The poverty rate shows a vast gap between this sub-group and the rest of the displaced group. While 49 per cent of self-identified displaced Roma fall below the PPP $4.30 poverty line, only 17 per cent of self-identified displaced non-Roma face poverty.

The data shown in Figure 2-2 indicate that IDPs are generally more vulnerable to poverty than refugees. This is particularly the case in Serbia and Montenegro – the state that faces the highest poverty rates for displaced persons. The dire situation of IDPs (even compared to refugees) is reflected in their income generation opportunities in the societies in which they now reside. On the other hand, IDPs tend to rely much more on irregular and informal incomes, which are more likely to go unreported. High levels of employment insecurity may reduce willingness to disclose incomes, which can drive a wedge between reported expenditures and incomes. As the contrast in the data shown in Figure 2-2 and Figure 2-3 shows, differences between income- and expenditure-based estimates are much more pronounced for IDPs than for other groups.[85]

84 Calculated using the daily PPP $4.30 equivalized expenditures poverty threshold. Total expenditures are based on responses to the question: "How much did your household spend last month in total?"

85 Total incomes are based on the sum of responses to the question "What sum was made by each of these kinds of income in the past month (including wages, benefits, remittances, informal earnings, etc.)?"

Poverty depth

There are also differences between and within groups in terms of poverty depth. While poor displaced households are, on average, living on PPP $1.60 a day less than the PPP $4.30 poverty line, poor majority households fall short of escaping poverty by just PPP $1.20 a day. Dividing the data into five quintiles based on equivalized household expenditures[86] shows that, while the distribution of displaced households across quintiles is broadly comparable to that of majority households, subtle differences are apparent (see Figure 2-4). In particular, 28 per cent of displaced households (compared to 25 per cent of majority households) fall into the bottom two expenditure quintiles, while 27 per cent of majority households (compared to 23 per cent of the displaced) fall into the top quintile. This suggests a moderately higher concentration of displaced relative to majority households in the middle or low expenditure groups, which in turn is responsible for the higher poverty rates shown in Figure 2-2.

Implications of poverty

Expenditure patterns

Differences between majority and displaced households in expenditure patterns, purchases and possession of certain household items are proxies for their social exclusion. While 28 per cent of majority households responded that they had purchased a consumer durable item in the past 12 months, just 15 per cent of displaced persons reported having made such a purchase. Given the similarity of expenditure patterns outlined in Figure 2-4, this difference can be attributed to the uncertain and unsettled status of the displaced.

The data in Table 2-3 show that displaced households have lower expenditures than majority households, both in total and on most items. Average monthly equivalized household expenditures of displaced households are 82 per cent of those of majority households. Given the similarity of other household characteristics, these data perhaps most appropriately show the levels of deprivation experienced by displaced households. The real differences between majority and displaced households can be seen in the structure of household expenditures (see Table A1 in the Annex).[87] In the case of purchases of small household appliances, such as radios or CD players, the difference is even

Table 2-3
Differences in average monthly household expenditures

	Majority (euros)	Displaced (euros)	Displaced (% of majority expenditures)
Food	338.4	266.9	78.9
Durable goods	70.0	48.4	69.1
Clothes	100.4	61.5	61.3
Housing and utilities	140.0	110.9	79.2
Alcohol and tobacco	48.2	41.2	85.5
Medicine	31.9	34.1	106.9
Transport	58.1	40.3	69.4
Household goods	46.1	38.5	83.5
Education*	8.6	18.1	210.5
Health care*	11.6	12.3	106.0
Entertainment	40.3	17.3	42.9
Total	893.6	689.5	77.2

* Derived from reported annual household expenditures

FIGURE 2 – 4

Distribution of expenditures by group
Percentage of displaced and majority household members falling within each equivalized expenditure quintile

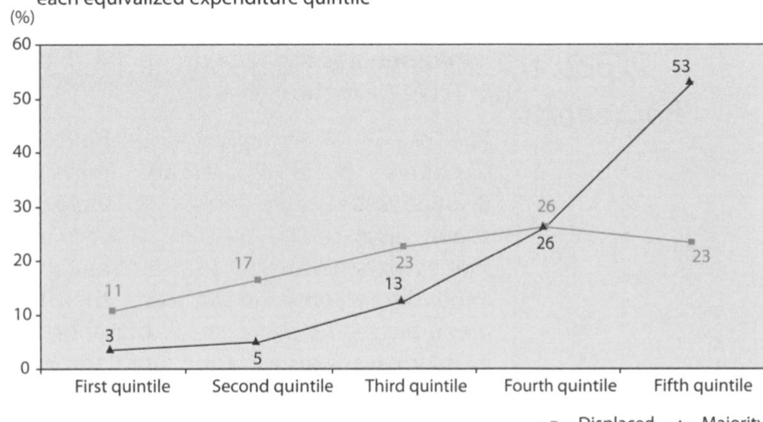

86 Households were ranked by equivalized household expenditures. The first 20 per cent of the households (those at the bottom of the distribution) fall into the first quintile, the second 20 per cent – into the second, and so on. Hence the first quintile constitutes the poorest one fifth of the sample; the fifth quintile constitutes the most affluent.

87 Here and elsewhere in the report, the regional averages for the three groups surveyed are given by the unweighted averages, unless otherwise stated.

> **Box 13: National MDG targets, vulnerable groups and poverty among the displaced**
>
> As this chapter shows, poverty disproportionately affects the displaced. The national MDG report for **Croatia** calls for halving relative poverty between 2001 and 2015. This corresponds to a reduction in the share of people at risk of poverty in Croatia from 18.2 per cent in 2002 to 9.1 per cent in 2015. This corresponds to annual average declines of 0.70 percentage points, relative to the 16.7 per cent level recorded in 2004. Moving at this rate, the displaced surveyed would reach the national target only in 2091. If the national target were to be achieved by 2015 for the displaced, the pace of poverty alleviation would need to be almost eight times higher than for the national average.

FIGURE 2 – 5

Outstanding debt

Outstanding household bills for water, electricity and other utilities as a percentage of monthly household expenditures

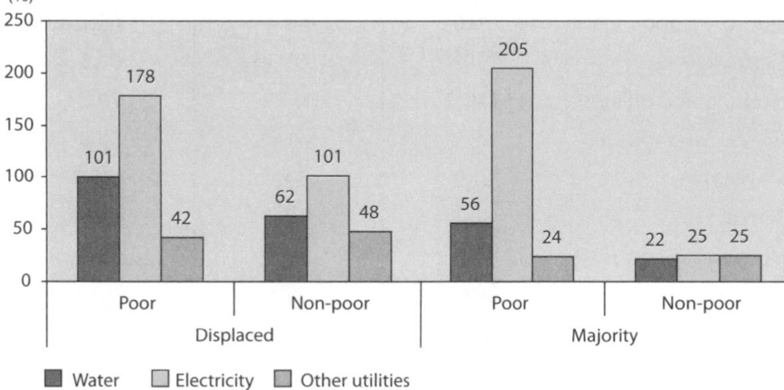

The young are dis–proportionately represented in poorer households

higher (only 8 per cent of displaced and 14 per cent of majority households have purchased these). This may reflect the more temporary nature of the housing arrangements for displaced person households. (Data on durable goods purchases by households for each group are shown in Table A2 in the Annex.)

The profile of equalized household expenditures (in euros) reveals interesting disparities between groups. As Table 2-3 shows, displaced persons are closer to majorities' expenditure patterns but still their expenditures on food are lower than the majorities' – 79 per cent. A big shortfall in their case is also in the 'durable goods' category (69 per cent of the level of majorities), which can be explained by their unresolved housing status.

Household indebtedness

As the data in Figure 2-5 show, irrespective of poverty level, displaced households appear to be more indebted than majority households with the exception of debts for electricity.[88] However, the magnitude of indebtedness is much lower than for Roma households. One possible explanation is that displaced households have higher incomes than Roma households do (equivalized household income of 132 euros versus 67 euros respectively). This simply means that, unlike Roma households, the displaced can still meet most of their utility payments and avoid accumulating large outstanding electricity, water or housing bills.

Correlates of poverty

Locational effects

The location of a household in an urban – rather than rural – area has been shown to have a significant positive relationship with the equivalent expenditures of that household (Revenga, Ringold and Tracy, 2002). Dividing households into capital, urban, and rural localities allow these locational effects to be clearly seen from the data (see Figure 2-6).

The data in Figure 2-6 show that, in contrast to majority households, poverty rates for displaced households appear to be highest in capital areas. This pattern probably outlines the unsettled status of displaced populations, and the fact that they end up living in refugee centres in capitals whereas those living in rural and urban (but not capital) areas most likely rely on extended family networks.[89] In rural areas displaced households appear even less poor than the majority. This could be explained by the access to state and charity support for displaced people providing some basic survival minimum – not available for the majority population in rural areas.

Number of children

The number of children in a household has an important effect on individual wel-

[88] Respondents were asked if they have outstanding payments for water, electricity, or other housing utilities. If they did, they were asked to assess roughly the amounts due for each category.

[89] No allowance has been made to account for the possible higher cost of living in urban areas, which might understate poverty in urban areas.

fare and has been shown to have a strong negative relationship with equivalized expenditures in some countries in the region (Revenga, Ringold and Tracy, 2002). The demographics of households within each expenditure quintile indicate that the young are disproportionately represented in poorer households (see Figure A1 in the Annex). This outlines the higher risk of poverty for children in larger households, even though the poverty risks associated with larger household size could be offset by potential economies of scale. This suggests that use of unified equivalence scales (like the OECD equivalence scale) for both vulnerable and non-vulnerable households may not be appropriate, and that the weight given to children should be increased.

The data in Figure 2-7 show a strong positive relationship between the number of children and poverty rates for both majority and displaced households. As would be expected, poverty rates for displaced households are in general higher than those for majority households. However, displaced households with 2 – 3 children have poverty rates that are closer to rates for majority households. This suggests that these households are able to implement some coping strategy – such as the inclusion of children in income-generating activities – while not suffering from the same financial burdens as larger families.

FIGURE 2 – 6

Location and poverty

Poverty rates by location (capital, rural, urban) for the displaced and majority

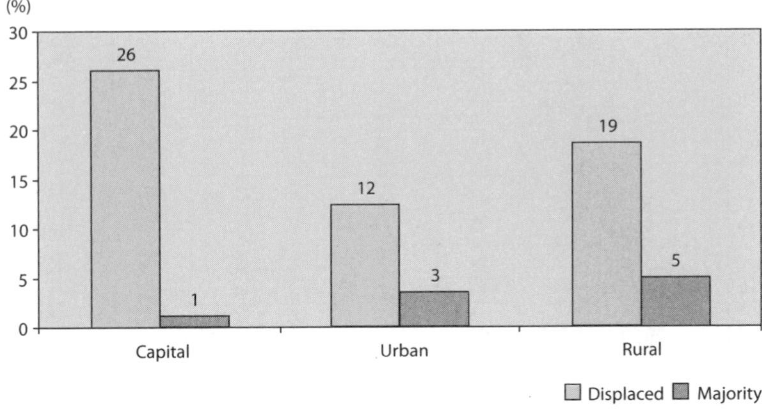

FIGURE 2 – 7

Household size and poverty

Poverty rates by number of children for the displaced and majority

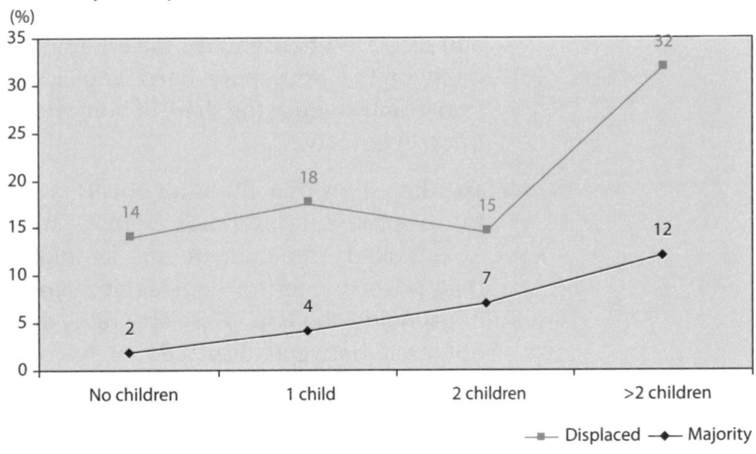

Education and skills

The survey data clearly illustrate the benefits of education in escaping household poverty. As shown in Figure 2-8, displaced and majority households whose heads have no education have a 40 and 19 per cent chance of living in poverty, respectively, while households whose heads have attained tertiary education have just a 5 or 1 per cent chance, respectively.

As shown in Figure 2-8, the biggest gaps between majority and displaced households in terms of poverty rates arise when the household head does not have a formal education. This suggests the concentration of displaced workers into middle-to-low-income employment requiring just elementary or primary education. As such, the displaced with no education whatsoever may be lacking marketable skills; while displaced workers with secondary and higher education may have skills that are poorly aligned with available employment opportunities.

FIGURE 2 – 8

Education and poverty

Poverty rates among adult household heads (over 16 years of age) for the displaced and majority by level of education

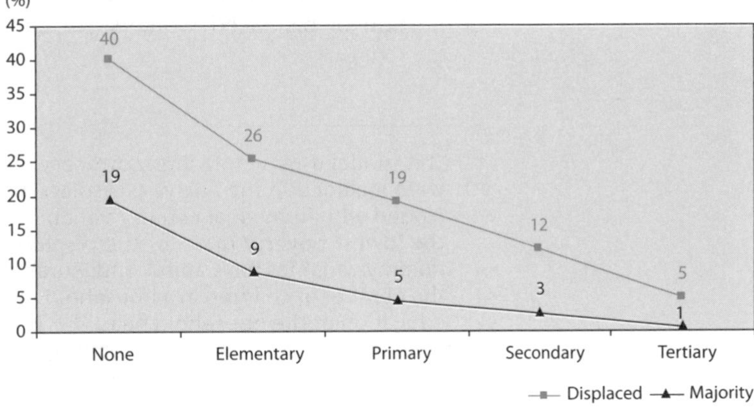

FIGURE 2 – 9

Employment and poverty
Poverty rates for displaced and majority households with skilled or unskilled heads

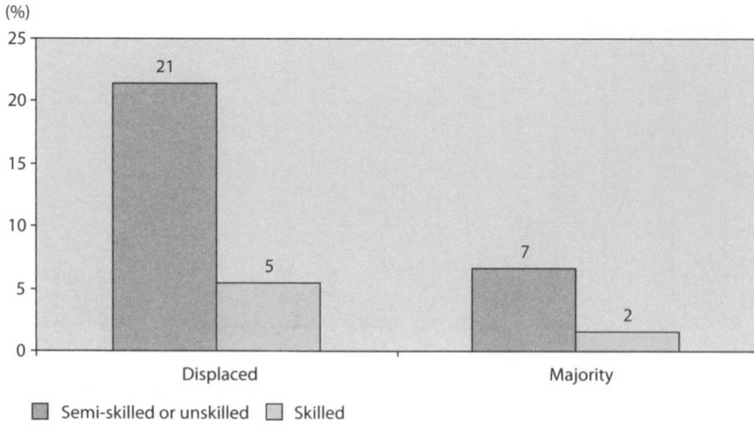

Employment

As shown in Figure 2-9, for both majority and displaced households, skilled employment of the household head appears to significantly reduce the share of households living in poverty.

The data show that although poverty rates for displaced households with a head in unskilled employment are far higher than poverty rates for equivalent majority households, the gap in poverty rates does not exist between displaced or majority households with heads engaged in skilled employment. This strongly suggests that lack of access to skilled employment is a major cause of the high poverty rates among the displaced.

As would be expected from the trend observed in the *Education* section above, the data in Figure 2-10 show that a far higher proportion of displaced workers are concentrated in low- or semi-skilled positions (26 per cent), in contrast to workers from majority households (9 per cent).

Determinants of poverty

In the *Correlates of poverty* section it was shown that, in addition to group status (displaced versus majority), a number of other factors affect poverty rates. It is therefore reasonable to ask about the extent to which higher poverty rates among the displaced can be understood in terms of these objective factors, as opposed to other factors associated with displacement such as discrimination or problems adapting to a new environment. In addition, the factors discussed above – locational effects, numbers of children, education levels, employment status – are all closely related. It is therefore necessary to ask whether these factors each have independent effects on poverty levels and if so, how large these effects might be.

To clarify this issue, the natural log of equivalized (PPP $) household expenditures was regressed against the factors mentioned above (locational effects, numbers of children, education levels, employment status).[90] The results of the analysis – shown in full in Table A17 in the Annex – show that only the capital-displaced interaction term and Croatian dummy variable failed to show a significant relationship with expenditures. A reduced form model excluding insignificant terms showed that 47 per cent of the variance in log expenditures can be explained with reference to just two principal factors: the household's location (the country of residence and location in urban, rural, or capital areas) and the status of the household head (in terms of education and employment).

[90] This model uses simple linear ordinary least squares (OLS) method. The following variables were included in the analysis: Displaced (1 = Displaced, 0 = Majority), country of residence (coded with individual country variables using Bosnia and Herzegovina – the country with the lowest poverty rates for the displaced – as a baseline), locality (coded using separate dummy variables for 'Capital' and 'Rural' localities and using an urban locality as a baseline), the number of children in a household (ordinal variable with five categories: 1, 2, 3, 4, or ≥5), education of the household head (1 = primary or above, 0 = elementary or below), and skill level of the household heads' employment (1 = skilled, 0 = unskilled). A capital*displaced interaction term was also included in the analysis to capture the differing effect of a capital location on expenditures of the displaced. Simple descriptives for continuous and ordinal variables in the analysis and the frequencies for the dummy variables are included in Table A16 in the Annex. The pooling of majority and displaced samples was deemed permissible on the basis of a Chow test (see Chow, 1960) performed on the residual sums of squares of separate regressions conducted separately for the majority and displaced samples (F=0.19). Details of these analyses are in the text.

As predicted, displacement, the number of children in a household, living in a rural area or outside of Bosnia and Herzegovina[91]—these all had negative effects on household expenditures. Similarly, in line with the analysis presented above, the presence of a well-educated household head, or of a household head with skilled employment, was shown to have individual and positive effects on household expenditures. Overall, residing in a capital area was shown to have a positive effect on expenditures, but the interaction between residing in a capital and displacement was not statistically significant. The finding of no relationship for the interaction between the capital and displaced variables and expenditures suggests that the unusually high poverty rates among the displaced in capital areas (discussed in the *Correlates of poverty* section) are due to other factors such as the education and skill levels of household heads.[92]

FIGURE 2 – 10

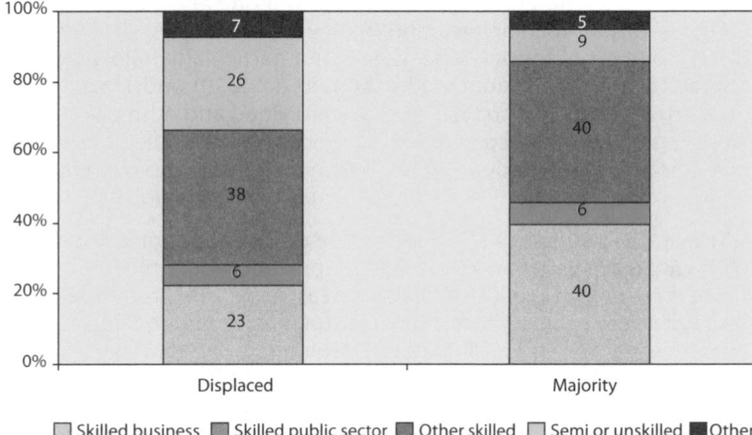

The results show that education and employment opportunities can play a major role in lifting displaced households out of poverty. Predicted expenditures for displaced households located in urban areas with an average number of children and well-educated heads in skilled employment are 180 per cent higher (PPP $435 per month) than those with a poorly educated head, and even 107 per cent higher than majority households with a poorly educated household head employed in unskilled labour. (Issues concerning education and skill levels of displaced workers are discussed in the following chapter.)

However, the results also indicate that lower welfare levels among the displaced cannot be explained by education and employment status alone. For majority households located in urban areas with an average number of children and a well-educated head in skilled employment, the predicted average monthly expenditures would be PPP $587 - 134 per cent more than that of displaced households with analogous locational, family size, skill and education level profiles. This suggests that factors other than education and skill level - such as unequal opportunities - are at least partially responsible for the welfare gap between the two groups outlined in the *Poverty status* section above. Studies such as those investigating the attitudes of majority communities vis-à-vis Roma (see World Bank, 2005) should also be carried out vis-à-vis the displaced, in order to identify and respond to obstacles to overcoming barriers to their integration.

Lack of access to skilled employment is a major cause of the high poverty rates among the displaced

Barriers to opportunities among displaced households are shown by separate regressions for displaced and majority samples,[93] which show that displaced expenditure levels in displaced households are more dependent on the level of education of the household head than in majority households. An urban displaced household with an average number of children with a highly educated head (irrespective of the type of employment) predicted expenditures would be 207 per cent higher than those of analogous households with a poorly educated head. For majority households, the predicted expenditures associated with a well-educated household head is somewhat lower (168 per cent). As the analysis in the *Education and Employment* chapter (Chapter 2.3) shows, these impressive increas-

91 With the exception of Croatia.

92 It seems likely that the relationship between capital areas and poverty in displaced households can be understood with reference to country of origin. Seventy-four per cent of the displaced living in capital areas live in Serbia or Montenegro (compared to 46 per cent of the displaced living outside capital areas). These territories are associated with relatively high poverty rates (see Figure 2-3).

93 These models use a simple linear ordinary least square (OLS) method. With the exception of the group-membership variable, all other variables are the same as in the previous model. Simple summary statistics and frequencies for all variables are included in Table A18 in the Annex.

Box 14: **Area-based development in Southern Serbia**

Area-based development programmes usually address multi-sectoral development challenges that require local-level cooperation between various actors who are often estranged from one another. Southern Serbia is exactly such an area (International Crisis Group, 2003). After the dissolution of former Yugoslavia – and particularly following the military conflicts in neighbouring Kosovo (in 1999) and Macedonia (in 2001) – many local communities were divided and ethnic tensions were high. In such circumstances, development activities targeting one social or ethnic group, and eschewing a holistic approach to the region, could contribute to further hostilities and even violence.

UNDP and its partners responded to these threats by designing and implementing a series of area-based development programmes in Southern Serbia, starting in 2001.[94] The main local partners in these initiatives, which delivered some $27 million in programming during 2002 - 2007, are municipalities and local NGOs. In addition to UNDP monies, funds were provided by the EU's European Agency for Reconstruction, the Swedish International Development Agency, and the Governments of Austria and Norway, as well as by the Government of Serbia.

The focus of these activities evolved over time. Initial objectives emphasized peace building and reconciliation, as well as support for local economic development, and rapid employment activities targeting the unemployed, minorities and ex-combatants. Subsequent phases focused on better local governance and cooperation among South Serbian municipalities. The impact of these programmes is perhaps best seen in the fact that the dire forecasts about tensions and conflicts in Southern Serbia did not materialize. Indeed, relations within the 400 communities/municipalities participating in these programmes often improved. Following the March 2004 events in Kosovo (when Serbs in the territory were targets of a renewed wave of ethnic cleansing), protests and unrest broke out in Belgrade and Nis – but not in Southern Serbia.

UNDP's experience with area-based development in Southern Serbia suggest several important conclusions. First, area-based development programming can indeed provide the right format for preventing conflict and ameliorating the consequences of displacement and vulnerability in the Western Balkans. The programmes introduced under the UNDP umbrella contributed to local-level social cohesion that reinforced multiple identities and community (rather than ethnic) affiliations. Post-conflict reconciliation measures are now giving way to local-level sustainable development as the major programming priority in this area. This change is intended to bring communities in Southern Serbia farther from conflict and closer to the "European standards" to which the government in Belgrade aspires. Establishing a regional development agency to support all the municipalities covered by this project is the next envisaged milestone in this regard.

es in displaced household incomes are from a much lower base. Similarly, although the engagement of displaced household heads in skilled (rather than unskilled) employment can lead to an expected 70 per cent increase in expenditures (compared with a 66 per cent increase for majority households), the expenditures in displaced households with a head engaged in such employment remains far lower than those of majority households (38 per cent and 23 per cent lower for households with educated or uneducated household heads, respectively). In other words, irrespective of the type of employment in which displaced household heads are engaged, they earn lower incomes than majority household heads in otherwise analogous situations. (Barriers to employment and incomes among the displaced are discussed in the following *Education and employment* chapter.)

Conclusions from Chapter 2.2

This chapter emphasizes the importance of the unresolved legal status of displaced persons, and of its links to poverty and exclusion. It suggests that, while Roma need priority attention in terms of poverty reduction efforts, it is not just Roma who need such attention. Refugees and internally displaced persons are also vulnerable groups who face greater-than-average risks of poverty and social exclusion. Data also support the findings of other research that, within the 'displaced group' IDPs are often in much more difficult positions than refugees, and as such deserve particular policy attention.

Such factors as group status, country of residence, age, education level, and skill level of employment, significantly affect a household's vulnerability to poverty. Although displaced persons have lower poverty rates than Roma, the analysis also shows that in terms of the above mentioned factors, displaced households are vulnerable to poverty, i.e. they have a high risk of falling into poverty in the future given their household characteristics and their unsettled status. Also, the magnitude of the decline in status experienced by the displaced (most of whom were not vulnerable prior to the conflict) suggests that subjective perceptions of poverty and vulnerability may be particularly acute.

It should be kept in mind that some of the IDPs are Roma. On the other hand, the issue of the adaptation capabilities of the Roma IDPs as compared to those of the other IDPs should be considered.

[94] These were the South Serbia Municipal Improvement and Recovery Programme, and the companion Rapid Employment Programme, during 2001 – 2003; and the Municipal Improvement and Recovery Programme I and II during 2003 - 2007.

CHAPTER 2.3

Education and employment

Summary

Unemployment is a major determinant of vulnerability, and employment can provide the income needed to escape poverty. This chapter looks at both the frequency and the quality of employment of displaced persons in the region, with a particular focus on the educational determinants of employment.

The survey data show that education is not the problem for the displaced that it is for Roma, as differences in education levels between displaced and majority respondents are generally insignificant. However, while education per se is not a major problem for displaced persons, levels of education do affect employment opportunities. Important gender differences do appear in terms of tertiary education, with displaced women much less likely to continue their education after secondary school. Literacy rates are similar, as are enrolment rates at the secondary level, but enrolment rates in primary schools are a little lower for the displaced.

While unemployment rates are consistently higher for displaced than majority workers, in contrast to Roma, subjective unemployment rates are lower for the displaced in some West Balkan countries. This may reflect a greater reluctance to accept the stigma that can come with declaring oneself to be unemployed. The displaced are mainly employed in low-skilled manual jobs, and they are more likely to work in the informal sector to a greater extent than are members of majority communities. Income levels for the displaced are lower than for majority households but, unlike Roma, the displaced derive almost all of their income from labour (rather than social benefits, begging, or other forms of income generation).

Self employment and access to credit: more majority households try to start a business than do displaced, but the differences are not great. As with Roma and the poor in general, the displaced find it hard to get bank credit, although there was little difference in the average value of loans between displaced and majority households. Displaced households are more likely to borrow from friends, relatives and NGOs and are less likely to be members of credit cooperatives or credit unions than majority households. Collateral is a major constraint and, whereas nearly all majority households live in housing that belongs to them or their family members, fewer than half of displaced households do. The displaced are also less likely to own land. A large share of displaced households borrows for home improvements and this may help explain banks' reluctance to lend.

Age: youth unemployment is slightly higher among displaced than majority households, though rates are very high in both communities.

Gender: unemployment rates for women are higher than for men across the region, and the gap between the rates are higher for displaced than for majority communities. And whereas employment rates for displaced men exceed the Lisbon employment rate targets (70 per cent overall), those for majority and especially displaced women fall short.

Location: unemployment rates among the displaced are higher than among majority communities in both urban and rural areas, with rates for both groups higher in rural areas than in towns and cities. Unemployment is also influenced by the extent to which the displaced live in mixed communities; unemployment rates are higher in segregated communities.

Despite having education levels similar to those of majority households, the displaced do not have the same employment opportunities. As might be expected, unemployment falls in both communities at higher levels of education, although the labour market advantages for displaced persons with higher education are smaller than for majority workers. In addition, improvements in education for the displaced do not lead to commensurate increases in wages.

Displaced women are much less likely to continue their education after secondary school

The displaced are mainly employed in low-skilled manual jobs, and they are more likely to work in the informal sector

Education status

The survey data indicate that education is the area in which the profiles of displaced and majority respondents coincide most closely (see Figure 2-11). This suggests that weak education backgrounds do not pose the major problem for displaced persons that they pose for Roma.

FIGURE 2 – 11

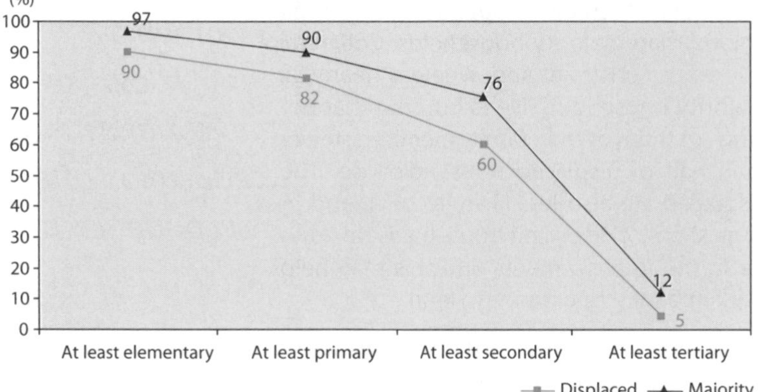

However, there is a small gap in education status between majority and displaced household members. As with the Roma, lower attainment rates among the displaced reflect their lower enrolment rates, particularly at the secondary level (see Figures 2-12 and 2-13).

FIGURE 2 – 12

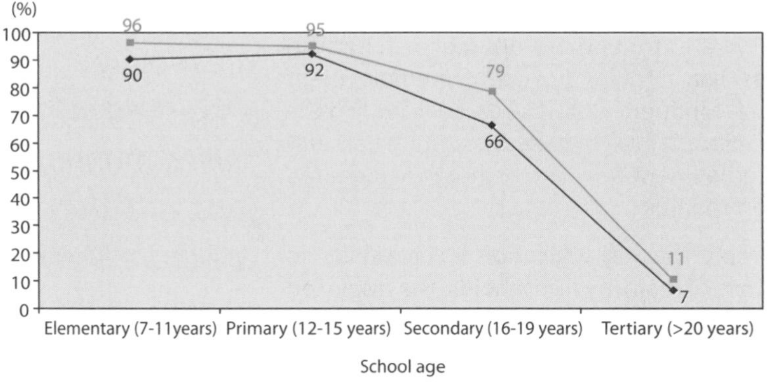

Lower enrolments among the displaced are reflected in the number of years they spend in education. While the majority spends an average of 10 years and nine months in education, displaced persons spend just nine years.

Lower enrolment and attainment rates among the displaced, along with problems (for some respondents) associated with learning new languages, are reflected in the lower literacy rates among this group (see Table 2-4), which (with the exception of Bosnia and Herzegovina) fall below national literacy rates.

Demographic differences

Although the above suggests that the education status of displaced and majority communities is broadly comparable, at least at the elementary and primary levels, it is clear that important pockets of vulnerability are present among the displaced. In particular it is important to distinguish between the displaced whose schooling was disrupted by displacement, versus those who either completed school before they were displaced or have begun/renewed education since the displacement. As shown in Chapter 2.1 (see Figure 2-1), the two largest waves of displacement followed shortly after the Croatian and Bosnian conflicts in 1991, and the armed resistance movement in Kosovo which took hold after 1997. The data show that for displaced persons of secondary-school or prime university age (16-21 years), there were major drops in education levels, particularly for those at the older end of this range and who may have been less able to pick up their education in another environment following displacement (see Figure 2-14). These differences in education status can be explained by the turbulent and uncertain circumstances in which displaced children often find themselves (see Box 19). This underscores the importance of policies to ensure improved educational support for those whose education has been disrupted by displacement.

The survey data also suggest that displaced women are particularly vulnerable. Not only is the gap in attainment larger in the case of displaced women than displaced men (see Figure 2-15)—it increases with the level of education. The data indicate that displaced men are 15 per cent less likely to obtain secondary education than men from majority communities, while displaced women are 27 per cent less likely to obtain secondary education than displaced men. Overcoming the lower education status of the displaced requires interventions sensitive to the vulnerable state of displaced women.

Employment status

Despite broad comparability in the education status attained among displaced and majority communities (see Figure 2-11), there are major differences in the employment opportunities available to the two groups.

Unemployment rates in Southeast Europe

As in the *Employment* chapter on Roma, unemployment rates can be assessed based on both subjective reports of working status and objective measures based on responses to the question of whether the respondents earned any income in the previous month, and if so, how. As before, given the problems associated with using a subjective active job search criterion (see, for instance, Micklewright and Nagy, 2002) the condition of actively seeking employment – included in the ILO definition of unemployment – was not considered in calculating unemployment rates.

The data show that unemployment rates and subjective perceptions of unemployment are far higher among displaced than among majority respondents, and in most cases more than twice as high (see Figure 2-16).[95] In contrast to majority respondents, whose subjective perceptions of unemployment and reported unemployment rates are fairly close, relatively high proportions of the displaced perceive themselves as being unemployed when they are in fact involved in some form of income generation. This most likely reflects the fact that employment for the displaced is concentrated in the informal sector, involving irregular or poorly paid work. Although such activities may generate income, they may not be regarded as 'employment'.

Differences in types of employment and sources of income

The data in Figure 2-17 show that, in comparison with workers from majority communities, displaced workers are overrepresented in sectors dominated by manual labour and low-skill work – such as trade and construction – and underrepresented in public sector employment in such areas as public utilities, health care, education and science. This is most probably caused by both an aversion to lower-skilled employment among the ma-

FIGURE 2 – 13

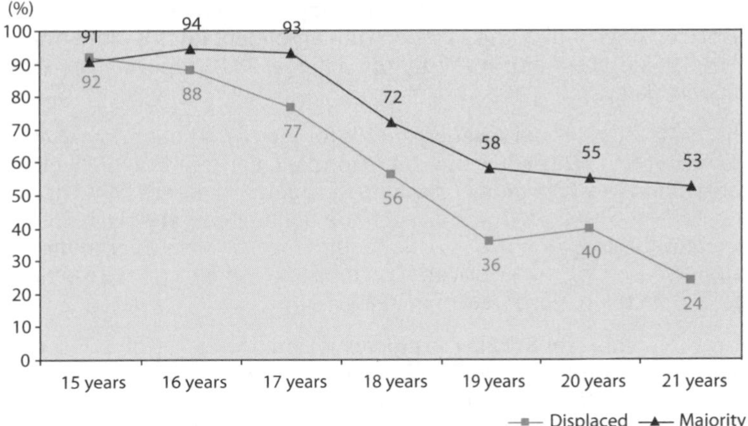

FIGURE 2 – 14

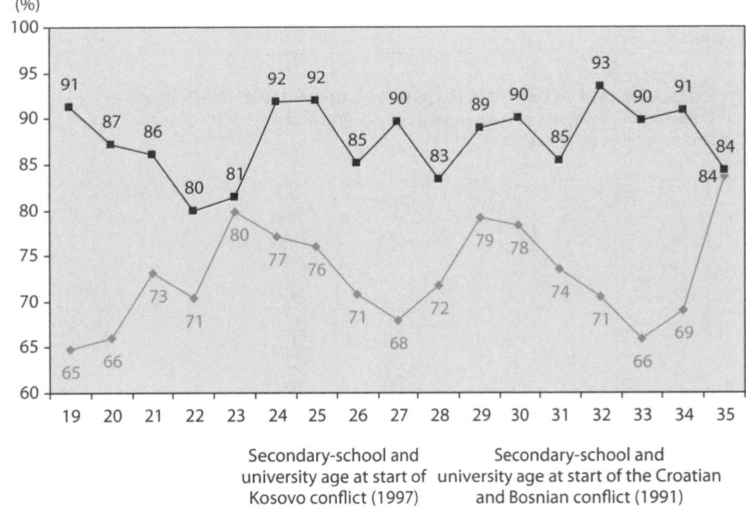

Table 2-4

Adult literacy gap

Percentage of displaced and majority respondents over 15 years of age who read and write and national adult (over 15 years) literacy rates.

	Displaced	Majority	National averages (2003)[96]
Bosnia and Herzegovina	95.0%	97.8%	94.5%
Croatia	93.0%	98.6%	96.1%
Serbia	94.2%	98.9%	
Montenegro	95.6%	99.5%	96.4%[97]

95 It should be emphasized again that the majority populations used as the basis of comparison are those living in proximity to the displaced sites selected for the survey, as opposed to the overall average for the country as a whole. In this way, we can compare groups that are similarly vulnerable due to their isolation in deprived areas.

96 Source: UNESCO Institute for Statistics, 2005: http://www.uis.unesco.org/.

97 Data for Serbia and Montenegro are combined.

Box 15: National MDG targets, vulnerable groups and primary education for displaced children

The survey data suggest that, while literacy is not a major problem for displaced households, the situation with enrolment rates is more troubling. This point is also made by the national MDG reports from the Western Balkans.

The MDG report for **Montenegro** calls for increasing net primary enrolment rates to 99 per cent by 2015, from 97.6 per cent in 2005 (which corresponds to 0.14 annual percentage-point increases). Moving at this pace, the displaced would reach the national target only in 2090. Meeting this target by 2015 would require that the pace of enrolment rate increases for the displaced would have to be almost eight times faster than the national rate of increase.

The MDG report for **Serbia** calls for achieving universal (100 per cent) net primary enrolment by 2015, from 97.9 per cent in 2002 (which corresponds to 0.16 annual percentage-point increases). Moving at this pace, the displaced would reach the national target only in 2097. Meeting this target by 2015 would require that the pace of enrolment rate increases for the displaced would have to be almost nine times faster than the national rate of increase.

FIGURE 2 - 15

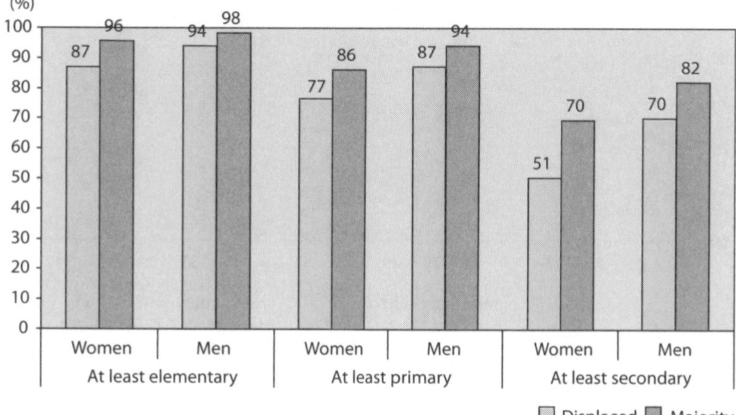

FIGURE 2 - 16

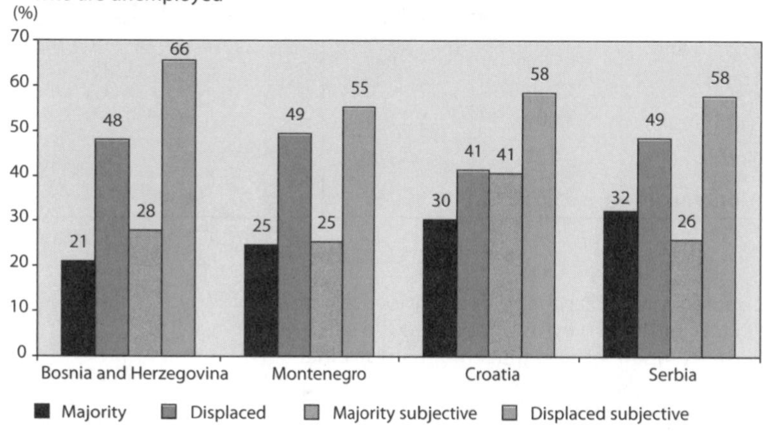

jority, combined with a lack of public-sector opportunities for the displaced due to their largely 'provisional' and 'unresolved' status.

The 'provisional' status of the displaced seems to affect their ability to obtain skilled employment: just 15 per cent of displaced workers are in skilled employment, compared with 31 per cent of workers from majority communities. Differences in levels and types of unemployment among the displaced have a major impact on their incomes. Average monthly incomes from wages among majority households (363 euros) are nearly double those of displaced households (191 euros).

Moreover, it does not appear that this wage gap is fully offset by either social benefits or such coping strategies as subsistence farming. The average income derived from unemployment benefits among displaced households was only 5.49 euros. Although the percentage of displaced respondents with access to agricultural land (18 per cent) is similar to the share of majority respondents (17 per cent), the average monthly net income derived from agricultural production is only 1.42 euros, compared with 4.76 euros among majority respondents. This may reflect the fact that 35 per cent of the displaced pay some form of rent on this land (compared with 13 per cent of majority respondents).

Perhaps because of their lower income levels, the displaced are disproportionately involved in informal-sector activities, which are often associated with poor job quality and weak social protection (ILO, 2002). As the data in Figure 2-18 show, employment in such activities for displaced workers (for which income was not reported for tax and social purposes) was high (and higher than for workers from majority communities) in all countries of the region, with the exception of Croatia.

Self-employment and access to credit

As mentioned in the *Employment* chapter on Roma, promoting the development of small- and medium-sized enterprises (SMEs) is a central aim of the Central European Initiative involving Bosnia and Herzegovina, Croatia, and Serbia and Montenegro (along with 12 other European states) (UNECE, 2001). However, the level of activity among the displaced in such activities is relatively low. The data show that, while attempts have been made to establish businesses in 17 per cent of majority households, this was the case in less than 9 per cent of displaced households.[98] As with Roma, relatively poor access to capital in general and bank credit in particular is a serious barrier to self-employment and entrepreneurial activities among the displaced. Thirty per cent of the majority households surveyed said they had used some type of credit, compared to 19 per cent of displaced households. The average loan size among the displaced was around 2,629 euros, compared to 3,344 euros among majority borrowers.

The data in Figure 2-19 show that, like Roma, displaced households are far less likely to use banks or credit unions/cooperatives, and more likely to use friends, relatives, and NGOs, as a source of credit than are majority borrowers. They are less engaged in credit cooperatives or credit unions, which further limits their access to microfinance services. The inability to provide collateral appears to be a central barrier to obtaining credit from banks or credit cooperatives. Private ownership of property or land is an important source of collateral. While 88 per cent of majority households live in properties that belong to them or to family members, just 40 per cent of the displaced are in such a position. Similarly, 36 per cent of majority households own the land on which the property is located, compared to just 22 per cent of displaced households.

Displaced households' poor access to formal sources of credit underscores the importance of microfinance programmes that focus on facilitating lending to vulnerable groups such as the displaced. The projects in Bosnia and Herzegovina (described in Box 16) can be used as an example for future programmes in the region.

Although these microfinance programmes have been largely successful (see Box 16), their long-term sustainability means ensuring that lending is increasingly directed to productive activities. The survey data show that, while similar proportions of displaced and majority households borrow for business purposes (around 6 per cent), a much lower proportion of the displaced borrow to purchase durable goods, which can boost labour market competitiveness and productivity (10 per cent as compared to 18 per cent for majority households). A much higher proportion of displaced households borrow for the less productive purpose of

FIGURE 2 – 17

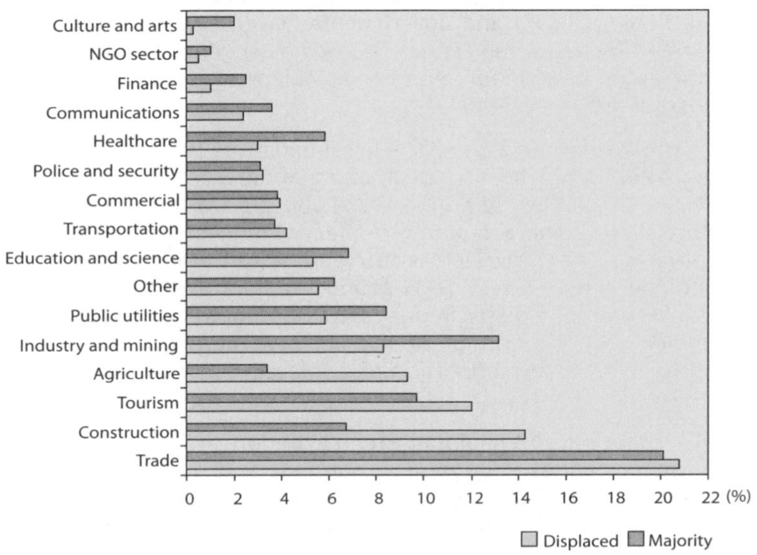

FIGURE 2 – 18

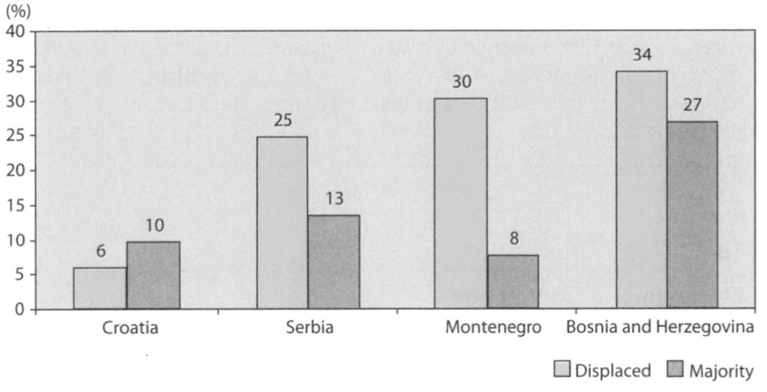

FIGURE 2 – 19

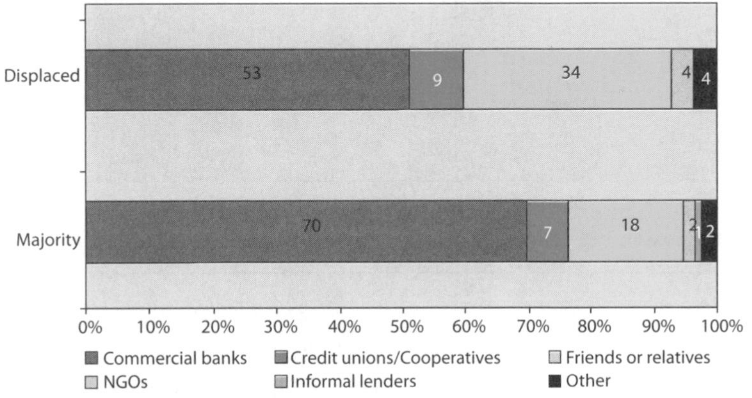

98 This is lower even than the proportion of Roma households in Bosnia and Herzegovina, Croatia, and Serbia and Montenegro, in which one or more household members have made efforts to establish their own businesses (13 per cent).

Box 16: The seeds of new business - microfinance programmes in Bosnia and Herzegovina

A number of microfinance initiatives, supported by multilateral agencies (including UNDP) and governments, have been introduced in Bosnia and Herzegovina. These initiatives have generally sought to improve access to credit for communities in depressed areas with large numbers of displaced residents.

The first phase of the $22 million Local Initiatives Project, financed by the World Bank, UNHCR, UNDP, and a number of donor governments, was implemented during 1996-2000. It provided over 50,000 micro loans to vulnerable and war-affected individuals that would not otherwise have had access to credit. A study of the project's second phase (during 2002-2005) found that improved access to micro credits led to increases in per-capita household income, quality of employment and entrepreneurial activity. The project was also found to increase the proportion of displaced that registered their businesses.

UNDP's Srebrenica[100] Regional Project, begun in 2002, targeted three municipalities – Srebrenica, Bratunac and Milici – that had suffered combinations of serious wartime damage and economic decline. Although the project included elements of support for local governance, infrastructure and housing development, its main focus was on post-conflict economic recovery by helping to improve access to finance through micro-credits for new businesses. An evaluation of the programme concluded that the provision of micro-credits had been highly successful, and had contributed to the restoration of basic commercial services in Srebrenica. By 2005, some 16,000 loans had been contracted and almost $20 million dispersed. Some $3 million of this was lent to displaced in the region – mostly to Bosniak returnees, but also to displaced Bosnian Serbs. The loans have had 100 per cent repayment to date; no defaults have been reported.

FIGURE 2 – 20

Employment rates by age

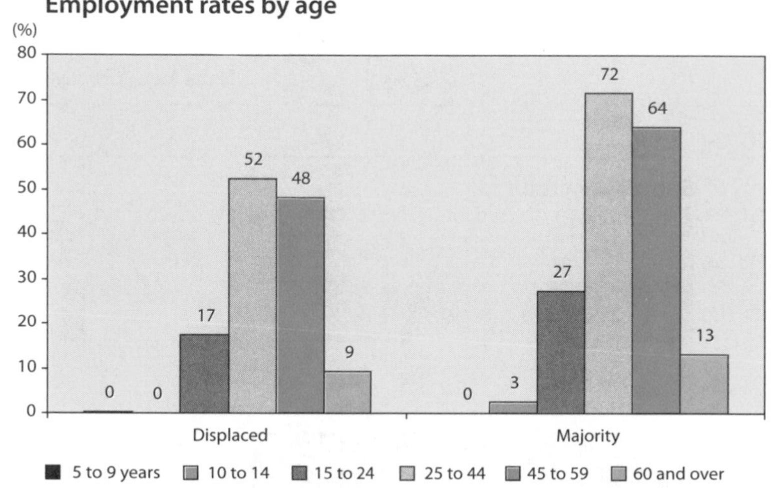

home improvement (33 per cent, compared to 19 per cent of majority households). This suggests that new micro-finance projects in the region should include business training and other business support components.

Correlates of employment

Age

The MDGs identify youth unemployment as a special cause for concern. As can be seen from the data shown in Figures A2 to A4 in the Annex, unemployment rates among young adults are above national averages for both majority and displaced households across the region.[99] Although (as in majority communities) unemployment rates are lower among displaced persons of 'prime age' (25-44 years old), unemployment rates for this age group remain high – between 32 and 45 per cent across the region – suggesting poor labour market conditions for even prime-age displaced adults.

Gender

Disaggregating unemployment rates by sex highlights the doubly vulnerable position of displaced women. The data show that majority and displaced women across the region have higher unemployment rates than men (see Figure 2-21). As discussed in the *Employment* chapter on Roma, this might be related to the greater probability that women will withdraw from conventional labour market activities to engage in activities such as housework and/or looking after children.

However, as shown in Figure 2-21, the gap in unemployment rates between displaced and majority workers is less pronounced in the case of men than of women. Likewise, the gap between majority and displaced workers in terms of employment rates is larger in the case of displaced women than men (Figure 2-22). Although employment rates among displaced men are low (just three quarters that of the EU Lisbon target of 70 per cent), the employment rates among

---

99 O'Higgins (2003, 2004) provides a description and some discussion of youth unemployment in transition countries as a whole. O'Higgins (2001) discusses in more detail why young people face higher unemployment rates than other age groups.

100 Srebrenica was the site of the execution of some 8,000 Bosnian Muslims in 1995 (see http://en.wikipedia.org/wiki/Srebrenica_massacre). Recovery and community rehabilitation efforts in this region therefore have particular significance.

displaced women are even lower – less than half the EU Lisbon target of 60 per cent.

Locational effects

The survey data show that unemployment rates are marginally higher in rural areas for both majority and displaced workers (see Figure 2-23). This is due entirely to higher unemployment rates among rural women for both groups, which underscores the labour market vulnerability facing rural displaced women.

Unemployment rates can also be influenced by the degree of ethnic segregation or integration. The survey approached this issue by posing questions about the ethnic mix of the respondents' settlement, village, town, city, or immediate neighbourhood. The data show that unemployment rates are highest among the displaced living in areas predominantly containing the displaced, and lowest among those living in mixed areas (see Figure 2-24). The extent of ethnic mixing does not appear to have a significant impact on the employment prospects of majority workers. This suggests that initiatives to reduce unemployment among displaced persons should focus on increasing their integration into majority communities and on providing living opportunities outside of refugee centres.[101]

Education

Education clearly affects employment status. But despite achieving education levels that are broadly comparable to those of majority workers, displaced workers do not have the same employment opportunities (see Figure 2-25). Whereas unemployment rates for both displaced and majority workers generally decline with increasing education levels, this relationship for displaced workers is not monotonic. While unemployment rates are higher among well-educated displaced (i.e., with a primary education or above) than well-educated majority workers, for poorly educated workers (i.e., with an elementary education or less) this situation is reversed: unemployment rates are higher among majority than among displaced workers. The relative labour market advantage accruing to those with higher levels of

FIGURE 2 – 21

Unemployment rates by sex

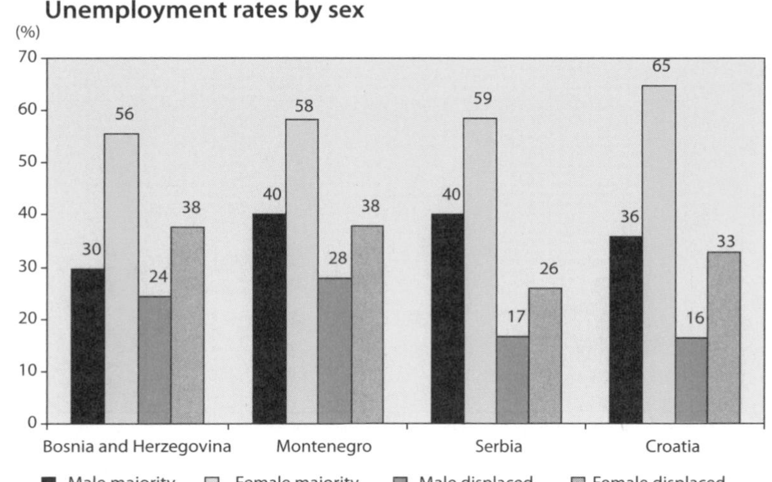

FIGURE 2 – 22

Employment rates by sex

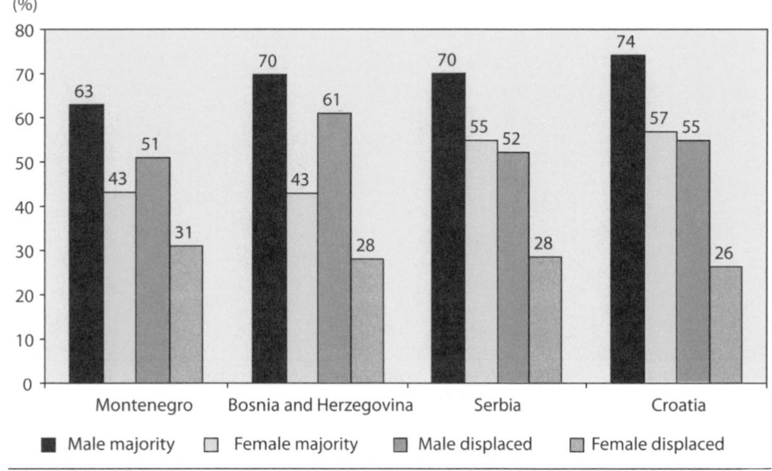

FIGURE 2 – 23

Unemployment rates by sex and location (urban and rural)

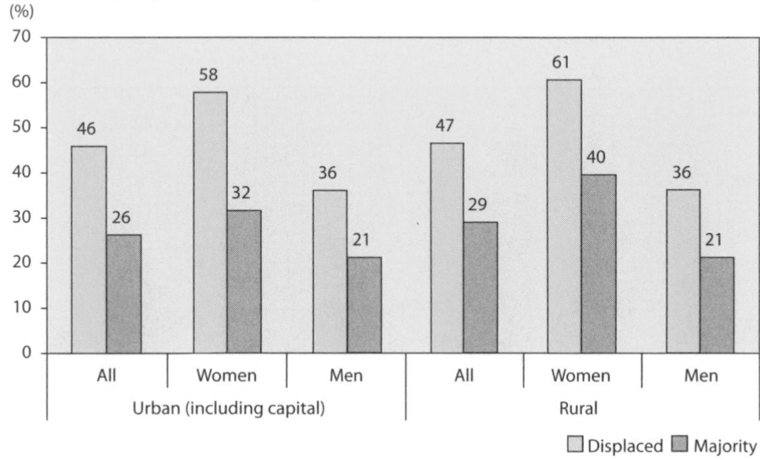

101 Although it might be assumed that mixed neighbourhoods tend to be more urban and that lower unemployment rates among the displaced therefore reflect the tendency for mixed neighbourhoods to also be urban ones – the data does not support this assumption. Fifty-six per cent of urban majority and 62 per cent of urban displaced live in neighbourhoods occupied by the same group compared with just 50 and 61 per cent of rural majority and displaced persons respectively.

FIGURE 2 - 24

Unemployment and ethnicity
Unemployment rates for the displaced and majority by ethnic mix of the neighbourhood

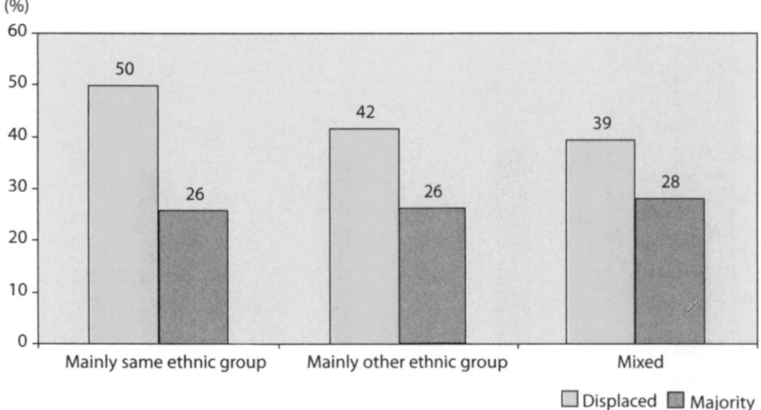

FIGURE 2 - 25

Education and unemployment
Unemployment rates by level of education

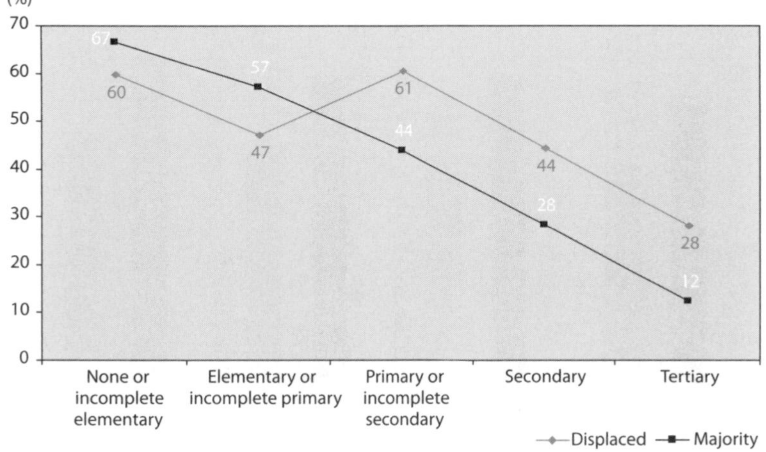

FIGURE 2 - 26

Education and the probability of employment
Expected probabilities of employment for majority and displaced men and women with each level of education

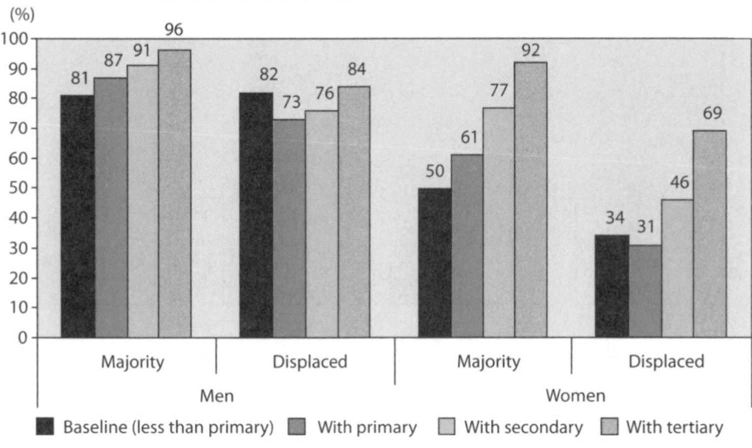

education is therefore less pronounced for displaced than for majority workers. Indeed, the unemployment rate for displaced workers with a primary education (61 per cent) is actually higher than the rates for displaced workers with an elementary education (47 per cent).

The lack of a relationship between education levels and employment opportunities for the displaced was shown clearly through a simple probit model. The results of the probit analysis show that for majority workers, completing any level of education leads to large and significant increases in the probability of employment for both men and women (see Table A13 in the Annex). However, for the displaced, only the completion of primary education in the case of men or the completion of secondary or tertiary education in the case of women had any impact on the probability of employment. These findings are shown in Figure 2-26, which displays the estimated percentage-point improvement in employment prospects for each increase in the level of education for majority and displaced workers.[102]

This hypothetical simulation indicates that, while the probability of employment generally increases with each level of education, for displaced men and women the impact of education on employment is only felt for workers with secondary or tertiary education, respectively. This suggests that displaced persons must have high (at least secondary) levels of education to 'prove' themselves to prospective employers.

Once employment has been secured, education has a differential impact on employment quality and income levels for majority and displaced workers. As shown in Figure 2-27, education substantially increases the numbers of both majority and displaced workers who find skilled employment. However, there are notable differences between displaced and majority workers in this respect. Greater proportions of majority workers are involved in skilled labour than displaced workers, irrespective of education levels. Moreover, while attaining elementary education substantially increases the proportion of majority workers in obtaining skilled employment (from 20 to 57 per cent), it has no effect on prospects for displaced workers, whose chanc-

[102] The calculation makes use of the statistically significant results from Table A13 in the Annex and uses the employment rates for poorly educated (i.e., without primary education) majority and displaced men and across the region as baselines.

es of finding skilled employment appear to increase substantially only after secondary education is attained.

This suggests that, thanks to their local work experience and networks, workers from majority communities can obtain skilled employment irrespective of their education level. Displaced workers by contrast do not have these connections and local experience. In the face of distrust from majority communities, only the very educated displaced seem able to obtain skilled employment. This is apparent in the fact that education does not lead to wages for displaced workers that are equivalent to those of similarly educated workers from majority communities. The results of a returns-to-education estimation[103] show that increases in education levels do result in significant wage gains for displaced workers (with the exception of primary education in the case of women). However, these gains are from much lower wage levels than those received by workers from majority communities (see Table A14 in the Annex). Presenting the wages associated with each education level as a percentage of the wages earned by a non-educated worker from the majority community shows that increasing the level of education for displaced men or women does not, with the partial exception of Bosnian women, bring their wages in line with similarly skilled majority workers. Thus, displaced workers too often do not have access to the employment and wages that are commensurate with their level of education (see Figure 2-28).

FIGURE 2 – 27

Education and type of employment

Percentage of the displaced and majority (over 15 years of age) with each level of education employed in a skilled profession

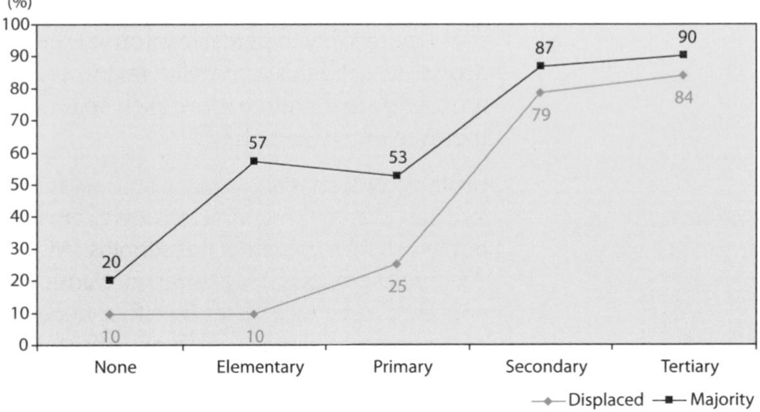

FIGURE 2 – 28

Relative returns to education

The estimated wages of majority and displaced men and women with primary, secondary or tertiary education as a percentage of the average wage of the uneducated majority

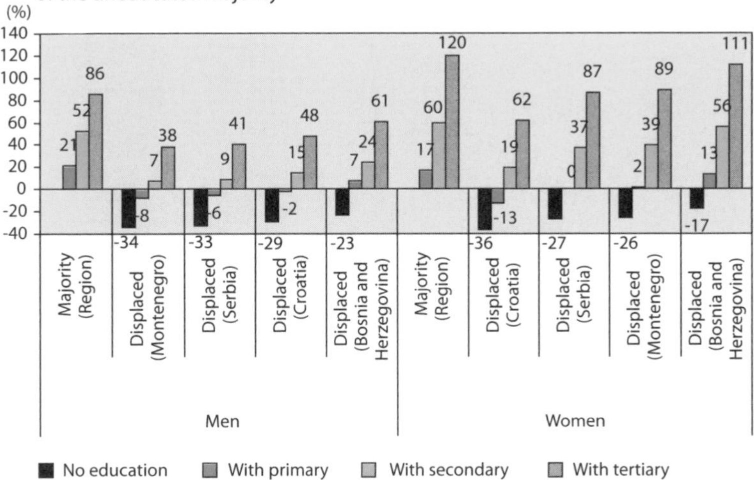

Conclusions from Chapter 2.3

Data analyzed in this chapter suggest that the educational and literacy status of displaced workers is very close to that of workers from majority communities. For the displaced in the Western Balkans, the concept of 'educational vulnerability' does not make much sense. This means that the barriers to education faced by displaced persons are quite different from the barriers Roma are facing. This underscores the need for specific, group-targeted measures for decreasing vulnerability. For the displaced, this means measures within a comprehensive national strategy for displaced populations, implemented at the level of (and often by) the communities affected.

Box 17: National MDG targets, vulnerable groups and displaced youth unemployment

In **Bosnia and Herzegovina**, the National MDG report calls for reductions in youth (15-24 year-old) unemployment rates to 12 per cent by 2015. Assuming progress towards this target is calculated from the 34.8 per cent rate estimated in 2001, the youth unemployment rate in Bosnia and Herzegovina would have to decline by 1.63 percentage points annually. At this rate, the displaced would reach this 12 per cent target only in 2036. Achieving the target by 2015 would require annual reductions in the unemployment rate for displaced youths three times larger than the national figure.

[103] A basic Mincerian regression in which the natural log of wages was regressed against age, age-squared and education level. The model was estimated separately for men and women and for each of the groups.

Data show that the subjective perception of unemployment among the displaced is higher than among majority communities – even when the former are involved in some form of income generation. The displaced seem more likely to perceive informal sector economic activities as unreliable and short-term, and are therefore more likely to regard themselves as unemployed.

Unstable employment is associated with low incomes that are substantively lower among displaced than majority households. Moreover, inter-group discrepancies in wages do not seem to be fully offset by either benefits or by coping strategies such as subsistence farming. Displaced workers are overrepresented in sectors dominated by manual, low-skill labour, and are underrepresented in public-sector employment. This is largely consistent with their 'provisional' and 'unresolved' status. The displaced face also limited opportunities for self-employment and access to credit. Like Roma, the displaced tend to rely on family and other informal credit sources.

Unemployment rates among young displaced workers are higher than for older adults among both majority and displaced households. Displaced women also have higher unemployment rates than displaced men. Unemployment rates for both displaced and majority households drop with education levels, but unemployment rates are higher among well-educated displaced than well-educated majority workers. This may well be further evidence of the influence of displaced workers' unresolved status, as jobs requiring higher education are less available in the informal sector. However, for poorly educated workers this situation is reversed: unemployment rates among majority workers are higher than for displaced workers.

CHAPTER 2.4

Health and security

Summary

In the previous chapters, vulnerability was approached sectorally, in terms of poverty, employment and education. Human security (as an antidote to vulnerability) can also be defined to include health status and nutrition security, community relations, access to social services and threat perception.[104]

This chapter analyses housing conditions, threat perceptions, and health and nutrition conditions for displaced as opposed to majority households. The displaced face a very insecure housing situation: most live in accommodations for refugees with substandard sanitation infrastructure. These conditions, and the fact that they often have left much behind in the places from which they fled, mean that the displaced possess fewer basic household items, such as furniture or books. Access to information and communication technologies is often inadequate as well.

The displaced rate their health status worse compared to one year earlier. Some important gender differences exist in terms of incidence of chronic illnesses: more women are affected by chronic illnesses among both displaced and majority households. The displaced are more likely to suffer from neuroses and disorders related to the psychological trauma of displacement. Large physical distances to health facilities, low incomes, and lack of proper identity documents, are major barriers to access to health services for displaced households. Insufficient vaccination coverage (most often due to inadequate identity documents) is a major determinant of vulnerability, particularly for displaced children. Like Roma, displaced households are much more likely than majority households to go to bed hungry because they cannot afford food. Displaced children are particularly susceptible to nutrition risks.

The most common threat reported by both displaced and majority households is 'lack of sufficient incomes'. However, while large proportions of displaced households view hunger, poor sanitation and inadequate housing as the greatest threats to their households, majority respondents are more concerned with such issues as crime and corruption. When asked who would be the best placed to handle these threats, both groups responded that the family should handle problems of low incomes, hunger and inadequate housing. Poor sanitation and corruption, by contrast, were seen by both groups as requiring the intervention of the police, NGOs or local government.

Housing status

While almost all majority households live either in apartments or houses considered to be in good condition, almost two fifths (38 per cent) of displaced households live in camps and other accommodations specifically for refugees, or in dilapidated houses and shacks (see Figure 2-29).

FIGURE 2 – 29

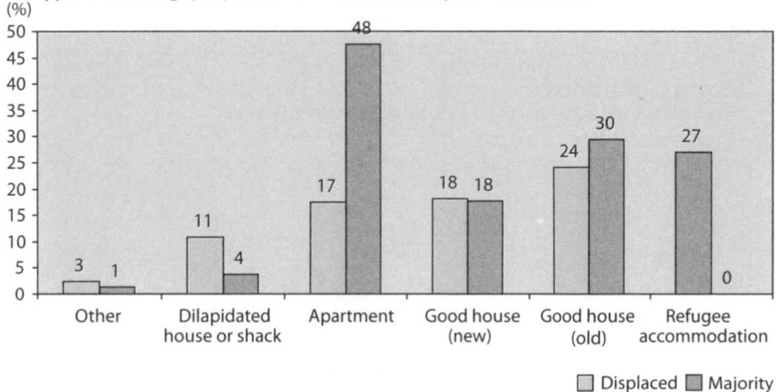

[104] The survey did not ask questions related to violence, though it is confirmed that violence, including inter-personal violence, is a major health threat that particularly affects women.

Table 2-6

Gender aspects of health status

	Majority		Displaced	
	Male	Female	Male	Female
Average score on self-assessment of improvement/deterioration of health in the last year (with '5' representing 'much worse' and '1' meaning 'much better')	3.1	3.2	3.2	3.4
Incidence of chronic illnesses (percentage of those who reported having chronic illness)	16	20	19	23
Average number of days of normal activity lost as a result of illness	13.9	11.2	18.4	17.5

Differences in the housing status of majority and displaced households are also reflected in crowding. While majority households can expect to have an average of three rooms in their homes, displaced households have an average of just two. Similarly, while majority households enjoy an average of 27 square metres per household member at home, displaced persons have just 17 square metres. Access to basic infrastructure is an additional useful proxy of household vulnerability, and displaced households are extremely vulnerable in this respect. The data show that almost a quarter of all displaced households live without access to an indoor toilet; similar proportions live without access to a bathroom or sewerage for waste disposal in their homes (see Figure 2-30).

FIGURE 2 – 30

Basic household conditions

Percentage of displaced and majority households without basic amenities

(%)
30
25
20
15
10
5
0
4
1
18
2
22
7
23
4
25
6
No electricity
No kitchen
No sewerage
No bathroom
No toilet
Displaced
Majority

FIGURE 2 – 31

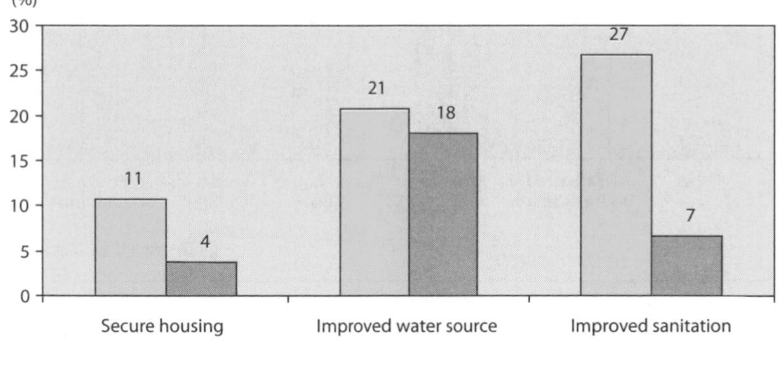

Examining the data according to MDG indicators shows that the proportions of displaced households without access to secure housing (i.e., living in dilapidated houses or shacks), improved water sources (i.e., piped water within the dwelling or garden/yard), or improved sanitation (i.e., toilet or bathroom inside the house), are far higher than the proportions of majority households, and far below MDG targets for countries in the region (see Figure 2-31).

The data show that, relative to majority households, the displaced lack access to such household items as washing machines, ovens, refrigerators, and in many cases even a bed for each member of the household (see Figure 2-32). They also show that displaced households are far more likely to use wood for either heating or cooking than majority households (Figure 2-33). The displaced are less likely to have the use of either central heating or piped gas to heat their homes, or electricity or gas to cook with.

Health and nutrition

Halting or reversing the spread of disease and eliminating hunger are central components of the MDGs. The data suggest that displaced households in the Western Balkans are particularly vulnerable to poor health and malnutrition, and illustrate the need for disaggregated health data to monitor their status. The data show that displaced respondents lost an average of 17 days of normal activity as a result of illness, compared to just 12 days for majority respondents. This seems to be related both to the higher incidence of illness among displaced respondents and their less satisfactory access to healthcare. As the data in Table 2-6 show, women in both groups of households report somewhat worse health during the last year than men. Differences in incidence of chronic illnesses are particularly pronounced. Despite this, women from both majority and displaced communities report fewer working days lost than men. This suggests that women are either more likely to report their illness to be 'chronic', are less likely to let illness affect their everyday activities, or are engaged in everyday activities that are less disrupted by illness.

Twenty-two per cent of displaced respondents (compared to 18 per cent of majority respondents) report suffering from some form of chronic illness. This may be due to the lower quality of housing: the incidence of diseases among displaced households associated with dust and other lung irritants that are attributable to poor housing conditions, such as bronchitis or emphysema, is higher than among majority households (14 per cent of the displaced compared to 8 per cent of the majority). The data also support one of the more alarming findings often reported by qualitative research – the frequency of neuroses and psychological trauma.

Just 35 per cent of displaced households have access to a family doctor, compared to 43 per cent for majority households. The data suggest that such limited access to health care for displaced households is caused by their remoteness: 35 and 36 per cent of displaced households reported living more than three kilometres from a primary medical centre or general practitioner respectively, compared to 17 and 24 per cent for majority households. (However, 39 per cent of displaced households reported living within three kilometres of traditional healers, compared to 30 per cent of majority households—see Figure 2-34). These data suggest that, in light of the scarcity of modern medical care in the vicinity of the camps in which they live, displaced households turn more to traditional – largely unregulated – forms of health care.

In addition to their physical isolation, low incomes and inadequate identity documents are also barriers to adequate health care for displaced persons. Thirty-eight per cent of displaced households reported periods during the past 12 months in which they could not afford to purchase medicines prescribed to a member of the household (compared to 20 per cent for majority households). Although throughout the former Yugoslavia displaced persons were officially given ID cards entitling them to health care, 9 per cent of displaced respondents reported having been denied medical service due to lack of proper docu-

FIGURE 2 – 32

Home amenities

Percentage of displaced and majority households without various items

(%)	Refrigerator	Oven	Adequate bedding	Washing machine
Displaced	11	15	23	30
Majority	2	3	5	6

FIGURE 2 – 33

Type of fuel used

Share of displaced and majority households using a given fuel for heating or cooking

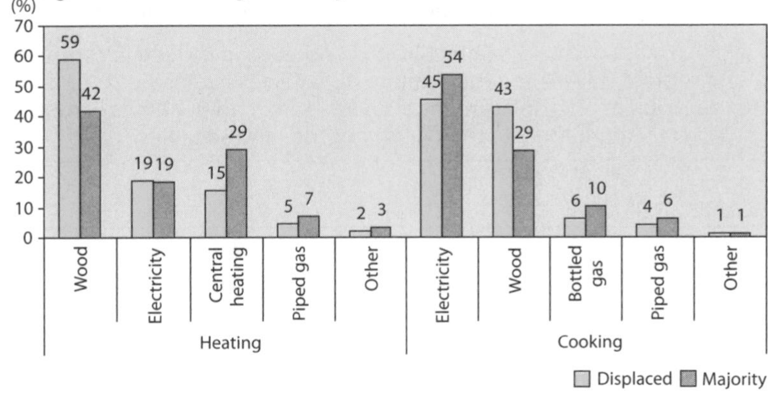

FIGURE 2 – 34

Access to health services

Share of displaced and majority households by distance from health services

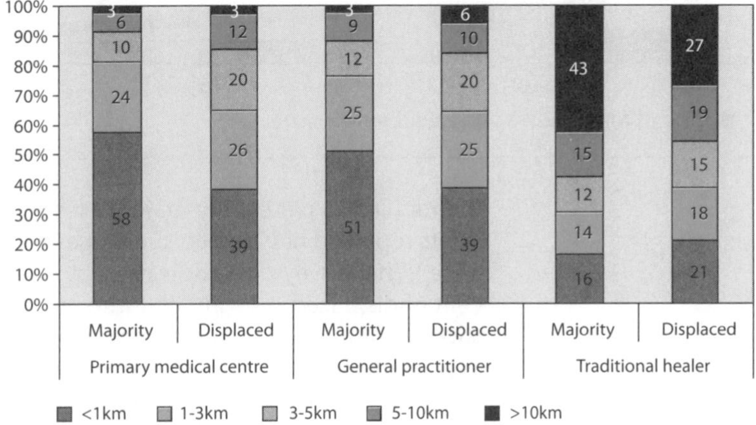

Box 18: National MDG targets, vulnerable groups and displaced households' access to improved sanitation

Improved sanitation is often used to measure countries' progress toward reaching MDG 7. In the case of displaced persons, this indicator reflects the quality of housing and associated infrastructure in the settlements where these households reside.

In **Montenegro**, the national MDG report calls for universal access to improved sanitation by 2015, up from 98.5 per cent in 2005. At the national level, meeting this goal would require annual increases in such access of 0.15 percentage points. But for displaced households, progress at this rate would mean that the target would only be met in 2137. If the government wishes to achieve improved sanitation by 2015 for all displaced households, the pace at which access to improved sanitation is growing would need to be increased by over 12 times.

In **Serbia,** the national MDG report likewise called for achieving full access to improved sanitation by 2015, up from 88.3 per cent in 2000. At the national level, meeting this goal would require annual increases in such access of 0.78 percentage points. But for displaced households, progress at this rate would mean that the target would only be met in 2049. If the government wishes to achieve improved sanitation by 2015 for all displaced households, the pace at which access to improved sanitation is growing would need to be increased by over four times.

Because these indicators reflect living conditions in collective centres, real progress is likely to require more definitive, sustainable solutions to the problems of displacement, such as return to their homes or more complete integration into their new countries and societies.

FIGURE 2 – 35

Nutrition vulnerability

Percentage of households in which a member went to bed hungry in the past month because he or she could not afford food

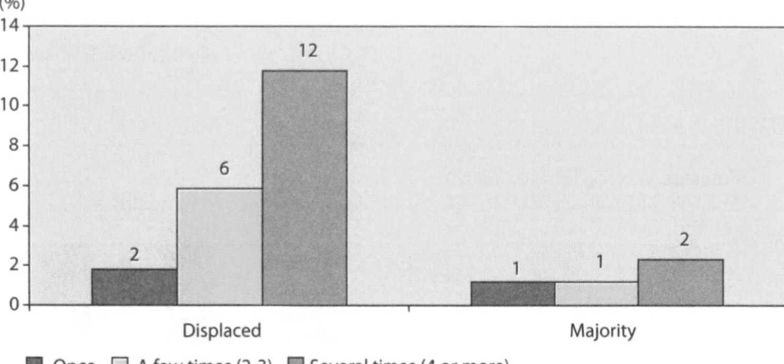

ments. (Only 3 per cent of majority respondents reported having had such an experience.) The survey data indicate that 6 per cent of displaced persons' children are not vaccinated against such common diseases as polio, diphtheria, tetanus, and whooping cough, with a lack of medical identity cards (ID) given most frequently (38 per cent) as the reason for this. Although 5 per cent of children under 14 years of age from majority households also do not receive vaccinations, the most common reason given for this is that vaccinations are 'not considered important'. Thus, although the total number of children who are not vaccinated is not large, and caution should be exercised in interpreting these findings, these results point to the unresolved status of displaced persons as a major determinant of their vulnerability.

Health status is directly related to nutrition, which in turn is influenced by expenditures (i.e., poverty). The data show that although the reported differences in nutrition security for Roma households are much more pronounced than for majority and displaced households, the latter still face considerable risks. As much as 12 per cent of displaced households (versus 2 per cent of majority households) reported experiencing four or more cases within a month when they went to bed hungry because they couldn't afford food. Almost one fifth of displaced households face nutrition risk, compared with 4 per cent of majority households (Figure 2-35). For children from displaced households, this figure rises to 27 per cent, compared to just 7 per cent for children from majority households.

Political participation and access to information

Political participation is essential for ensuring that the needs of the displaced are met. However, the survey data show that displaced households have much lower social or political engagement than majority households. Just 13 displaced households surveyed (1 per cent of the total sample) reported having at least one household member who is a member of the local municipal council or assembly, compared to 35 majority households (3 per cent of the total sample). Limited access to information, which is an important component of social and political participation, might be a contributing factor. The data show that the displaced are far less likely than the majority to have access to various sources of information in their homes.

Threat perceptions

In light of their higher rates of poverty and unemployment, their poorer housing conditions and health and nutrition status, it is not surprising that the largest threats perceived by displaced households are those of insufficient incomes, inadequate housing, crime, hunger, conflict or physical insecurity, and sanitation-related diseases (see Figure 2-36). On the other hand, majority communities are more likely to perceive threats in terms of such governance-related issues as corruption and environmental pollution. This reflects majority communities' deeper integration into economic and political processes, as described in the *Political participation and access to information* section above.

When asked who is best placed to manage the response to threats, answers varied according to the threat in question. Across both groups, respondents who reported low incomes, hunger, or inadequate housing to be the greatest threats to their households tended to believe that their family would be best placed to manage these threats. Of those who emphasized corruption or poor sanitation as the greatest threats, the highest proportion of both groups responded that the police, NGOs, or local governments were best placed to tackle them. For those who viewed environmental pollution as the worst threat to their households, the preferred response agent varied across groups. It is indicative that the highest percentage of displaced persons and majority respondents indicated that NGOs would be best placed to respond.

Conclusions from Chapter 2.4

The survey data point to considerably different profiles of household vulnerability and security in the case of displaced versus majority households. While both groups complain about insufficient incomes, displaced households face additional challenges related to their unsettled status, and more frequently emphasize such issues as inadequate housing, the absence of household goods, and nutrition insecurity in their subjective threats assessment. Perhaps surprisingly, displaced persons do not frequently mention such threats as ethnic-related violence or threats to their possessions. These threats may have been associated with the conflict phase, which for most households was over by 2000. By the same token, the absence of on-going conflicts in the Balkans means that less attention is focused on the plight of the displaced and their families. This disinterest does not help attract the broad support needed to improve their situation. Indeed, the biggest threat to displaced persons at present may be the lack of imminent 'televizable' threats that can

FIGURE 2 – 36

Perceived threats

Percentage of the displaced and majority reporting each threat to be the most serious facing their household

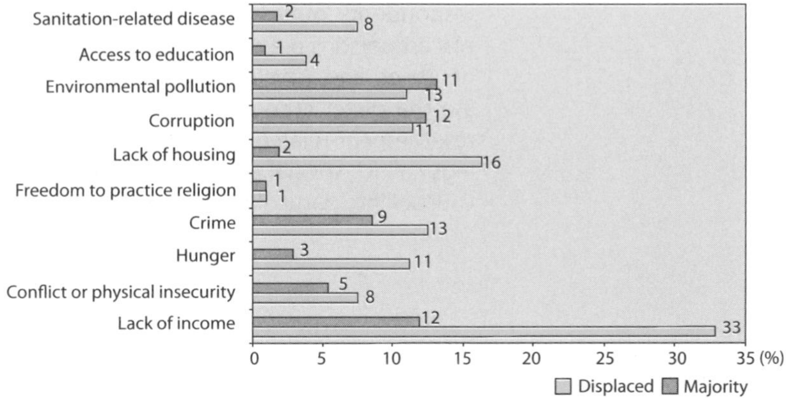

Box 19: Displaced children in Serbia – struggling for survival, far from development

Nominally, education in all Southeast European countries is free and available to all. In reality, however, different groups face different problems in exercising their right to education.

Children of displaced families are particularly vulnerable to educational risks. In some cases, collective centres are far from schools, making it difficult for children to attend. A Norwegian Refugee Council report on internally displaced persons found that 20 per cent of displaced children in Serbia do not attend school. Those who attend often do so in classes with over 50 children per classroom.

Language can also be a barrier, particularly for Albanian- or Roma-speaking children. Chronic illnesses, lack of proper clothing, and intolerance from local children can add further difficulties. Most of the displaced Roma children from Kosovo have either never been to school or dropped out before completing the fourth year. Even when children show an interest in school, cultural attitudes to education compound the practical and psychological barriers to school attendance.

Some of the children are in orphanages, others are in foster care, others live with close or distant relatives. Twelve per cent of children in Serbian orphanages are displaced. Life for these children has been described as "only survival, no development". Nutritional risks are also present: to date, school meals have not been part of the education programmes. While such risks are present for the entire population, they can be particularly difficult for displaced children. Border communities and other strategically located municipalities can be hit by large influxes of displaced persons, putting the educational system and other public services under severe stress. For example, in certain areas of Vojvodina and Kraljevo, 42 per cent of the people are refugees and IDPs.

UNICEF plays a leading role in providing education for these children, organizing 'catch up' classes for approximately 30,000 displaced children of primary school age (some 1,000 of whom are Roma) in collective and community centres and in Serbian primary schools. Most of the assistance for children has gone to education for younger children. UNICEF reports that more than 8,000 children in Serbia have lost a parent or been orphaned during the decade of wars. Their lack of prospects makes youth understandably angry and prone to destructive behaviour. If they are left without positive role models and opportunities to constructively craft their future, displaced children are at risk of growing into angry young people who perpetuate cycles of violence and retaliation.

Box based on "Refugee and Internally Displaced Women and Children in Serbia and Montenegro". September 2001. Women's Commission for Refugee Women and Children (WCRWC). New York: WCRWC.

generate attention and precipitate decisive action. International organizations can do much in this respect.

Health status data reported by displaced respondents outline worrying trends. Displaced persons are most heavily affected by neuroses and psychological disorders that are the direct consequence of conflict and resettlement-related trauma. These findings call for special attention like psychiatric counselling, particularly for children. Lack of appropriate medical identification is another problem detected by the survey. Registration-related barriers are a formal obstacle that can prevent access to primary health care and hospital services. Since these barriers are closely related to questions of the status of displaced households, resolving these 'status issues' should be a matter of international concerted action. Addressing discrepancies between legislation and its implementation should be particular concerns.

Policy recommendations

This chapter focuses on the policy implications of the preceding chapters and links them to the broader conceptual and policy frameworks in Southeast Europe vis-à-vis the Roma, the displaced and other vulnerable groups. These policy recommendations are not meant to be a comprehensive 'catechism on issues of vulnerability'. The regional analysis presented here does not lend itself to country-specific recommendations; these are the domain of the national vulnerability reports.[105] The recommendations of this chapter, as with the rest of this report, focus on more general framework issues that can contextualize policy at the national level.

General principles of intervention

Policies intended to decrease vulnerability during the last 15 years in Southeast Europe have too often suffered from the absence of two critical components: a comprehensive human-centred conceptual framework, and clear, measurable objectives. Policies have too often focused on treating symptoms rather than causes, and have been developed on a case-by-case basis (often in response to humanitarian disasters) without a clear conceptual underpinning. Policies tend to be group-oriented, contributing to the fragmentation of local communities. In the countries of the Western Balkans, where millions of people experienced the horrors of ethnic cleansing, policy approaches that emphasize ethnicity are unlikely to be sustainable.

The analysis presented here points to large similarities – as well as important differences – in the extent, determinants, and types of vulnerability between Roma and displaced peoples in Southeast Europe. Some of these determinants are group-related, others are (income) status related. Careful combinations of different policies (group-centred and status-centred) are needed to decrease overall vulnerability levels. These policies need to be fitted to different national contexts, reflecting various levels of overlap between different groups and differences from country to country. But policies should also reflect certain general principles, as well as the specifics of different vulnerable groups. This section deals with these general principles/conceptual foundations that should underpin successful approaches to vulnerability. These building blocs are subsequently elaborated in group-specific policies reflecting the particular challenges Roma and vulnerable groups are facing.

Non-discrimination and equality before the law

Non-discrimination should be a foundation of inclusive policy frameworks

Non-discrimination should be a foundation of inclusive policy frameworks. Legal frameworks for non-discriminatory policies exist in all Southeast European countries, and are undergoing further development, particularly as the *acquis communautaire* is transposed into national legislation during EU accession processes. At present, however, these frameworks are not fully developed, and capacity gaps in state institutions (particularly the courts) and civil society limit their implementation. Also, not all aspects of anti-discrimination policies are universally accepted. The concepts of positive discrimination (or affirmative action) and indirect discrimination (where discrimination is held to occur even if the intent to discriminate is absent), are not always supported by majority populations. So do propositions concerning the desirability of state intervention to prevent discriminatory practices in private contracting. However, under human rights law, the State has an obligation to ensure that no one under its jurisdiction is discriminated against, regardless of whether the act of discrimination is committed by State or private actors. This is why both the State and private sector should be involved in consultations towards an anti-discrimination strategy (Kälin, 2006).

105 Albania, Serbia and Montenegro have already elaborated such reports using the UNDP vulnerable groups survey data. In other countries (Macedonia and Croatia) such reports are being drafted. All the reports are available at http://vulnerability.undp.sk.

Efforts to design and implement anti-discrimination laws across the region should be strongly encouraged and supported by donors

Still, the belief that legal and policy frameworks should ensure fair treatment *regardless of ethnicity*, in order to encourage *equality of opportunities* (as opposed to equality of outcomes) seems widely held in Southeast Europe. This can be channelled into support for social policies focusing on vulnerability (as opposed to ethnic) criteria. One concrete – and important – precondition for non-discriminatory policy regimes is proper anti-discrimination legislation. Not all countries of the region have adopted them – and those that have need to improve enforcement. Fragmentary anti-discrimination references in various specific pieces of legislation do not constitute a comprehensive anti-discriminatory framework. Efforts to design and implement anti-discrimination laws across the region should be strongly encouraged and supported by donors.

Positive discrimination is more likely to be accepted, and its possible abuses attenuated, if it is accompanied by 'equality before the law' as a second non-discrimination principle. Equality before the law means that support for vulnerable groups should not lead to double standards with different legal regimes applying to different ethnic (or other vulnerable) groups. These problems are illustrated by the issue of the large debts for housing, electricity and communal services accumulated by many Roma households, which have acquired explosive political dimensions in many Southeast European countries. Tensions around these issues are too often resolved either by local utility companies writing off these debts—thereby provoking angry claims of 'preferential treatment for Roma' from nearby majority communities—or by cutting Roma households or communities off from electricity, heating or water grids.

Roma and the displaced should receive state support first and foremost not because of their ethnic or legal status, but because they are victims of social exclusion

Debts cannot be simply written off on the grounds that households are desperately poor. Bankruptcy reform (to protect the rights of both delinquent household debtors and their creditors),[106] and the introduction of transparent debt swapping schemes and household solidarity debts funds, can fill in the missing pieces of the institutional puzzle. Such funds can be capitalized by households and NGOs, and can be integrated with projects for community support, microlending schemes and the like. Rather than seeing areas of vulnerability and insecurity as short-term problems to be solved by special initiatives, they should be understood as outcomes of inadequate policy reform, in which the full benefits of anti-discrimination laws and market-friendly social policy mechanisms have not yet been fully captured.

Recognition of joint interest

Recognition of joint interest in mutually acceptable solutions to problems of vulnerable groups is an obvious precondition to finding these solutions. This recognition must form the basis of any dialogue, in order to gain the support of the broadest set of constituencies and avoid the perception that solutions are being imposed from above or in response to the demands of one group or another. Majorities and minorities alike could start by recognizing that diversity can be an asset for any society. Two inter-related issues are crucial here: positive discrimination, and social policy targeting according to criteria of vulnerability and not ethnicity.

The deep exclusion from formal labour markets, educational and other mainstream institutions experienced by Roma (and, to a lesser extent, the displaced) suggest that some amount of positive discrimination is needed to redress the legacies of discrimination and intolerance. But as the growing concerns of at least some majority communities concerning the allegedly 'privileged' status of Roma suggest (see Box 20), the introduction of positive discrimination in Southeast Europe could be fraught with difficulties. Growing numbers of vulnerable individuals among majority communities already believe that their governments are implementing poverty reduction strategies for Roma, but not for them. Roma-targeted assistance therefore risks a backlash that could make such measures self-defeating, or worse.

If possible, measures that would further fragment societies along ethnic lines should be avoided. Instead, it is vulnerability—along the dimensions set forth in this report—that should be targeted, rather than ethnicity. Roma and the displaced should receive state support first and foremost not because of their ethnic or legal status, but because they are victims of social exclusion,[107] and

106 Personal bankruptcy recommendations for vulnerable groups have been developed as part of UNDP research on barriers to Roma employment in the Czech Republic (see http://undp.org/europeandcis).

107 "Most Roma are vulnerable, but not all vulnerable are Roma".

because EU integration and national legislation requires that anti-discrimination laws and social policy address their plight. Since vulnerability in many Southeast European countries is shared across ethnic groups, majority and minority communities have a common interest in addressing it.

As painful as these issues are in the Roma/majority context, they can be even more painful in the context of displaced persons, who often face legacies of ethnic cleansing and victor/vanquished dynamics. In some countries, the wounds of previous conflicts make the vulnerability of the displaced even more acute than the vulnerability of the Roma. Rebuilding fractured communities is a long and painful process, and can only be done when joint interests in living together are recognized.

Welfare-to-work programmes and labour market reform

The importance of increasing employment for Roma and displaced workers in Southeast Europe raises questions about the effectiveness of active labour market policies and programmes for vulnerable groups. Such policies seek to reduce unemployment by addressing skill and spatial mismatches, and improving information, on the labour market. In addition to reducing poverty, active labour market policies can support the adoption of more pro-active labour market postures by vulnerable workers and help alter passive, defeatist mindsets that can come with long-term unemployment and social marginalization. Moreover, when employment subsidies are smaller than the unemployment benefits that would otherwise be paid, active labour market policies can be cost-effective social policy instruments, even in the short term.

'Welfare to work' measures—under which unemployed workers engage in publicly-funded employment in lieu of receiving cash payments, sometimes in partnership with private employers—are close to the spirit of active labour market policies. Not all countries in Southeast Europe (or their employment support activities) are well prepared in this regard, however. Most labour offices continue to function primarily as unemployment registration bodies, rather than as brokers who link job seekers with private-sector employment opportunities. Unfortunately, the high rates of unemployment of-

Box 20: **Backlash against positive discrimination: ATAKA in Bulgaria**

In Bulgaria's 2005 parliamentary elections, ATAKA, an openly anti-Roma party, received 8.93 per cent of the votes, which translated into 21 seats in the parliament out of 240. The party's success reflected a general decline of sympathy vis-à-vis Roma among other voters. The mean values of a 'sympathy scale' (where 10 means strong sympathy and 1 means strong antipathy—see below) declined from 4.1 in 1994 to 2.9 in 2004 (the year preceding the elections) and 3.5 in 2005 (right after the elections). While many aspects of this scale remained constant over time, tolerance by non-Roma respondents of their children studying in classes where the majority of children are Roma declined sharply. (This may have more to do with justified concerns about the quality of education in Roma-dominated schools than with intolerance vis-à-vis Roma *per se*). These data also show a near tripling of support for the argument that 'Roma are privileged in Bulgaria'. That is, despite compelling evidence of Roma poverty and social exclusion in Bulgaria, the growing public perception that Roma are 'privileged' boosted support for ATAKA. (It is difficult to imagine the successful introduction of policies based on positive discrimination in such circumstances.)

"Yes" responses to questions of: "Would you accept..."

	1994	1997	2000	2003	2004	2005
... living in the same town/village with Roma?	57%	51%	54%	55%	59%	63%
... working together with Roma?	49%	41%	38%	40%	41%	47%
... living in the same neighbourhood with Roma?	38%	32%	27%	28%	33%	37%
...your children attending classes in which there are a few Roma children?	65%	62%	65%	66%	66%	65%
...your children attending a class in which half the children are Roma?	22%	12%	11%	12%	12%	12%
...your children attending a class in which the majority of children are Roma?	13%	7%	5%	5%	3%	5%
Do you think that "Roma are privileged in Bulgaria?" - completely agree or rather agree	23%	25%	32%	31%	65%	-

Data from regular surveys conducted by GALLUP for the Ivan Hadjiyski Institute of Social Values and Structures, based on identical sampling methodology and questionnaires over the years.

What are the roots of such misperceptions? Is it the plethora of Roma projects - many of which have been something less than robustly successful? Is it the increasingly visible cleavage between the rich 'Roma aristocracy' and their perennially impoverished Roma constituencies? Is it the 'writing off' of Roma household electricity debts - a practice not applicable to the non-Roma poor? Perceptions of increasing poverty among non-Roma vulnerable households?

The best answer to these questions is perhaps 'all of the above'. It may be that Bulgarian voters were not rejecting policies that seek to reduce vulnerability *per se*, but rather the ineffectiveness of such policies to date. Support for social inclusion may still be there, if measurable, sustainable results can be delivered.

ten prevalent in the areas where Roma and displaced households are concentrated can make this principle quite difficult to realize in the short run—particularly in countries with weak state capacity for effective social policies.

Recent World Bank research indicates that active labour market policies are more effective when the economy, and demand for labour, is growing (Betcherman, Olivas and Dar, 2004). The experience in Bulgaria reveals positive net impacts from all active labour market programmes tested, with the largest impact achieved from supporting self-employment, from wage subsidies, and from training and retraining (Ministry of Labour and Social Policy, Bulgaria, 2005). Although the impact of temporary employment initiatives is often small, when combined with training programmes, temporary employment schemes can provide significant benefits to the long-term unemployed, helping to improve qualifications and employability within practical skills-building projects. Active labour market policy beneficiaries with primary education (or less) seem to benefit more than other groups – and Roma clearly would fit into this group.

Reform of employment protection legislation likewise has implications for active labour market policies and their ability to address labour market vulnerability. Employment protection legislation seems to have the reverse of the intended effect in many Southeast European countries, by discouraging companies from hiring workers whom they may not be able to dismiss subsequently. Recent research (World Bank, 2005d) suggests that strong employment protection legislation limits job creation in Southeast Europe (Croatia is a good example of the impact of strong employment protection legislation on vulnerable groups). While the impact of this 'protection' on vulnerable groups has not yet been thoroughly investigated, their high unemployment rates and generally weak labour market positions strongly suggest that the interests of workers from vulnerable communities are poorly served by such measures. Simply put, they have fewer jobs to be protected, and are less likely to get a new one (Rutkowski, 2003). (There may also be many other benefits to labour market deregulation: one study suggests that greater labour market flexibility is associated with larger FDI inflows, particularly in transition economies (Javorcik and Spatareanu, 2004).

Recent research (World Bank, 2005d) focusing on changes in the length and scope of fixed-term (as opposed to permanent) contracts suggests that young workers, and those employed in the informal sector, are the chief beneficiaries of reforms in this area. These changes can reduce youth unemployment rates by allowing wages and employment protection standards to fall below national minimum levels for a defined period, in order to provide new labour market entrants with needed experience, skills and training. After such apprenticeships, younger workers can more easily find regular employment. The same applies to allowing flexible working hours, which helps accommodate changes in labour market demand without increasing unemployment, and can be especially important for women and working parents. Their high unemployment rates and extensive engagement in the informal sector suggest that Roma and displaced workers would stand to benefit from labour market reforms in these areas as well.

When it comes to addressing labour market insecurity for Roma and displaced workers, it is clear that no silver bullet exists, and various instruments must be used in various combinations depending on the specific national (and even local) context. Still, growing numbers of countries in Southeast Europe (as well as EU member states) are experimenting with labour market deregulation, welfare-to-work programmes, and other reforms to increase the effectiveness of active labour market policies. The labour market vulnerability experienced by Roma and displaced workers suggests that these policy reforms could be used with great effect in addressing the needs of these (and other vulnerable) groups. The guiding principles behind such policy reforms should be sustainability, an appropriate human development focus, engaging the private sector as partners, and ensuring better coordination between the various government agencies involved in benefits provision and other forms of social protection. The development of better data on poverty and social exclusion, disaggregated by ethnicity, displacement status, gender, region, and other dimensions of vulnerability, is also extremely important in this respect.

Involving the private sector

When facing challenges of high unemployment and poverty rates, governments often succumb to the temptation of increasing public spending for social assistance and public works programmes. These may be justifiable as short-term emergency measures, particularly in circumscribed post-conflict regions where the area-based development paradigm may be usefully applied (e.g., in South Serbia). In the longer run, however, it is the market and the private sector, not governments, that must create jobs for Roma, displaced and other vulnerable workers. Governments' role is primarily in helping vulnerable workers to improve their employability, rather than in providing direct employment opportunities. Public works can be useful in this respect – but rather as an opportunity to improve skills, and less so as direct employment provision.

This means that private employers must be at the heart of any long-term sustainable strategy to reduce unemployment for Roma and displaced workers.[108] Growing numbers of companies increasingly understand that consigning millions of Roma and displaced households to the socio-economic margins is bad for business. While unemployment rates are quite high in some parts of Southeast Europe (e.g., Kosovo, Macedonia), in others (e.g., Romania) they are well below European averages, and labour shortages are sharpening. With training in the right skills, Roma workers could increasingly fill these gaps. Likewise, since the skills of the displaced generally do not differ dramatically from national profiles, displaced workers could make an important contribution to many companies' business plans. Companies that take the trouble to recruit workers from these communities and adopt employee diversity programmes to keep those workers who have been recruited can realize gains that are well in excess of the costs incurred. Social policy incentives—particularly within the welfare-to-work framework—to defray the risks private employers take in pursing these measures could be critically important.

Involving the private sector also means the appropriate application of business criteria to social programmes and projects targeting vulnerability. Competition between social service providers and local implementing partners should be promoted, whenever possible. Measurable quantitative deliverables should be defined and applied when determining development priorities and policies, on the basis of cost/benefit analysis.

Self-employment and access to microfinance

Self-employment can play an important role in moving vulnerable workers from passive dependency to active income generation. As with labour market deregulation, reforms to improve business environments must wrestle with a number of trade-offs. Improvements in the business environment may have mixed consequences for Roma and displaced workers, particularly if job creation rates lag behind overall economic growth, or if the benefits of employment growth are concentrated at the top of the labour market. In order to ensure that benefits from improvements in the business climate do reach vulnerable households, measures to improve access to credit and capital necessary for small business start-ups are important.

As discussed, microlending can be particularly important in this regard. For that purpose, however, several rules should be followed. First of all, loans should be clearly distinguished from grants. Many vulnerable communities receive social assistance in the form of cash transfers that do not need to be paid back. When community development projects are implemented in parallel with microlending, the distinction between grants and loans is blurred, and incentives to borrow (and repay) are weakened. (Why should individuals borrow when they can obtain a risk-free grant?) In order to avoid misleading beneficiaries, the 'rules of the game' should be clear, which means clearly distinguishing subsidized from non-subsidized elements, and being sure that beneficiaries understand the risks associated with various forms of financial assistance.

When grant schemes are involved, they should envision a clear time horizon for a gradual transition to loans. This is central to prospects for long-term microfinance project sustainability, and often for financial-system deepening in rural or low-income urban areas.

This means that private employers must be at the heart of any long-term sustainable strategy to reduce unemployment for Roma and displaced workers

When grant schemes are involved, they should envision a clear time horizon for a gradual transition to loans

[108] For more on this, see UNDP/Ernst&Young, 2005b.

The positive externalities of employing Roma or displaced workers who would otherwise not have a job should be also reflected when assessing a project's viability

Soft loans should be avoided. Financial markets do not work when creditors' leverage over debtors is excessively weak. In the context of microcredits for Roma and the displaced, this comes down to answering the following question: *what to do in the event of default?* Answers should start with an emphasis on formalizing the informal property rights that vulnerable groups often enjoy vis-à-vis their dwellings—but rights that are too often not reflected in law, due to exclusion from formal legal systems.[109] They should include the introduction or strengthening of personal bankruptcy mechanisms that would protect the interests of both vulnerable debtors (Roma, the displaced) and creditors (bank or microfinance institutions) in a transparent, regularized manner. Where possible, microcredits can also be distributed to groups of vulnerable individuals; creditors can rely on reputational factors and peer pressure to ensure repayment.

The positive externalities of employing Roma or displaced workers who would otherwise not have a job should be also reflected when assessing a project's viability. Aligning project finance with market principles is critically important in microfinance. However, this should not preclude the use of subsidies in microfinance projects, in order to ensure that what is socially desirable is also profitable for implementing partners. In the case of projects targeting vulnerable communities, these subsidies should allow implementing agencies to internalize at least some of the positive externalities associated with their activities. These include helping to reverse the consolidation of perpetually vulnerable and dependent underclasses. In addition to donors (working in the project management framework), these subsidies can come from government agencies under welfare-to-work and public-private partnership schemes.

Microfinance is effective only if applied in combination with other approaches and policies

Finally, a dose of realism regarding microfinance is necessary. The survey data show that microfinance is effective only if applied in combination with other approaches and policies. It is not equally applicable to the most marginalized and excluded. The impact on the most vulnerable can be indirect – through improved local economic opportunities using microfinance to support members of the community who are not at the very bottom.

Evidence-based policies

UNDP has invested heavily in improved data capacity for evidence-based social policy making. The survey on Roma in five Central European countries conducted in 2002 and the *Avoiding the Dependency Trap* report based on these survey data was a breakthrough in this regard. The "Vulnerable Groups in Southeast Europe" data collection project was the logical next step, expanding this work both territorially (to the rest of Southeast Europe) and beyond the Roma (to displaced persons).

While data collection should be a priority and responsibility of national statistical agencies and governments, they face some problems. Some are constitutional in nature – many countries' data protection legislation limits the official collection of data by ethnicity, thereby complicating the task of measuring the ethnic dimension of vulnerability. Also, given the variety of criteria for defining vulnerability (in addition to ethnicity), the number of surveys and related costs could be prohibitively high.

On the other hand, policies that are not based on reliable data can be even more expensive. In the absence of such data, priorities are difficult to determine—particularly when choices need to be made at the local level. Cost/benefit analysis of different policy options, progress monitoring, impact assessment—all this is impossible. Data that are disaggregated by relevant vulnerability criteria must be collected, in order to make possible in-depth monitoring of the standard MDG frameworks and social inclusion indicators, particularly within the framework of the joint inclusion memoranda that the European Commission has concluded (or is now negotiating) with the countries of Southeast Europe. Only then vulnerability analysis will facilitate targeted area-based interventions.

---

[109] In addition to missing identity papers, this exclusion takes the form of the absence of Roma landholdings in cadastral registries, or the failure of local land use and zoning systems to officially recognize Roma dwellings as properties. For displaced households, the 'provisional' nature of their legal status can act as an additional constraint on their ability to collateralize their dwellings and other property.

Possible ways to overcome existing barriers in vulnerability data collection, in terms of capacity, legislation, and political commitment, include the following:[110]

- The capacity of statistical institutions needs to be strengthened, in order to meet the needs for improved MDG and social inclusion indicators disaggregated by sex, age, ethnicity, and to make possible sub-national target setting and MDG monitoring.
- The use of vulnerability statistics for formulating, monitoring and evaluating MDG-related policies should be encouraged. Awareness of the importance of evidence-based-policy making should be cultivated.
- Existing instruments (like labour force and household budget surveys) should be extended to provide better coverage of vulnerable groups. People from these groups should be involved in the process of data collection, processing and analysis to ensure broader ownership of the data and reduce the possibility of mistrust.
- For vulnerable groups that are difficult to capture in household budget and labour force surveys (such as people with disabilities or living with HIV/AIDS), specialized thematic surveys (e.g., in education, health) seem best able to provide the data needed. In order to ensure that the various statistical instruments are used in a complementary manner, better coordination between organizations involved in data collection is needed. Open access to primary data by all researchers and other interested parties is particularly important in this respect.
- When legal obstacles exist, legal frameworks need to be modified, in order to ensure a better balance between the need to identify vulnerability on the one hand and to protect privacy (associated with individual data) on the other.

Policies specifically targeting Roma

The general principles outlined above should be translated into group-sensitive policies, programming, and projects, which in turn should often be conducted within an area-based development framework. This section outlines the Roma-specific elements that should complement the general framework of policies targeted at decreasing vulnerability.[111]

Reducing dependency

Roma are particularly vulnerable to dependency traps. With limited development opportunities and few successful role models from their own communities, Roma can easily reduce their professional aspirations to the point where survival on social welfare is an acceptable option. Reliance on welfare payments can exacerbate problems of vulnerability by weakening incentives to improve labour market competitiveness. The failure to leave social safety nets today can reduce the likelihood of breaking this dependency cycle in the future. But because Roma participation in the formal economy is often limited, relatively large numbers of Roma do not pay the social security taxes needed to fund these benefits. This 'asymmetrical' participation in social welfare systems (active regarding benefits, limited regarding contributions) can further promote exclusion and ethnic intolerance. Once they are stuck in dependency, aspirations can fall further, making escapes from poverty and dependency even more improbable. Discrimination by majority communities may be an important determinant of Roma vulnerability, but it is certainly not the only one.

In order to break this 'culture of dependency', social welfare systems should seek to avoid weakening work incentives by reflecting the principle of 'positive net benefits for positive net efforts'. Social assistance should therefore be conditional on attempts by beneficiaries to leave the social safety net-

'Asymmetrical' participation in social welfare systems can promote exclusion and ethnic intolerance

Discrimination by majority communities may be an important determinant of Roma vulnerability, but it is certainly not the only one

110 The recommendations resulted from the first Experts' Group meeting entitled 'Measuring vulnerability: Problems and possible approaches to ethnically sensitive statistics', that was organized as part of the Decade of Roma Inclusion on 27-28 July 2004. The group, which consisted of representatives from national statistical offices, governments and Roma groups, discussed how to improve such data collection instruments as the census, household budget and labour force surveys, in order to collect ethnically disaggregated data.

111 These recommendations can be found in the concept paper prepared for a conference on Roma inclusion organized by UNDP and the Friedrich Ebert Foundation in Brussels in November 2005, which can be downloaded from http://europeandcis.undp.org.

work, and improve labour market competitiveness, in a reasonable period of time. Likewise, social welfare should not be perceived as an unconditional entitlement that is paid irrespective of income earned in the informal sector. Engaging private employers and welfare-to-work schemes can make it easier to 'escape the dependency trap'.

Long-term focus on education

Policies and projects should focus on improving access to elementary education for Roma children

The survey data show that broader education and employment opportunities can reduce poverty, and vice versa. Building on this link must be at the core of breaking the vicious cycles of poverty and exclusion. Ambitious initiatives in education, in terms of desegregation, more resources, and reform of educational curricula, administration and finance are needed for this.

As discussed in Chapter 1.3, the conflicts in the Balkans and related dislocation of transition in Southeast Europe have been accompanied by dramatic declines in education levels for Roma, who report large reductions in educational attainment and literacy rates for individuals 25 years of age or younger. Policies and projects to address these gaps should therefore focus on improving access to elementary education for Roma children. The reinvigoration of pre-school preparatory classes ('zero classes'), combined with additional support for learning the languages of majority communities, should be a priority for central and municipal governments. Appropriate incentives for families to participate in such schemes, such as linking parental eligibility for social benefits to their children's school attendance, should be designed and implemented.

The survey data also suggest that, while adequate education and skills are key to improved access to employment, they are not sufficient to bridge the employment and income gaps Roma are facing. Improving employment opportunities for Roma requires combining initiatives to improve their educational status (like the Roma Education Fund) with anti-discrimination measures addressed to majority communities, employers and others. Companies in particular need to become more involved, both to help create the positive role models needed to reduce workplace stereotypes and discrimination, and to raise expectations in Roma communities.

Employment promotion and social support are key to sustainable development that decreases dependency

The survey data indicate that the high poverty rates among Roma (and, to a lesser extent, the displaced) in Southeast Europe disproportionately affect education levels. In light of the importance of education for employment and incomes, cycles of poverty among Roma and the displaced can only be broken if access to quality education improves for those living in extreme poverty. The introduction of grants to cover out-of-pocket educational expenses (e.g., for the purchase of suitable clothing, books, computers)—which would be conditional on school attendance by the students in question—seems particularly important in this respect. The resources of the Roma Education Fund could be effectively deployed in this area, but there is no substitute for better alignment of government social and education policies with the needs of vulnerable communities.

The introduction and expansion of weekly boarding schools, as a form of educational assistance for poor families, should also be considered. In addition to promoting educational inclusion for Roma children, these schools could increase aspiration levels and support health education, particularly regarding nutrition. Boarding schools are not without problems: the 'export' of bright children to boarding schools can weaken community ties, and the educational and socialization benefits they deliver are often weaker than those of regular schools. But if these schools function according to participatory and inclusive principles, they can offer superior educational alternatives.

Role models are part of escaping from poverty and vulnerability. Children often lack positive examples showing how and why education pays off. There is a strong correlation between educational levels of household heads, household status, and the educational achievements of household members.

Redefinition of existing structures for inclusion

The redefinition (not substitution) of national and sub-national structures for inclusion, employment promotion and social support are key to sustainable development that decreases dependency. This emerges as a key lesson from the sluggish implementation of the Decade of Roma Inclusion. Three years after the Decade was initiated and year and a half after it was officially launched, real progress is still to come. Too many government structures and NGOs charged with addressing Roma development issues are still unable to reflect the needs of Roma communities. Political will needs to be matched with the national and sub-national institutional capacities needed to map Roma development challenges into the administrative structures in which they work. For a community to feel the benefit of, say, pre-accession funds, proper projects should be defined, and included into the relevant development strategies at national and local levels.

Projects should be defined, and included into the relevant development strategies at national and local levels

The successful operationalization of the Decade of Roma Inclusion is still to come. When the Decade was formally launched at the beginning of 2005, national action plans (NAPs) had already been adopted in each participating country, so that implementation could begin thereafter. Unfortunately, those plans were not translated into operational programmes and projects that could reach the community level. The expected outcomes of the Decade (articulated in its objectives and the NAPs) were not linked to all outputs, activities and the necessary inputs. The absence of explicit activities and inputs made costing impossible. Without financial information, Decade-related initiatives cannot be included in budget planning. Last but not least, the Decade's general targets were not accompanied by the specific indicators needed to monitor the progress (or its absence) of the Decade implementation.

These problems reflect inadequate capacity to translate general political commitments into pragmatic action, to identify needs and allocate resources, to monitor progress, and to modify initial project design when necessary. But they also reflect the fact that the Decade is still insufficiently results-oriented. Interim evaluations of the Decade in the countries involved, that would complement the NAPs with progress indicators and align them with national development priorities, would therefore seem extremely important.

Aligning the Decade of Roma Inclusion with the area-based development paradigm

The Decade of Roma Inclusion has created an inter-governmental framework, within which specific actions and commitments can be designed and implemented. In many countries, however, the Decade's substantive content is not yet fully defined, particularly at the local level. Area-based development can be of assistance here, in a number of respects. Many of the development challenges facing Roma are seen most clearly at the local level. This reflects both the concentration of Roma communities in certain geographic areas, and the fact that responsibility for delivery of the most necessary services – particularly education, employment facilitation and health care – is at least partly decentralized. As such, their quality dramatically varies depending on locality, ethnic structures, local poverty rates and the like. School desegregation means more than just issuing regulations in the national capital—it also means implementing them in schools in concrete locations. Similarly, increasing employment opportunities requires dialogue between local labour offices and local businesses, local-level facilitation of new start-ups, and local microfinance activities. Moreover, area-based programming can promote the local-level integration of Roma and other communities. By contrast, narrow group- (rather than area-) defined interventions may further isolate Roma from the social mainstream.

The Decade of Roma Inclusion national action plans and feasibility studies therefore need to be implemented via area-based and community development programmes that address the needs of these communities, including both their Roma and non-Roma constituencies. These programmes should be expressed in terms of clear targets, budgets, and monitorable indicators. Otherwise, these plans will remain hollow declarations that are likely to increase frustration among both Roma and majority communities. Such area-based approaches could be closely linked to regional development planning, and through this to the relevant pre-accession and EU funding instruments. In many respects, area-based approaches may be the only realistic vehicle for targeted use of EU funds to address Roma development needs.

Area-based programming can promote the local-level integration of Roma and other communities

Genuine representation of Roma and reliable partnerships at the local level

Genuine representation of Roma communities as counterparts in useful dialogue with governments is a precondition for their productive involvement in the design and implementation of Roma-targeted policies. 'Nothing for Roma without Roma' has already become a standard requirement. Unless genuine representation of Roma communities is achieved, this powerful message may be little more than tokenism that camouflages exclusionary approaches to policy formulation.

Box 21: Feasibility study on the national action plan in Romania

Romania has the largest Roma community in Southeast Europe. It has also been holding the Presidency of the Decade of Roma Inclusion during 2005-2006. For these reasons the drafting of Romania's National Action Plan (NAP) was particularly important. UNDP's Country Office in Bucharest therefore supported the National Agency for Roma in developing a feasibility study for the Decade in Romania. The feasibility study sought to: (1) clarify the relationship between the NAP and other related initiatives (national and international); (2) facilitate inter-ministerial coordination concerning NAP implementation; and (3) define realistic results indicators, based on available statistical data. This last point was particularly important in terms of increasing the monitoring capacity of the government institutions charged with NAP implementation.

The NAP in its initial format was essentially a list of declarations, rather than a set of objectives with activities that could be budgeted, monitored and distributed among relevant agencies and partners. The first step in drafting the feasibility study was therefore defining a new structure for the NAP, to address the gaps apparent in the initial draft. The objectives under the four main NAP components (education, health, employment and housing) were therefore analyzed according to:

- Outcomes
- Targets
- Key actions
- (revised) Indicators
- Timeframe
- Responsible bodies (administrative bodies and organizations carrying out activities)
- Estimated costs involved
- Implementing and monitoring arrangements

All objectives, outcomes and targets were restructured, and clear indicators for results and monitoring instruments for each outcome and target were specified. This made possible the provision of realistic estimates of the timeframe, resource requirements, and other elements of a decent business plan.

The final outcome was not so much a better document, but rather a better understanding among the key players involved in the Decade implementation, in terms of specific objectives, numbers and indicators. This was definitely a lesson worth replicating in other countries of the Decade.

Representatives of Roma communities and government agencies are indeed engaged in dialogue. But this dialogue too often takes the form of parallel monologues in which expression does not necessarily lead to communication, or the finding of a common language or joint interest. The Decade of Roma Inclusion, which was nominally initiated by the governments of the participating countries, occurred thanks to the pressure and persistence of outside actors. The dialogue conducted within the Framework of the Decade has too often been limited to mutual recriminations.

These problems are sometimes exacerbated by the weak legitimacy of national and local Roma elites. Efforts to facilitate the formation of Roma elites during the 1990s often had a top-down character. These new leaders made Roma issues more visible internationally; the European Roma Forum, with which the Council of Europe concluded a partnership agreement in December 2004, is perhaps the best-known success story in this area. However, at least some of the challenges of complementing this political presence with legitimacy vis-à-vis the constituencies the international Roma organizations claim to represent, remain unresolved.[112] While these 'boosted elites' may be better than no elites at all, the tasks of ensuring their accountability to their constituencies remain before us. Research shows that many Roma do not trust Roma NGOs or Roma political parties; cooperation among Roma NGOs is too often absent when it would be useful (Boscoboinik and Giordano, 2005).[113]

Area-based development projects must be implemented locally. Reliable partners – organizations that can deliver – are needed for that purpose. Donors and international organizations can play a key role in identifying and supporting such partners. In many respects, the credibility of donors engaged in such projects is also at stake. Their inability to focus on project and policy impact erodes trust in donor assistance, and undermines support for Roma projects among Roma and majority communities. Projects that inadvertently enrich certain Roma families or intermediaries without generating meaningful long-term development results are, regrettably, not rarities. At the same time, the successful design and implementation of policies and projects

[112] The Forum, as its official site states, "is, at heart, a body of community leaders and policy experts who shall be elected by Roma and Traveller institutions across Europe" [emphasis added]. The sequence of tenses is important – the Forum has been recognized by the Council of Europe as an international counterpart, even if its legitimization by Roma communities remains incomplete. Appropriate electoral procedures (concerning, for example, the determination of electoral lists) and other representational mechanisms have still to be decided.

[113] UNDP's Regional Human Development Report *Avoiding the Dependency Trap* also found that Roma respondents' trust in Roma NGOs was even lower than their trust in the state administration.

to reduce Roma vulnerability requires Roma participation. The programming frameworks employed by many donors too often do not lend themselves to this participation. The programme infrastructure for absorbing pre-accession EU funding does not permit regranting, for example. The logic of 'big projects implemented by big organizations' crowds out the smaller community-level organizations that can realize community-level outcomes. There should be real possibilities for local beneficiaries to participate in project development.

While the capacities of Roma NGOs need to be strengthened, traditional 'capacity development' projects are not always sufficient. Learning by doing should be encouraged, for example via involving Roma in internship programmes and international organizations. A core of young Roma meeting minimal education and skill requirements should be identified for this purpose. This long-term endeavour should be started now, with targeted work in schools with Roma children and in communities with their parents. Cooperation with Roma civil society, particularly community-level organizations, can also ensure Roma organizations' involvement in that process.

Learning by doing should be encouraged, for example via involving Roma in internship programmes and international organizations

The time frames for many Roma projects need to be lengthened, in order to train local Roma NGOs to the point where they can continue the project 'on their own'. Longer (4–5 year) project cycles and support from municipalities are therefore crucial to increasing the sustainability of project results. Project design should be flexible enough to reflect the needs of direct beneficiaries. Implementing partners should have vested interests in the project's sustainability, in order to continue project activities after the project officially ends. This is much more likely to be the case for local partners than for international or commercial consultancies.

Relationships with majority communities

Issues of majority community perceptions (inaccurate and otherwise) of Roma are becoming increasingly important. Funding for policies to address vulnerability may be small compared to the scale of the problems, but media 'attention' may inflate its significance in popular perceptions. This is particularly the case when projects are not robustly effective or whose impact is disputable. In extreme cases (see Box 20), Roma can even be perceived as privileged.

Such dual perceptions of vulnerability issues have become common in the last 15 years: majority and vulnerable communities increasingly view otherwise incontestable facts and events in diametrically opposed ways. Majority communities and Roma too often find themselves in a situation analogous to a husband and wife seeking a divorce: they bombard each other with accusations and grievances. The search for common interest – hard to achieve when policies and projects are designed along 'ethnic' lines – seems to have vanished. Whereas the behaviour of Roma communities (and their intermediaries from the 'development business') seems at times to reflect the belief that majorities should have a 'guilt complex' vis-à-vis the Roma, majority communities perceive Roma poverty and social exclusion as a voluntary choice, which can be described as 'the absence of responsibilities and having to pay taxes'. Both sides see the other as being wrong; notions of tolerance, common responsibility, and common interest are conspicuously absent.

Respect for gender issues and distinct cultures

As the survey data discussed in this report show, women are often more vulnerable than men, in both Roma and displaced communities. To some extent, this heightened vulnerability reflects traditional gender roles that are often related to cultural factors. Culture, however, evolves. It is therefore important to realize which components of 'traditional culture' are compatible with contemporary social standards – particularly regarding women – and which are not. For example, common-law marriages in Roma communities should be legalized, with all attendant rights and responsibilities for both partners. And Roma women who question or refuse to honour traditions of early marriage and childbearing deserve tolerance, if not support, from their communities, as well as from social service providers.

Majority communities often perceive Roma poverty and social exclusion as a voluntary choice

Roma women are particularly prone to lower educational attainment and literacy rates. The size of the pro-male educational attainment gap shows that Roma women are relatively more disadvantaged than women from displaced or majority communities. Since enrolment rates for Roma men and women do not differ markedly, this gap

'Improvements' within existing 'provisional' settings should not be seen as sustainable development options for the displaced

cannot be attributed to access to education *per se*. The greater burden for Roma women (relative to men) of childcare and household chores may affect their educational attainment rates. This suggests that measures to increase gender equality within Roma households—measures emanating from within Roma communities themselves—may be particularly worthy of support.

Policies specifically targeting displaced persons

Displaced communities in Southeast Europe also face some specific challenges that require appropriate policy and programming responses. The section below outlines some major proposals that could contribute to improving the status of these populations. The list is shorter than in the case of Roma, but the magnitude of the challenges these populations face in many respects is comparable.

The regional context is crucial here. The challenges displaced populations face in Southeast Europe may be insignificant from a global perspective. However, given the level of socioeconomic development of these countries, their aspirations for EU membership, and the resources available compared to those for other regions of the world, the issue of displaced populations takes on significant dimensions.

The displaced represent lost opportunities in the form of untapped human potential, talent and skills

The guiding principles on internal displacement

As the data suggest, the issue of IDPs in the region is of primary concern. This is why a major step towards improving the status of the displaced would entail applying the Guiding Principles on Internal Displacement. Adopted by the UN Economic and Social Council in 1998, the principles are based upon, reflect and are consistent with international human rights law. The document provides a consistent framework for identifying needs for planning, implementing and monitoring protection activities (Kälin, 2005). Hence implementing the 30 principles in the national contexts is a first step towards improving the status of the displaced in the region.

The Guiding Principles are not binding. They were written by a group of independent experts and have not been negotiated by states. However, since the "principles reflect and are consistent with international law" (OCHA, 2004), their non-binding character does not prevent them from being a powerful tool to press governments for more explicit progress in improving the status of displaced populations. In fact, in many cases the non-binding character of the Guiding Principles has been an advantage (Kälin, 2001). Governments in the region need to be encouraged to abide by the principles by aligning policies and national legislation accordingly. The international community can be particularly instrumental in this regard.

Moving from humanitarian assistance and crisis prevention to development[115]

Although most of the displaced in the Western Balkans are living in temporary accommodations or with 'host families' and not in displaced camps per se, their situation is often quite dramatic. Displaced households usually lack temporary employment opportunities or access to basic services. Seen from this perspective, 'improvements' within existing 'provisional' settings should not be seen as sustainable development options.
Real improvement can only come from displaced persons being fully integrated into society or enjoying sustainable opportunities upon their return to their places of origin. In either (or both) cases, the focus of the policy

---

The particular vulnerability of internally displaced people is highlighted also by UNHCR's last report on the status of world's refugees. See UNHCR 2006.

The need of an explicit development focus is a good example of why policies targeting displaced populations – similarly to MDGs targets – should have a clear regional focus reflecting regional specifics. In some countries an excessive development focus may prevent people from addressing issues of humanitarian concern and human rights violations. As the recent report on internal displacement trends published by the Norwegian Refugee Council and International Displacement Monitoring Centre states, "UN country offices often focus on development issues and find it hard to acknowledge and address the more sensitive humanitarian and human rights challenges connected to most IDP situations" (IDMC/NRC 2006).

This is reflecting the spirit of Principle 18 of the Guiding Principles on Internal Displacement. See also Recommendation 4, economic, social and cultural rights in Buscher, Lester and Coelho, 2005.

response to vulnerability needs to shift from humanitarian assistance to development.

The survey data on which this report is based and other sources suggest that addressing vulnerability in the Western Balkans is crucial for these societies' internal cohesion. Issues of displacement are particularly important, in the aftermath of the armed conflicts of the 1990s. Settling the problems of these groups has both humanitarian and symbolic significance; it is a page in the region's history that still is to be closed. As such, more effective approaches to issues of vulnerability, inclusion and reconciliation are closely linked to prospects for the successful attainment of other priorities, such as EU integration and, subsequently, accession. Sustainable solutions to the development challenges facing displaced communities must go beyond the humanitarian and symbolic. Large displaced communities that have lost livelihoods, skills and assets are in fact a double burden for the societies. In addition to the substantial fiscal costs of social assistance to these households, the displaced represent lost opportunities in the form of untapped human potential, talent and skills. This clearly points to the development challenges faced by the displaced.

International efforts that initially focused on the provision of humanitarian or post-conflict assistance in the Western Balkans are increasingly emphasizing the development aspects of reconstruction. UNDP is likewise increasingly involved in poverty alleviation and local economic development projects for displaced communities, in order to complement the humanitarian focus with sustainable development components (see Boxes 14 and 22).

Box 22: **Protecting the displaced and local economic development in an area-based context**

Defending or restoring the rights of the displaced often requires the rejuvenation of multiethnic communities and local economies in the areas to which the displaced seek to return. When displaced persons began to return to their pre-war homes in Bosnia and Herzegovina in 1996, property rights and repossession issues were at the top of the agenda. The intervening 10 years have shown, however, that property restitution does not recreate multiethnic communities. Nor does it guarantee sustainable economic livelihoods for returnees, or better development prospects for their communities. Ten years after Dayton, creating sustainable economic livelihoods remains the largest obstacle facing the displaced who seek to return. This is certainly one of the main reasons why—even according to optimistic estimates—less than half of Bosnia and Herzegovina's pre-war minority residents have returned to their homes.

UNDP's Srebrenica Regional Recovery Programme (SRRP) attempts to address these issues in communities that were devastated by ethnic cleansing. The SRRP takes an integrated, holistic approach to laying the basis for local economic recoveries and better local governance, and therefore for sustainable returns of displaced persons to the communities of Srebrenica, Bratunac and Milici. The SRRP has five interrelated components: economic development, local government, civil society, gender mainstreaming (female-headed households make up a large share of the returnees) and infrastructure; it places a heavy emphasis on community participation in its implementation.

The programme started in 2002 and is expected to continue until December 2008. It has an overall budget in excess of $24 million, funded by the governments of the Netherlands, Italy, Denmark, Norway, Canada, United Kingdom and Japan, as well as Republika Srpska (the relevant entity within Bosnia and Herzegovina). Additional support has also come from the UN Foundation, the International Fund for Agricultural Development, as well as UNDP. While it is unlikely to make the world forget the horrors of the Srebrenica massacre, the SRRP is helping to restore community links. The programme's partnership networks include the three municipal governments, the three local centres for social work, utility companies, the Srebrenica Business Centre, the Srebrenica Regional Extension Service for Agriculture, private companies, civil society organizations, local communities, international organizations, schools, outpatient health care centres and all relevant ministries.

However, despite the passage of 6-10 years since the conclusion of hostilities, development efforts do not always reach the displaced. To a significant degree, displacement issues in the Balkans continue to be addressed in terms of mitigating humanitarian disaster threats. They are also addressed within national (rather than regional) policy frameworks. In many respects, sustainable solutions to the problems require human development, human security, human rights and inter-governmental approaches. These challenges are not just sectoral – they are not 'just' about employment, access to education, or identity documents – they are about responding to the determinants of poverty, exclusion and vulnerability. Likewise, the inter-governmental nature of dis-

---

Combinations of these two options – in terms of repossessing their properties in countries of origin in order to sell them and invest the funds acquired in the country of (re)settlement – seem to be particularly attractive for displaced Serbs, many of whom have been displaced for a decade or more.

One example is the European Agency for Reconstruction (EAR) that is increasingly focusing on supporting economies and local societies. One of the major objectives of new EC-funded programmes managed by the Agency is supporting the development of a market economy while investing further in critical physical infrastructure and environmental actions at the local level. For more details see http://www.ear.eu.int/sectors/sectors.htm.

placement, combined with the recasting of the State Union of Serbia and Montenegro following the May 2006 referendum on Montenegro independence, as well as the changing status of Kosovo, underscores the desirability of regional solutions to problems of displacement.

Towards a regional 'Decade of the Displaced'?

Humanitarian assistance should be followed by comprehensive, sustainable integration programmes

As humanitarian assistance for displaced communities is phased out before appropriately crafted development policies and programmes have yet to come on line, a vacuum in policies vis-á-vis the displaced may emerge. Humanitarian assistance should be followed by comprehensive, sustainable integration programmes, or by targeted development aid that reflects the vulnerability characteristics faced by the displaced. While national governments and NGOs must play a key role in this next phase, the magnitude of the task – particularly in Bosnia and Herzegovina, Serbia, and Kosovo – may well be beyond the capabilities of national actors. Effectively addressing the vulnerability of the displaced in the Western Balkans may therefore require a broader framework of international support.

A 'Decade of the Displaced' could facilitate the creation of an overall mutually acceptable framework, into which the national policies would fit

Efforts to address Roma vulnerability have since 2005 benefited from the Decade of Roma Inclusion. By contrast, efforts to assist the displaced lack an overarching regional political commitment that could mobilize the governments to approach these issues in a systematic manner. A 'Decade of the Displaced', modelled (where appropriate) on the structures and lessons of the Decade of Roma Inclusion, could provide such a framework. Such an inter-governmental framework could provide a forum at which agreements on major priorities could be brokered, push governments to undertake explicit commitments, and ensure coordinated international support for their implementation. In fact, it would build upon the intergovernmental '3 x 3 Initiative' resulting in a Ministerial Declaration following the Regional Ministerial Conference on Refugee Returns in Sarajevo on 31 January 2005 (Morjane, 2005). As with the Roma Decade, a 'Decade of the Displaced' could facilitate the creation of an overall mutually acceptable framework, into which the national policies would fit.

Such an initiative should target all persons displaced by the conflicts in the Western Balkans. It would match regional visibility and international commitment with focused national action plans needed to better respond to the vulnerability challenges facing displaced communities – challenges that are generally common across the region, but also bear national characteristics that need to be taken into account. A regional strategy to set the principles for addressing the needs of displaced communities could be elaborated, with the active participation of governments, the international community, and representatives of the displaced themselves. Following the pattern of the Decade of Roma Inclusion, the regional principles could be translated into national action plans that could be rooted in (and co-financed from) the regional development priorities of the participating countries. This strategy should complement the Migration, Asylum, Refugees Regional Initiative of the Stability Pact for Southeast Europe. Also following the example of the Decade of Roma Inclusion, countries with national strategies for responding to issues of displacement could update and modernize these strategies, with a view to transforming policy frameworks and attitudes towards regarding the displaced, away from them as a burden for local communities, and towards becoming able to make best use of their 'human capital'.

Of course, such an initiative would face a number of difficulties. Characteristics of displaced communities and the challenges they face differ sharply from country to country. Multiple political challenges are also apparent, as the development challenges faced by the displaced may be closely linked to

---

"We, the ministers responsible for refugees and internally displaced persons in Bosnia and Herzegovina, Croatia, and Serbia and Montenegro, met today in Sarajevo to identify our individual and joint activities that should be undertaken in the forthcoming period with the assistance of the international community in order to ensure a just and durable solution to the refugee and IDP situation in our countries; [...] Pursuant to our country programmes, we are committed to solving the remaining population displacement by the end of 2006..." The fact that the issue of displaced populations is still on the table in 2006 is an additional argument in favour of a 'Decade of the Displaced' initiative.

See http://www.stabilitypact.org/marri/default.asp.

country-specific ethnic tensions or to Kosovo's unresolved status. Numerous technical issues would also need to be addressed (*Which institutions should compensate the victims of displacement? What role should be played by the local authorities, particularly for internally displaced persons? For which properties should the displaced be compensated? How should the value of these properties be assessed?*). But as serious as these difficulties may be, they are also why an overarching inter-governmental initiative may be the best, most sustainable way to provide international support for national (and bilateral when possible) efforts.

That many of international actors (including, but not limited to, the UN family) deal with issues of displacement is another argument in favour of such an initiative. In practice, however, many of these organizations pursue their own 'sectoral' priorities and resist coordination, making effective collaboration on the ground distressingly difficult. This is unfortunate, since responses to issues of displacement should be based on a clear and consistent business model within a protection framework based on applicable bodies of law – particularly if displaced communities are to make the transition from assistance and dependency to sustainable development. Emergency relief requires a different set of approaches and operational modalities than sustainable local integration efforts. A 'Decade of the Displaced' could provide the forum at which these transition modalities can be negotiated, agreed and coordinated. These include first and foremost a better division of roles and responsibilities between different agencies involved in displaced persons' issues.

Political participation of displaced communities and adequate representation

Although of different nature from the Roma, the problem of adequate representation of the displaced is not less acute. Displaced persons often face difficulties voting in elections. The survey data show that displaced persons are underrepresented and not sufficiently included in local policy-making that affects their interests and status. The displaced often find themselves in the role of 'project beneficiaries' with limited opportunities to influence the design and implementation of the policies that are meant to assist them.

The issue of adequate representation of the displaced may become particularly relevant if a regional initiative (along the lines outlined above) were to be launched. Adequate representation would also help the displaced articulate their interests at the local (community) level, and would reduce the chances of the problems of the displaced being misused in arguments between governments in the region. Stronger local representation would help implement rights-based approaches to development also in the case of displaced communities. With representative bodies in place that are capable of articulating and promoting displaced communities' interests, interaction and cooperation with local-level institutions and populations in host societies would be facilitated. This would reduce rejection (and sometimes stigmatization) of refugees and IDPs and would facilitate their sustainable integration, particularly of young people.

Adequate representation would help implement rights-based approaches to development in the case of displaced communities

[121] The overall UN response is coordinated by the Undersecretary-General for Humanitarian Affairs and Emergency Relief Coordinator who heads the Office for the Coordination of Humanitarian Affairs. In 2004, pursuant to a decision of the Secretary-General, the Inter-Agency Internal Displacement Division was established, housed within the Office for Coordination of Humanitarian Affairs (OCHA). The Division consists of international staff seconded by UNDP, UNHCR, WFP, UNICEF, OCHA, OHCHR, IOM, the NGO community and the Representative of the Secretary-General on the human rights of internally displaced persons. The Division works closely with members of the Inter-Agency Standing Committee (IASC) and Senior Network on Internal Displacement. It assists the Emergency Relief Coordinator in discharging his function to coordinate an effective response to the needs of internally displaced people (IDPs) worldwide. For more details see http://www.reliefweb.int/idp/partners/ian.htm.

[122] For example, a new role for UNHCR is being discussed with one of the possible options being transforming it into a 'displacement agency'. The Inter-Agency Standing Committee has agreed, as part of the humanitarian reform process that has been ongoing since the summer of 2005, that UNHCR will assume primary responsibility and accountability for the response to internally displaced persons and affected populations in complex emergencies in the areas or 'clusters' of protection, camp management and coordination, and emergency shelter. For further information on the reform process see www.humanitarianinfo.org/iasc.

For more details on the political participation and electoral rights of IDPs see IDMC/NRC, 2006.

Property and real estate swaps should be encouraged – but in ways that transparently recognize displaced households' legitimate ownership rights

Facilitating integration into new communities[124]

In accordance with the Guiding Principles and under the right to freedom of movement and choice of residence enshrined in human rights law, displaced persons must be protected from forced return to their place of origin, and from compulsory integration into their host country. In cases when integration in host societies is chosen, it should be facilitated by the active engagement of, and support for, local host communities. Integration of the displaced should not be seen as – or permitted to become – an additional burden on these local communities. Area-based projects that help communities integrate the displaced can be a particularly effective, sustainable response to the vulnerability associated with displacement. Such projects could begin by assessing the institutional capacity of municipalities to cope with significant inflows of displaced persons (whether for return, integration or both), in order to identify gaps for external support. Parallel assessments of the 'social capital' of the displaced could be conducted, to identify the appropriate sectoral areas of project support. In some cases this may be agriculture; in other cases displaced households may better fit into services or other sectors. Where possible, inter-municipal collaboration within and across national boundaries to facilitate the integration or return of the displaced should likewise be promoted. Donors should be encouraged to provide priority support for such projects. The guiding principle should be approaching the displaced as an asset (rather than as a burden) for local economies – but an asset that requires appropriate investments in order to generate significant returns.

Donor-funded property compensation funds for displaced persons could be established and managed within the framework of the 'Decade of the Displaced'

UNDP's experience with returnee projects points to the importance of working with central and municipal governments to build capacity for managing displacement issues. The 'Sustainable Transfer to Return-related Authorities' project implemented by UNDP in Bosnia and Herzegovina is a good example of this: it involves local authorities in all aspects of the return and reintegration of the displaced. These include the articulation of return needs, the design of relevant interventions and their funding, implementation and evaluation. National and local partners have been involved in project design and implementation. These partnerships have helped strengthen stakeholder ownership in the project, which bodes well for its success.

Property compensation and real estate swaps[126]

Many displaced households have experienced not just physical displacement (from their homes and communities), but also social displacement, being pushed from the security of middle-class status into socio-economic vulnerability. Once the conflict is over and when international frameworks for addressing displaced persons' problems are put in place, the restitution of property rights should be put on the table. Apart from the direct benefits for the affected populations, restitution of property rights may bring additional momentum to the returns process, encouraging other people and whole communities to follow. The process, however, should be nationally owned and nationally directed. Whenever possible, property and real estate swaps should be encouraged – but in ways that transparently recognize displaced households' legitimate ownership rights, rather than making them both victims and beneficiaries of non-transparent property confiscations. Compensation for lost and destroyed property should be available and negotiable within internationally agreed frameworks. Donor-funded property compensation funds for displaced persons could be established and managed within the framework of the 'Decade of the Displaced'.

Principle 28 of the Guiding Principles on Internal Displacement explicitly addresses the issue of voluntary resettlement in another part of a country.

The issue is also addressed in ECRE's *The Way Forward: An Agenda for Change* (ECRE, 2005). As stated in its background paper, " the displaced should also be afforded a long-term resident status granting them rights similar to those of nationals" (Hudson and Weiler, 2005).

Principle 21 of the Guiding Principles on Internal Displacement explicitly addresses the issue of property and possessions.

As the example of Bosnia and Herzegovina shows, local institutions have to be particularly instrumental in this regard since they are in control of municipal housing stock (Davies, 2004). On the other hand, the example of Kosovo underscores that "without adequate security guarantees, housing and property restitution will not result in return" (NRC, 2005). Other examples from the region (Croatia in particular) suggest that there are risks involved in basing post-conflict property restitution on a pure return rationale (Williams, 2004). On issues of post-conflict property restitution see also Phuong, 2000, Hovey, 2000 and Leckie, 2000.

Methodology annex

The survey questionnaire that was used to generate the data on which this report is based follows the philosophy of integrated household surveys, with separate components containing both household and individual modules. Within the individual module, each household member's profile was registered (demographic characteristics, economic status, education, health). The household module addresses issues related to the household in general (dwelling type, access to basic infrastructures, household items etc.). Questions related to incomes and expenditures were addressed in both modules, making it possible to crosscheck the results.

The primary universe under study consists of: (i) all the households in Roma settlements or areas of compact Roma population; (ii) displaced persons (IDPs/refugees); and (iii) non-Roma communities living in close proximity to Roma and the displaced. While Roma, refugees and IDPs are not Southeast Europe's only vulnerable groups, they are definitely among the most vulnerable.

The vulnerable group samples

The sampling of vulnerable groups in general and of Roma in particular is a major challenge in every survey targeting diversities and vulnerability. The first assumption of the survey was that major disparities in socio-economic status of the populations are most obvious (and can be explored best) at the level of municipality (or other relevant micro-territorial units). Since at this level vulnerability factors exist that affect both Roma and other communities, vulnerability profiles of the two groups (Roma and majority) in the same municipality were developed, in order to make possible the identification of those vulnerability factors that affect Roma.

The most difficult question in this regard is "Who is Roma?" and how to appropriately identify the survey respondents. The primary objective of the survey was to map the vulnerability of groups with common socio-economic, cultural and linguistic patterns – irrespective of how potential survey respondents might identify themselves. Since Roma identity is often associated with underclass status and discrimination, the decision to avoid self-identification as 'Roma' is not infrequent. Simply asking potential survey respondents "Are you Roma?" is therefore unlikely to yield unbiased survey data. These issues are further complicated by the multiple ethnic identities that are commonly found in Southeast Europe (and not only among Roma). The question "Are you Roma?" implicitly suggests its antithesis ("You are not Bulgarian, Romanian, Macedonian etc.?"). This extensive possible confusion between 'ethnicity', 'nationality' and 'citizenship' further argues against relying solely on self-identification. In most countries, therefore, Roma are underreported in censuses, and officially registered sizes of Roma populations often differ dramatically from experts' estimates.

While accepting the belief that censuses understate the absolute numbers of Roma, the survey accepted that the census data provide reasonably adequate pictures of the structure and territorial distribution of those individuals who identify themselves as Roma. Since the absolute number of Roma populations is not known, random sampling was not possible, so a 'pyramid' sampling model was used instead. Within this model, various estimates of Roma population (including census data) constitute different tiers of the pyramid. The bottom of the pyramid constitutes the total ('real') number of Roma in a country. The top represents the hypothetical situation of total exclusion in which not a single person would self-identify as Roma. Census data constitute one of the pyramid's tiers, with the pyramid's strata reflecting the structure of the population. Under this model, if the 'propensity to underreport' (i.e., the share of Roma not willing to identify themselves as Roma) is distributed similarly in different regions within a country, the structure of the population reflected in the census tier would be identical to the structure of the total population. This should be sufficiently unbiased to construct a representative stratified sample.

In practical terms, it was assumed that the propensity to underreport was identical for each region within an individual country. Based on this assumption, the Roma sample was taken as representative of the Roma population living in 'Roma settlements or areas of compact Roma population'. Those settlements and areas were defined as settlements where the share of Roma population equals or is higher than the national share of Roma population in the given country, as reflected in the census data. The share – not the absolute number – of Roma was used for identification of the sampling clusters. The knowledge that X per cent of Roma (as reported in the census) live in settlement Y was taken to mean that X per cent of the sample will be derived from settlement Y. In this way, the demographic structure of the sample reflects the demographic structure of the Roma population (as reflected in the census data in proportions).

At the first stage of the sample design the universe was defined as mentioned above, using 'average and above share of Roma in each settlement'. In the second phase, taking into consideration also Roma organizations' estimates of Roma populations, the distribution of the settlements and population sizes, sampling clusters were determined. Respondents were then identified using 'random route' selection processes (third stage).[128]

Internal (self-identification) and external (outsider's identification) modes therefore prevail at different stages of the sampling process. Self-identification (reported during the census) was used in the first stage; external identification (assessment of local people, NGOs, experts) was employed in the second stage. In the third stage (respondents' selection), the results of the first two stages were confirmed or rejected by 'implicit endorsement of identification'. In practice this meant that having identified the sample clusters and the households to be interviewed, the introductory sentence at the beginning of the interview was "Good morning/day, we are conducting a survey among the Roma population. Would you like to be interviewed?" In case of explicit denial ("I am not Roma, why should you interview me?") the interview was cancelled. Willingness to participate in the interview was interpreted as the household member's implicit endorsement of belonging to the universe under study.

In some cases (particularly in big cities and capitals), large Roma communities constitute relatively small shares of total populations. In such cases, the sampling methodology conformed to administrative subdivisions (usually the 'capital municipality' is divided into smaller municipalities and/or lower levels of self-government). These lower levels were then chosen as the sampling units. Such cases were also corrected typologically, introducing additional sampling points.

A similar approach was applied to refugees/displaced persons with the only difference that instead of census data for the first stage of the sampling design, official registries and data on refugees/displaced persons' distribution provided by relevant institutions dealing with displaced populations were used to outline the universe under study. In the second phase, based on these lists, the sampling clusters were determined through random sampling. At the third phase individual respondents were identified using 'random route' selection processes (third stage).

Control samples

In order to derive data for meaningful comparisons that would respond to the data needs of an area-based development approach, a control sample of populations that are not defined as 'vulnerable' in the context of this report (i.e. that are neither Roma, nor refugees/displaced) was constructed. Given the fact that the ethnic affiliation of those populations is diverse (in some cases they are a minority at the national level but constitute a local majority), their exact definition would be 'non-Roma and non-displaced persons living in close proximity to the two vulnerable samples'. The control groups' samples were constructed using similar procedures as for the two vulnerable groups. In the case of Roma, those are representative samples of non-Roma communities living in settlements with Roma communities of 'average and above' size. In the case of the displaced sample, the control

[128] To a certain extent the sampling process is similar to Leslie Kish's cluster sampling model.

group is non-displaced populations living in proximity. In the second stage of sampling (determining the size of the population and the sampling clusters), external identification was used to identify the 'proximity populations' (assessment of local people, local self-governments). In the third stage random route selection was also applied to select the individual households.

In cases of municipalities with a high share of Roma and the number of majority population not sufficient for creating a majority sample (for example, in cases of isolated Roma settlements or segregated neighbourhoods), a majority sample was based on a typologically similar settlement in the same district (administrative unit) with a Roma population equal to or higher than the national average. The criterion for choosing this settlement was that it be the 'closest village accessible by road connection'.

The desire to obtain comparable data for non-Roma and non-displaced populations living in close proximity to the two vulnerable groups surveyed reflected a major emphasis of the current analysis: its area-based development focus. The majority samples gave the survey the 'benchmark' needed for assessments of the depth of Roma and displaced persons' poverty and vulnerability vis-à-vis the control groups (non-Roma and non-displaced) living in similar socio-economic environments and sharing some of the challenges the two vulnerable groups are facing. Despite the sample design challenges it poses, this approach allows us to distinguish among various vulnerability factors, particularly those that are related to minority status (and hence can be attributed to various forms of discrimination), as opposed to manifestations of regional development disparities or depressed local economic circumstances. It also provides clues on how to tackle the issues of exclusion and marginalization. Although often determined by institutional factors and policies, exclusion occurs at the level of interaction. This is primarily the level of the community, where people have daily contact. Measuring the distance between Roma and non-Roma in areas they cohabitate could be an important clue of how to tackle challenges of social distance.

It is important to bear in mind that this approach does not attempt to guarantee national representativeness for majority communities. Because they share similar socio-economic circumstances, those populations may also be facing some vulnerability risks and thus also may be – but not necessarily are – vulnerable. If they are, the status of these populations would be worse than national averages – as is the case on some indicators compared to national averages. Whenever national indicators are available these are used as a benchmark to assess the vulnerability of the three groups covered in the survey.

Methodological costs and benefits of the Roma sample

The samples based on municipalities with average and above shares of Roma population are not fully representative for the entire Roma populations of the countries covered in this survey. They do, however, cover roughly 85 per cent of Roma in each country, and as such provide a good basis for developing quantitative socio-economic indicators of Roma welfare (quality of life, life expectancy, access to services, incomes etc.). The resulting samples are representative not just for residents of segregated Roma communities, but also for the majority of Roma.

The data generated by these samples are broadly consistent with census data, since this survey's data are based on relative numbers (structure and regional distribution) instead of absolute numbers of Roma registered in the censuses. This approach also gives some standardized criterion for majority sample selection. The major drawback of this sampling methodology is related to its application to municipalities where the share of Roma in the total population is below national averages. Because these municipalities effectively fall out of the scope of the sample, the conditions of Roma concentrated in 'mini-poverty pockets' or who are dispersed (presumably integrated with the majority) are not captured. Both groups are represented in the sample, however. In the first case, most of the 85 per cent of Roma who are captured by this survey methodology also live in similar poverty pockets, which benefit from representative sampling. In the second (integrated) case, this would be because a significant portion of the 85 per cent of Roma is functionally integrated (employed, maintaining contacts with majority communities and institutions) and thus typologically similar to dispersed (presumably integrated) Roma from the 15 per cent. Those of the 15 per cent who are 'dispersed and integrated' and self-identify themselves as Roma are typologically close to those who are integrated into the 85 per cent. Those who have been assimilated and do not self-identify as Roma fall out of the scope of the research, either because they don't meet the criterion of 'being Roma' (whatever that means) or because they don't meet the vulnerability criterion.

Looking at the self-identification done through the interview, asking each individual household member to state their ethnic affiliation, 16,198 Roma individuals declared Roma ethnicity out of 17,071 (95 per cent) individuals in the Roma sample. This proves that the sampling method chosen (indirect identification) corresponds very well to the self-identification method, without asking the question: "Are you Roma?".

Finally, it is important to realize that given the uncertainties concerning the size of Roma populations in these countries, the data and the analysis built on them have certain limitations. The survey does not provide precise answers to questions like "How many Roma live in poverty?" or "How many Roma have completed secondary education?". It instead gives answers to questions like "What share of Roma live in poverty?" and "What share of Roma have completed secondary education?". Based on these averages and using estimates of Roma population sizes, certain ranges for those variables can be provided. Such answers are useful for policy purposes because they outline the distance between various groups, highlight the causes of these differences, and provide benchmarks against which future trends can be assessed. These benchmarks can easily be much more relevant than those based on census data. From a policy perspective, such benchmarks are crucial. The allocation of resources based on official census data (which underestimate the size of Roma communities) inevitably falls short of the scale of needs. Using benchmarks—even in range formats, as presented in this report—can be an important step towards more realistic and adequate policies.

Fieldwork and partnerships

Given the nature of the survey – addressing the needs of groups that are not easy to identify – fieldwork was another major challenge. A high level of trust was needed on the side of respondents – particularly in the case of Roma. As a specific and unique minority group, Roma in some countries show certain levels of distrust towards other ethnical groups and the ethnical majority as well. In order to overcome the possible distrust to enumerators, Roma interviewers were used for the fieldwork where possible (in countries where a sufficient number of trained Roma was available). In other cases Roma intermediaries were used (following the pattern of 'Roma assistant teachers'). These were either Roma 'assistant interviewers' (a Roma representative accompanying the experienced pollster) or local social workers or representatives of Roma NGOs. In

Achieved samples

	Majority		Roma		Displaced		Total	
Country	House-holds	Household members	House-holds	Household members	House-holds	Household members	House-holds	Household members
Albania	450	1876	450	2479			900	4355
Bosnia and Herzegovina	404	1240	400	1941	398	1381	1202	4562
Bulgaria	500	1302	500	2176			1000	3478
Croatia	254	715	252	1252	197	656	703	2623
Kosovo	354	2275	354	2223			708	4498
Macedonia	377	1399	379	1836			756	3235
Montenegro	198	700	199	699	204	708	601	2107
Romania	601	1771	601	2905			1202	4676
Serbia	399	1270	399	1759	403	1553	1201	4582
Region	3537	12548	3534	17270	1202	4298	8273	34116

all cases the intermediaries were trained prior to the fieldwork (on the contents of the questionnaire, on general rules and procedures of an interview etc.). The general rule, however, was to approach the communities carefully, with respect and avoiding any suspicion about the purpose of the data collection. Since using 'assistant interviewers' or other intermediaries increased the costs of the survey substantially, this component was financed by the Council of Europe as a part of its "Roma under the Stability Pact" project.

The survey was executed by agencies-members of Gallup International, coordinated by the regional office of Gallup International in Sofia, which managed the data collection of the whole survey. Using Gallup International member agencies, this framework made possible applying similar standards and procedures in all countries covered by the project, making cross-country comparisons possible and reliable. After the fieldwork was completed a thorough check was run on 10-15 per cent of the sample depending on the country. All errors were cleared and in one case (Montenegro) re-interviewing was necessary. Data control and validation was conducted centrally by the regional office of Gallup International.

From the outset all agencies involved were working in a coordinated manner under the methodological and conceptual guidance of the UNDP Bratislava Regional Centre. The methodology of the survey, sampling and fieldwork were broadly discussed with colleagues from the World Bank and members of the Data Experts Group. Three consultants (Gabor Kezdy, Valerie Evans and Dragana Radevic) were particularly instrumental in the final design of the methodology and sampling models.

Data annex

Table A1

Average monthly household expenditure by category and country (euros)

		Transport	Food	Alcohol	Clothes	Housing	Medicine	Goods	Going out	Total
Albania	Roma	48.2	254.1	61.5	53.6	34.8	25.6	22.6	44.4	544.8
	Majority	51.4	391.2	67.4	133.6	97.5	35.0	35.5	63.4	875
Bosnia and Herzegovina	Roma	18.8	279.9	42.9	33.1	60.6	41.3	28.2	4.1	508.9
	Displaced	26.4	263.7	31.8	57.4	102.0	33.9	36.4	14.9	566.5
	Majority	142.8	286.1	34.0	66.4	106.3	29.3	38.8	25.7	729.4
Bulgaria	Roma	6.0	166.3	25.8	14.8	29.1	15.1	13.4	7.8	278.3
	Majority	18.6	133.3	17.8	24.5	53.2	27.9	12.0	8.0	295.3
Croatia	Roma	56.7	579.8	81.0	147.3	130.0	38.4	109.8	33.8	1176.8
	Displaced	64.1	303.7	56.5	54.0	143.0	20.3	54.7	18.4	714.7
	Majority	85.0	442.3	64.4	131.1	239.9	29.0	70.5	47.2	1109.4
Kosovo	Roma	69.7	347.1	95.8	173.5	158.2	121.5	59.1	48.1	1073
	Majority	128.1	580.2	120.7	261.0	209.1	123.3	73.7	91.4	1587.5
Macedonia	Roma	13.3	238.3	35.4	18.3	61.4	34.7	13.3	3.0	417.7
	Majority	36.7	279.3	28.5	52.7	118.2	30.7	35.2	13.6	594.9
Montenegro	Roma	28.2	323.3	63.6	98.9	63.2	35.2	37.6	31.0	681
	Displaced	47.5	314.0	63.2	94.6	125.0	60.0	37.2	57.0	798.5
	Majority	96.0	466.7	72.5	170.6	187.9	60.0	45.2	85.8	1184.7
Romania	Roma	42.7	193.9	50.9	68.6	52.0	42.1	21.0	42.7	513.9
	Majority	36.6	148.2	42.7	67.2	66.3	31.1	18.7	28.5	439.3
Serbia	Roma	43.0	206.3	35.2	46.5	58.2	31.9	38.5	13.0	472.6
	Displaced	41.9	222.1	36.7	61.9	93.0	31.7	31.8	17.0	536.1
	Majority	44.6	263.1	44.4	86.2	83.4	24.7	37.5	47.1	631

Table A2

Percentage of households owning each durable good

Household items	Majority	Roma	Displaced
Radio receiver	83	60	84
Refrigerator	94	59	89
Oven	83	53	86
TV set	96	80	86
Telephone	70	23	44
Car	45	13	30
CD player	30	8	17
Computer	22	2	13
Internet connection	12	1	7
Satellite dish	21	12	9
Mobile phone	62	29	56
Washing machine	71	31	69
Bed for each household member	90	47	77
Thirty and more books	61	9	28
Generator	7	3	2

Table A3

Household expenditures on bills in euros, with percentage of household total expenditures in parenthesis, by expenditure quintile

Sample	Quintile-group	Water	Electricity	Rent
Majority	1	96.9 (15%)	262.2 (22%)	79.8 (8%)
	2	195.0 (15%)	443.7 (18%)	99.3 (5%)
	3	87.0 (13%)	315.4 (20%)	102.2 (8%)
	4	95.1 (17%)	337.1 (20%)	115.7 (10%)
	5	55.0 (11%)	219.7 (15%)	105.2 (8%)
Roma	1	178.2 (28%)	343.8 (34%)	152.4 (6%)
	2	157.5 (32%)	322.8 (34%)	131.9 (9%)
	3	228.2 (35%)	398.3 (39%)	122.1 (12%)
	4	188.7 (34%)	325.6 (37%)	121.9 (11%)
	5	253.3 (29%)	303.3 (40%)	259.7 (10%)

Table A4

Inter-group inequality

Gini indices, calculations based on total monthly expenditures per equalized capita in euros (number of observations).

	All .4335 (7706)	Majority .3939 (3372)	Roma .4383 (3315)	Displaced .3475 (1019)
Albania	.4783 (891)	.4082 (442)	.3860 (449)	N/A
Bosnia and Herzegovina	.3648 (1171)	.3154 (398)	.3983 (382)	.3051 (391)
Bulgaria	.3405 (935)	.2948 (468)	.3094 (467)	N/A
Croatia	.3805 (612)	.2863 (241)	.3773 (240)	.3767 (131)
Kosovo	.3796 (706)	.3427 (354)	.3866 (352)	N/A
Macedonia	.3446 (732)	.2859 (359)	.3140 (373)	N/A
Montenegro	.3236 (446)	.2551 (144)	.3596 (155)	.2829 (147)
Romania	.3401 (1157)	.3002 (587)	.3188 (570)	N/A
Serbia	.4051 (1056)	.3097 (379)	.4746 (327)	.3551 (350)

FIGURE A1

Linear relationship between log equivalent expenditures and number of children

For Roma and majority combined samples as well as displaced and majority pooled samples

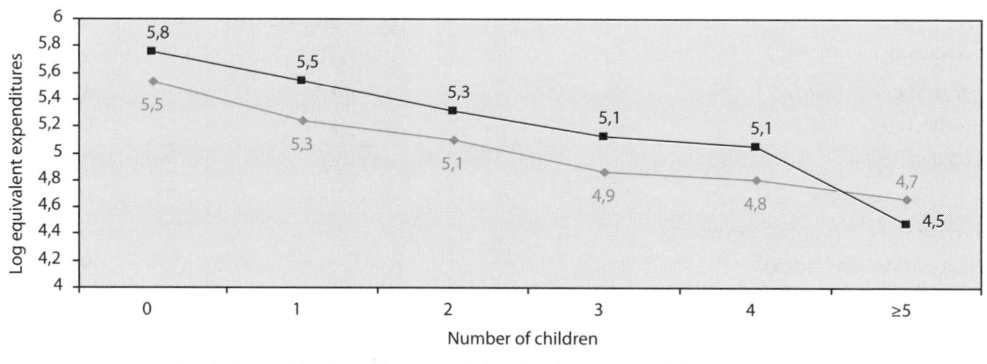

Table A5

Description of variables

(Used in group-related determinants of poverty regression)

Variable	**Mean** (Standard deviation in parenthesis)
Household expenditures equivalized	627.5 (622.5)
Log expenditures equivalized	5.3 (0.8)
Number of children	0.9 (1.3)
Dummy Variable	**Percentage of Sample**
Skill level of household head	
- Skilled	63.3
- Unskilled	36.7
Education level of household head	
- Well educated	62.5
- Poorly educated	37.5
Country of residence	
- Albania	14.6
- Bosnia and Herzegovina	10.7
- Bulgaria	11.7
- Kosovo	15.1
- Macedonia	10.8
- Montenegro	4.7
- Romania	15.7
- Serbia	15.1

Table A6

Group-related determinants of poverty

Coefficients for linear regression analysis of log equivalized expenditures with membership of the Roma sample, country of residence, capital or rural locality, number of children in household, and the skill and education level of household head

Roma	-0.42***
Rural	-0.23***
Capital	0.19***
Number of children	-0.10**
Skill level	0.32***
Education level	0.39***
Albania	-1.08***
Bosnia and Herzegovina	-0.01
Bulgaria	-0.62***
Kosovo	-0.78***
Macedonia	-0.53***
Montenegro	-0.50***
Serbia	-0.84***
Romania	-0.82***
A	5.87***
R-squared	0.53

***p<0.01, **p<0.05

Table A7

Description of variables

(Used in regression analysis of determinants of poverty within each group)

	Mean (Standard deviation in parenthesis)	
Variable	Roma	Majority
Household expenditures equivalized	73.5 (89.1)	140.7 (132.1)
Log expenditures equivalized	4.98 (0.79)	5.7 (0.70)
Number of children	1.24 (1.50)	0.53 (0.97)
	Percentage of Sample (with each level of variable)	
Dummy Variable	Roma	Majority
Skill level of household head		
- Skilled	33.1	84.2
- Unskilled	66.9	15.8
Education level of household head		
- Well educated	38.8	85.9
- Poorly educated	61.2	14.1
Country of residence		
- Albania	14.4	15.0
- Bosnia and Herzegovina	11.2	9.9
- Bulgaria	12.6	10.4
- Kosovo	12.9	18.1
- Macedonia	10.6	11.1
- Montenegro	4.0	5.6
- Romania	16.8	14.1
- Serbia	10.2	10.1

Table A8

Determinants of poverty within each group

Coefficients for linear regression analysis of log equivalized expenditures for Roma and majority households with the country of residence, locality, and number of children in a household and the skill level and level of education of the household head

	Roma	Majority
Rural	-0.75***	-0.29***
Capital	0.00	0.24***
Number of children	-0.10*	-0.00
Skill level	0.32***	0.35***
Education level	0.39***	0.42***
Albania	-1.14***	-1.00***
Bulgaria	-0.51***	-0.70***
Bosnia and Herzegovina	0.00	-0.00
Macedonia	-0.45***	-0.55***
Serbia	-0.97***	-0.75***
Montenegro	-0.38**	-0.55***
Romania	-0.72***	-0.91***
Kosovo	-0.61***	-0.86***
A	5.43***	5.85***
R-squared	0.35	0.43

***p<0.01, **p<0.05, *p<0.1

Table A9

Description of variables used in the Roma determinants of education logistic regression

Mean and standard deviation (in brackets) for continuous variables	
Age (years)	21.4
Age-squared	723.4
Percentage of each sample with each level of dependent variables used in logistic regression analyses	
Elementary to primary education	
- Elementary	56.9
- Primary	43.1
Primary to secondary	
- Primary	79.6
- Secondary	20.4
Percentage of each sample with positive responses for the explanatory dummy variable	
Role-model (positive)	34.9
Male	42.4
Poor	51.6
With chronic illness	16.1

Table A10

Odds ratios for explanatory variables in the Roma determinants of education logistic regression (standard errors shown in parenthesis)[129]

	Elementary to primary	Primary to secondary
Male	1.53*** (0.07)	1.48*** (0.13)
Age	0.89*** (0.01)	0.90*** (0.03)
Age-squared	1.00*** (0.00)	1.00*** (0.00)
Poor	0.66*** (0.06)	0.51*** (0.14)
Household head's education	1.69*** (0.07)	1.97*** (0.14)
Illness	0.82** (0.09)	1.48 (0.00)
R-squared[130]	0.10	0.08

***p<0.01, **p<0.05, *p<0.1

[129] Due to the small number of Roma with secondary or tertiary education, logistical regression analyses were not performed for individuals with secondary or tertiary education.

[130] Using Nagelkerke R-squared value.

Table A11

Description of variables used in group-related determinants of education logistic regression analyses

Mean and standard deviation (in brackets) for continuous variables	
Age	24.5 (18.0)
Age-squared	924.1 (1258.6)
Percentage of total sample with positive responses for dependent dummy variable	
Elementary to primary dummy	
- Elementary	52.8
- Primary	47.2
Primary to secondary dummy	
- Primary	52.7
- Secondary	47.3
Secondary to tertiary dummy	
- Secondary	83.9
- Tertiary	16.1
Percentage of total sample with positive responses for the explanatory dummy variable	
Roma	60.4
Well-educated head	49.4
Male	40.8
Poor	37.2
With chronic illness	15.5

Table A12

Increase in odds of increasing education from one level to the next associated with each explanatory variable in the group-related determinants of education logistic regression analyses (standard errors shown in parenthesis)

	Elementary to primary	Primary to secondary	Secondary to tertiary
Roma	0.36*** (0.08)	0.20*** (0.08)	0.22*** (0.70)
Male	1.53*** (0.06)	1.58*** (0.08)	0.82 (0.13)
Age	0.90*** (0.00)	0.85*** (0.01)	0.88*** (0.03)
Age-squared	1.00*** (0.00)	1.00*** (0.00)	1.00*** (0.00)
Poor	0.68*** (0.06)	0.37*** (0.09)	0.18*** (0.42)
Household head's education	1.53*** (0.06)	2.53*** (0.09)	3.33*** (0.34)
Illness	0.78*** (0.08)	0.82* (0.11)	0.66** (0.18)
R-squared[131]	0.12	0.33	0.14

***p<0.01, **p<0.05, *p<0.1

FIGURE A2

Youth unemployment rates across the region

Percentage of 15-24 year-olds who are unemployed by country

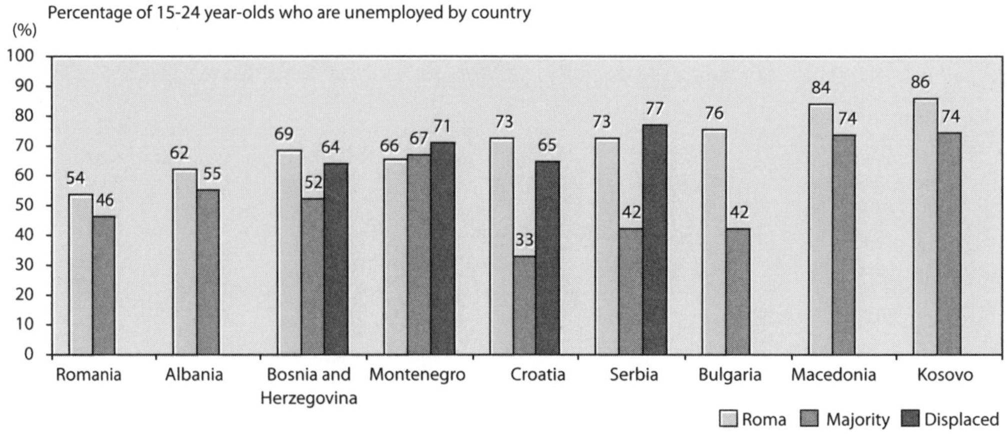

(%)	Roma	Majority	Displaced
Romania	54	46	
Albania	62	55	
Bosnia and Herzegovina	69	52	64
Montenegro	66	67	71
Croatia	73	33	65
Serbia	73	42	77
Bulgaria	76	42	
Macedonia	84	74	
Kosovo	86	74	

131 Using Nagelkerke R-squared value.

FIGURE A3

Prime-age unemployment rates across the region
Percentage of 25-44 year-olds who are unemployed by country

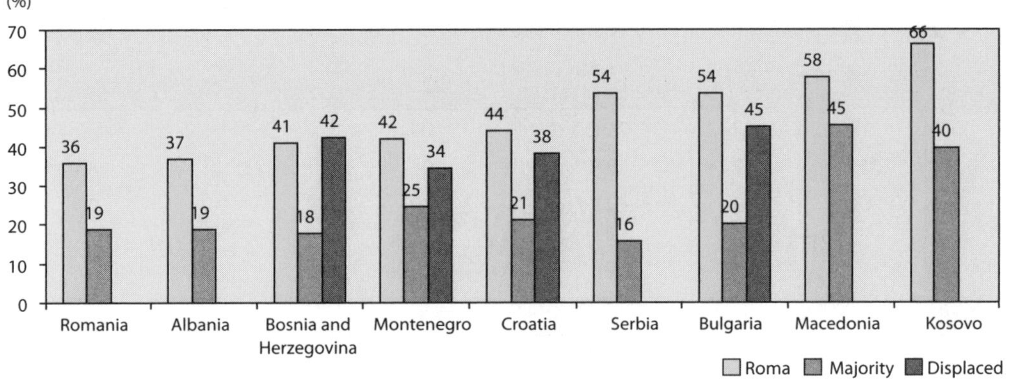

FIGURE A4

Older-worker unemployment rates across the region
Percentage of 45-59 year-olds who are unemployed by country

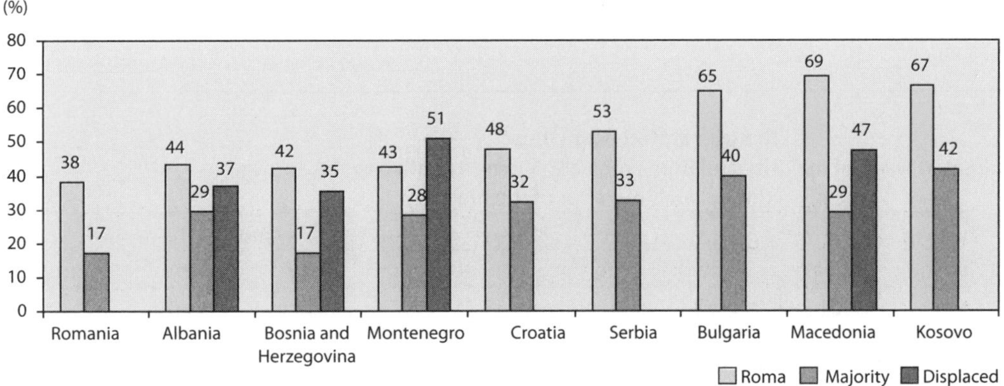

Table A13

The effect of education on the probability of employment[132]

	Majority		Roma		Displaced	
Coefficients on schooling (compared to the base category: no schooling, elementary or incomplete primary education)	Effect	Std. error	Effect	Std. error	Effect	Std. error
Men						
Completed primary	.23*	.13	.06	.04	-.30*	.18
Completed secondary	.45***	.12	.37***	.07	-.20	.16
Completed tertiary	.90***	.04	.69***	.25	.07	.18
N	3446		4865		1195	
Pseudo-R^2	.15		.10		.12	
Women						
Completed primary	.28**	.13	.28***	.05	-.09	.17
Completed secondary	.72***	.12	.49***	.09	.31**	.15
Completed tertiary	1.39***	.13	.53*	.29	.89***	.18
N	2928		3727		908	
Pseudo-R^2	.19		.10		.07	
Baseline employment probability	.61		.28		.41	

*p<0.1, **p<0.05,***p<0.01

[132] The table reports the effects, in terms of the percentage point improvement in employment probability, of raising one's education level from no- or elementary-education level to a primary, secondary or tertiary level, respectively. The probit model was estimated separately for adult men and women (16 years and above). Apart from the education variables, the model also included country-specific intercepts and age and age-squared variables.

Table A14

The returns to education by ethnic group

	Majority		Roma		Displaced	
Percentage change in wage arising from increasing one's educational level from	% change	Std. error	% change	Std. error	% change	Std. error
Males						
Elementary to primary	.18	.13	.29***	.04	.39***	.15
Primary to secondary	.25**	.12	.18***	.06	.23*	.13
Secondary to tertiary	.23*	.13	.62***	.19	.48***	.14
N	2173		2244		598	
R^2	.92		.93		.81	
Females						
Elementary to primary	.17	.15	.24***	.07	.37	.25
Primary to secondary	.38***	.14	.41***	.11	.51***	.22
Secondary to tertiary	.37***	.14	.21	.28	.67***	.24
N	1420		880		301	
R^2	.93		.93		.77	

*p<0.1, **p<0.05,***p<0.01

Table A15

Group-related wage gap

The estimated wage of majority and Roma men and women relative to the average wage of an uneducated member of the majority

	Men				Women			
	No education	Primary	Secondary	Tertiary	No education	Primary	Secondary	Tertiary
Majority – region	0	21	52	86	0	17	60	120
Roma – Bulgaria	-41	-24	-11	4	-34	-18	9	23
Roma – Kosovo	-46	-31	-18	-5	-37	-22	4	17
Roma – Serbia	-43	-27	-14	1	-45	-32	-9	2
Roma- Croatia	-14	11	31	53	-47	-34	-13	-1
Roma – Macedonia	-51	-37	-25	-13	-48	-35	-14	-3
Roma – Romania	-43	-27	-14	0	-53	-41	-22	-12
Roma – Montenegro	-46	-31	-19	-5	-63	-54	-38	-30
Roma – Albania	-61	-50	-41	-32	-64	-55	-40	-32
Roma – Bosnia and Herzegovina	-55	-42	-31	-20	-71	-64	-52	-45

Table A16

Description of variables

(Used in the group-related determinants of poverty regression)

Variable	**Mean** (Standard deviation in parenthesis)
Household expenditures equivalized	136.6 (122.5)
Log expenditures equivalized	5.7 (0.7)
Number of children	0.4 (1.0)
Dummy Variable	**Percentage of Sample**
Displaced	25.3
Capital	17.5
Rural	29.8
Well-educated head	85.6
Skilled head	82.7
Country of residence	
- Bosnia and Herzegovina	31.9
- Croatia	16.7
- Montenegro	17.1
- Serbia	34.3

Table A17

Group-related determinants of poverty

Coefficients for linear regression analysis of log equivalized expenditures with membership of the displaced sample, country of residence, capital or rural locality, number of children in household, and the skill level and level of education of the household head

	Original model	Reduced form model
Displaced	-0.30***	-0.30***
Rural	-0.12***	-0.12***
Capital	0.12**	10^{-2}x-9.8**
Capital*Displaced	10^{-2}x-6.0	
Number of children	10^{-2}x-9.9***	10^{-2}x-9.9***
Skill level	0.38***	0.38***
Education level	0.65***	0.65***
Croatia	10^{-2}x-5.4	
Montenegro	-0.46***	-0.45***
Serbia	-0.83***	-0.79***
A	5.66***	5.65***
R-squared	0.47	0.47

***p<0.01, **p<0.05

Table A18

Description of variables

(Used in the regression analysis of determinants of poverty within each group)

	Mean (Standard deviation in parenthesis)	
Variable	Displaced	Majority
Household expenditures equivalized	708.8 (547.5)	1020.9 (730.4)
Log expenditures	5.56 (0.87)	6.10 (0.65)
Number of children	0.82 (1.13)	0.51 (0.82)
	Percentage of sample (with each level of variable)	
Dummy variable	Displaced	Majority
Locality		
- Rural	32.0	16.7
- Capital	16.1	23.7
- Urban	51.9	59.6
Skill level of household head		
- Skilled	71.8	90.3
- Unskilled	28.2	9.7
Education level of household head		
- Well educated	84.6	91.8
- Poorly educated	15.4	8.2
Country of residence		
- Bosnia and Herzegovina	33.0	32.0
- Croatia	16.4	20.4
- Montenegro	16.9	15.7
- Serbia	33.6	32.0

Table A19

Determinants of poverty within each group

Coefficients for linear regression analysis of log equivalized expenditures for displaced and majority households with the country of residence, locality, and number of children in a household and the skill level and level of education of the household head

	Displaced	Majority
Rural	-0.15**	-0.10*
Capital	$10^{-2}\times4.5$	0.12**
Number of children	$10^{-2}\times-5.1$*	-0.15***
Skill level	0.36***	0.42***
Education level	0.73***	0.52***
Serbia	-0.91***	-0.71***
Montenegro	-0.43***	-0.46***
A	5.29	5.74
R-squared	0.45	0.40

***p<0.01, **p<0.05

Bibliography

Akim, V. 2002. *Ciganite v istoriyata na Romania (Roma in the History of Romania).* Sofia: Infonet 2000.

Alwang, J., P.B. Siegel and S.L. Jørgensen. 2001. *Vulnerability: A View From Different Disciplines,* Social Protection Discussion Paper Series No. 0115. Washington, D.C.: The World Bank.

Antic, P. 2005. *Roma and the Right to Health Care in Serbia.* Belgrade: Minority Rights Centre.

Bagshaw, S. and D. Paul. 2004. *Protect or Neglect? Towards a More Effective United Nations Approach to the Protection of Internally Displaced Persons.* Washington: Brookings.

Betcherman, G., K. Olivas and A. Dar. 2004 *Impacts of Active Labour Market Programmes: New Evidence from Evaluations With Particular Attention to Developing and Transitional Countries.* World Bank, Social Protection Discussion Paper Series No.0402.

Bojic, M. 2001. *Historija Bosne i Bosnjaka* (*History of Bosnia and Bosniaks*). Sarajevo: TKD Sahinpasic.

Boscoboinik, A. and C. Giordano. 2005. "Roma's Identity and the Political Arena", in: Memedova, A. et al. *Roma's Identities in Southeast Europe: Macedonia.* Rome: Ethnobarometer.

Bougarel, X. 1996. *Bosnie - Anatomie d`un Conflit* (*Bosnia – Anatomy of a Conflict*). Paris: La Decouverte.

Buscher, D., E. Lester and P. Coelho. 2005. "Guarding Refugee Protection Standards in Regions of Origin". *The Way Forward. An Agenda for Change. Europe's Role in the Global Refugee Protection System.* London and Brussels: ECRE.

Center for Reproductive Rights and Poradňa pre občianske a ludské práva (CRR and POLP). 2003. *Body and Soul. Forced Sterilization and Other Assaults on Roma Reproductive Freedom in Slovakia.* CRR and POLP.

Chow, G. 1960. "Tests of Equality Between Sets of Coefficients in Two Linear Regressions." *Econometrica.*

Commission on Human Security. 2003. *Human Security Now: Protecting and Empowering People,* New York: Commission on Human Security.

Consultative Group to Assist the Poor (CGAP). 2002. *Microcredit: One of Many Intervention Strategies.* Donor brief # 2. April 2002.

Coudouel, A., J. Hentschel, and Q. Wodon. 2002. "Poverty Measurement and Analysis." *The PRSP Sourcebook,* pp. 29-74. Washington, DC: The World Bank.

Csongor, A., Gy. R. Lukacs and N. O'Higgins. 2003. *Labour Market Programmes for the Roma in Hungary.* Budapest: ILO.

Davies, A. 2004. "Restitution of Land and Property Rights." *Forced Migration Review.* Vol. 21. September 2004.

De Soto, H. 2003. *The Mystery of Capital: Why Capitalism Triumphs in the West and Fails Everywhere Else.* New York: Basic Books.

Dimitrijevic, N. and P. Kovács. 2004. *Managing Hatred and Distrust: the Prognosis for Post-Conflict Settlement in Multiethnic Communities in the Former Yugoslavia.* Budapest: LGI/OSI.

Dordevic, D. 2004. *Romi od Zaboravljene do Manjine u Usponu* (Roma From a Neglected Minority Towards a Group in Focus). Nis: Odbor za gradansku inicijativu.

EMS Consortium. 2004. *Review of the European Union's Assistance to Roma Minorities – Interim Evaluation of Phare Support Allocated in 1999-2002 and Implemented Until November 2003,* Thematic Evaluation Report.

European Commission (EC). 2004. *The Situation of Roma in an Enlarged European Union.* Brussels: EC. Directorate-General for Employment and Social Affairs.

European Council on Refugees and Exiles (ECRE). 2005. *The Way Forward "An Agenda for Change. Europe's Role In The Global Refugee Protection System.* London and Brussels: ECRE.

European Roma Rights Centre (ERRC). 1997. *No Record of the Case, Roma in Albania.* Country Reports Series. No. 5. ERRC.

ERRC. 2004. *Stigmata: Segregated Schooling of Roma in Central and Eastern Europe, a survey of patterns of segregated education of Roma in Bulgaria, the Czech Republic, Hungary, Romania, and Slovakia.* Budapest: ERRC.

Forster, S., S. Greenne and J. Pytkowska. 2003. *The State of Microfinance in Central and Eastern Europe and the Newly Independent States.* CGAP.

Fraser, D. 1992. *The Gypsies.* Oxford: Blackwell.

Hannum, E. 2002. "Educational Stratification by Ethnicity in China: Enrollment and Attainment in the Early Reform Years". *Demography.* Vol.39. No.1. Feb 2002. pp.95-117.

Hoogeveen, J., E. Tesliuc, R. Vakis and S. Dercon 2004. *A Guide to the Analysis of Risk, Vulnerability and Vulnerable Groups*. Social Protection Unit. Human Development Network. Washington, D.C.: The World Bank.

Hovey, G. 2000. "The Rehabilitation of Homes and Return of Minorities to Republika Srpska, Bosnia and Herzegovina." *Forced Migration Review*. Vol. 7. April 2000.

Hudson, D. and R. Weiler. 2005. "Towards the Integration of Refugees in Europe." Background paper to *The Way Forward. An Agenda for Change. Europe's Role In The Global Refugee Protection System*. London and Brussels: ECRE.

Hyde, A. 2006. "Systematic Exclusion of Roma from Employment." *Roma Rights*. No.1. 2006.

International Crisis Group. 2003. *Southern Serbia's Fragile Peace*. International Crisis Group. (http://www.crisisgroup.org).

International Displacement Monitoring Centre (IDMC), Norwegian Refugee Council (NRC). 2006. *Internal Displacement. Global Overview of Trends and Developments in 2005*. Geneva: IDMC. NDC.

ILO. 2002. *Decent Work in the Informal Economy*, Report VI to the 90th International Labour Conference. Geneva.

ISVS. 2004. *Romas and Others - Others and Romas. Social Distance*. Sofia: Ivan Hadjiyski Institute for Social Values and Structures.

Ivanov A. 2002. *On Roma, Agriculture and Integration – Concretely and in Essence*. Sofia: C.E.G.A.

Ivanov, A. and N. O'Higgins 2006. "Education and Employment Opportunities for the Roma." *Comparative Economic Studies*. Vol.48. No.1. March 2006. pp.6-20.

Ivanov, A. and S. Tursaliev. 2006. "Microlending to the Roma in Southeastern Europe." *Comparative Economic Studies*. Vol.48. No.1. March 2006. pp.36-50.

Jaksic, B. 2002. *Roofless People*. Belgrade: Republika.

Javorcik, B. and M. Spatareanu. 2004. *Do Investors Care About Labour Market Regulations?* World Bank Policy Research Paper 3275. Washington DC: April.

Johnson S. and B. Rogaly. 1997. *Microfinance and Poverty Reduction*. UK: Oxfam.

Kälin, W. 2001. *How Hard Is Soft Law? The Guiding Principles on Internal Displacement and the Need for a Normative Framework*. Presentation at Roundtable Meeting, Ralph Bunche Institute for International Studies, December 2001. (http://www.brookings.edu/fp/projects/idp/articles/wk20011219.htm).

Kälin, W. 2005. *The role of the Guiding Principles on Internal Displacement*. Forced Migration Review Supplement, October 2005.

Kälin, W. 2006. *Specific Groups and Individuals: Mass Exoduses and Displaced Persons. Report of the Representative of the Secretary-General on the Human Rights of Internally Displaced Persons. Mission to Bosnia and Herzegovina*. New York: UN.

Kenrick, D. 1998. *Historical Dictionary of the Gypsies*. London: The Scarecrow Press, Inc.

Kenrick, D. and G. Puxon. 1995. *Gypsies under the Swastika*. University of Hertfordshire Press.

Kiers, J. and I. Zoon. 2005. *Roma Access to Employment in SEE. Croatia, Bosnia and Herzegovina, Serbia and Montenegro, and the former Yugoslav Republic of Macedonia*. Strassurg: Council of Europe.

Koytcheva, E. 2005. *Social-Demographic Differences of Fertility and Union Formation in Bulgaria Before and After the Start of the Societal Transition*. Ph.D. thesis. Rostock: MPIDR.

Krištof, R. 2004. "Romové, Evropa a Mezinarodní Instituce" (Roma, Europe and International Institutions), in: Jakoubek, M. and T. Hirt (ed.). 2004, *Romové: Kulturologické Etudy (Roma - Cultural Sciences Writings)*. Plzeň: Aleš Čeněk.

Leckie, S. 2000. "Resolving Kosovo's housing crisis." *Forced Migration Review*. Vol. 7. April 2000.

Liègeois, J.P. 1994. *Roma, Gypsies, Travellers*, Strasbourg: Council of Europe Press.

Liègeois, J.P. 2006. *Roma in Europe*. Strasbourg: Council of Europe Press.

Lippman, B. and S. Malik. 2004. *"The 4Rs: The Way Ahead?"* Forced Migration review. Vol. 21. September 2004.

Lippman, B. and J. Rogge. 2004. *"Making Return and Reintegration Sustainable, Transparent and Participatory"* Forced Migration review. Vol. 21. September 2004.

Maksimovic, A. 2004. "Refugees in Serbia: A Case Study of the Zabucje Collective Center", in: Dimitrievic, N. and P. Kovac (ed.). 2004. *Managing Hatred and Distrust: The Prognosis for Post-Conflict Settlement in Multiethnic Communities in Former Yugoslavia*. Budapest: LGI Books.

Malcolm, N. 1994. *Bosnia. A Short History*. London: Macmillan Publishers Lmt.

Malloy, T. 2003. *The Lisbon Strategy and Ethnic Minorities: Rights and Economic Growth*. Flensburg: European Centre for Minority Issues (ECMI).

MAR, 2005. *Minorities at Risk Project*. College Park, Maryland: Centre for International Development and Conflict Management. (http://www.cidcm.umd.edu/inscr/mar/).

Marushiakova, E. and V. Popov.2001a. *Gypsies in the Ottoman Empire*. Hatfield: University of Hertfordshire Press.

Marushiakova, E. and V. Popov. 2001b. "Historical and Ethnographic Background: Gypsies, Roma, Sinti", in: Guy, W. (ed.) 2001.

Between Past and Future. The Roma of Central and Eastern Europe. Hatfield Hertfordshire: University of Hertfordshire Press. pp.32-53.

Marushiakova, E., H. Heuss, I. Boev, J. Rychlik, N. Ragaru, R. Zemon, V. Popov and V. Friedman. 2001. *Identity Formation among Minorities in the Balkans: The Cases of Roms, Egyptians and Ashkali in Kosovo.* Sofia: MSS *Studii Romani.*

McNamara, D. 2005. Who Does What? *Forced Migration Review Supplement.* October 2005.

Micklewright, J. and Gy. Nagy. 2002. "The Informational Value of Job Search Data and the Dynamics of Job Search: Evidence from Hungary". *Acta Oeconomica.* Vol 52. No. 4. pp. 399-419.

Milcher, S. 2006. "Poverty and the Determinants of Welfare for Roma and Other Vulnerable Groups in Southeastern Europe." *Comparative Economic Studies.* Vol.48. No.1. March 2006. pp.20-36.

Milicevic, N. 2003. Polozaj Nacionalnih Manjina u Bosni I Hercegovini (The Status of National Minorities in Bosnia and Herzegovina), in: *Democracy and Multiculturalism in South East Europe.* Beograd: Ethnicity Research Center.

Milner, J. and P. Coelho. 2005. "Towards a European Resettlement Programme." Background paper to *The Way Forward. An Agenda for Change. Europe's Role in the Global Refugee Protection System.* London and Brussels: ECRE.

Ministry of Labour and Social Policy, Bulgaria. 2005. *Evaluation of Net Impact of Active Labour Market Programmes.* Sofia: Ministry of Labour and Social Policy.

Mizsei, K. and N. Maddock. 2005. *Unemployment in the Western Balkans: A Synoptic Diagnosis.* UK: Edward Elgar.

Morjane, K. 2005. *Regional Ministerial Conference on Refugee Returns.* Sarajevo. UNHCR.

Moser, C. 1998. "The Asset Vulnerability Framework: Reassessing Urban Poverty Reduction Strategies". *World Development.* Vol. 26. No 1. pp. 1-19.

Nash, C. and S. Kok. 2005. Background paper to *The Way Forward. An Agenda for Change. Europe's Role in the Global Refugee Protection System.* London and Brussels: ECRE.

Nimal A. F. 2004. *Micro Success Story? Transformation of NGOs into Regulated Financial Institutions.* Asian Development Bank.

Nincic, R. and B. Vekic. 1995. *Serbs in Croatia.* Vreme News Digest Agency. No. 204.

Norwegian Refugee Centre (NRC). 2004. *Trapped in Displacement. Internally Displaced People in the OSCE Area.* Geneva: NRC.

Norwegian Refugee Council (NRC). 2005. *Property Restitution in Practice: The Norwegian Refugee Councils' Experience.* Geneva: NRC.

O'Higgins, N. 2001. *Youth Unemployment and Employment Policy: A Global Perspective.* Geneva: ILO. (www.ilo.org/public/english/employment/skills/youth/publ/).

O'Higgins, N. 2003. *Trends in the Youth Labour Market in Developing and Transition Countries,* Social Protection Discussion Paper Series. No. 0321. Washington, D.C.: The World Bank.

O'Higgins, N. 2004. *Recent Trends in Youth Labour Markets and Youth Employment Policy in Europe and Central Asia,* CELPE Discussion Paper. No. 85. University of Salerno.

OCHA, United Nations Office for the Coordination of Humanitarian Affairs. 2004. *Guiding Principles on Internal Displacement.* New York: United Nations. (http://www.reliefweb.int/ocha_ol/pub/idp_gp/idp.html).

Oprea, A. 2005. "Child Marriage a Cultural Problem, Educational Access a Race Issue? Deconstructing Uni-Dimensional Understanding of Romani Oppression." *Roma Rights,* 2/2005.

OSCE/ODIHR 1999. *Report on the Joint OSCE/ODIHR - Council of Europe Field Mission on the Situation of the Roma in Kosovo.* (http://www.coe.int/T/DG3/RomaTravellers/documentation/fieldvisits/missionkosovo99_en.asp).

OSCE/UNHCR 2003. *Tenth Assessment of the Situation of Ethnic Minorities in Kosovo.* Period covering May 2002 to December 2002. (http://www.unmikonline.org/press/reports/MinorityAssessmentReport10ENG.pdf).

Pamporov, A. 2003. "The Marital Pattern in Romany Communities." *Naselenie.* No. 1-2/2003. pp.164-178 (in Bulgarian, summary in English).

Pamporov, A. 2004. *The Romany Family: Everyday Life Aspects.* Sofia: Effect.

Peng, C-Y., T-S. So, F. Stage and E. St. John. 2002. *The Use and Interpretation of Logistic Regression in Higher Education Journals: 1988-1999.* Human Sciences Press, Inc.

Phuong, C. 2000. "At the heart of the return process: solving property issues in Bosnia and Herzegovina." *Forced Migration Review.* Vol. 7. April 2000.

Phuong, C. 2004. *The International Protection of Internally Displaced Persons,* Cambridge: University Press.

Population Reference Bureau. 2005. *Population and Health Data.* Available at: http://www.prb.org/datafind/datafinder6.htm.

Revenga, A., D. Ringold and W.M. Tracy. 2002. *Poverty and ethnicity: A Cross-Country Study of Roma Poverty in Central Europe.* Washington, DC: The World Bank.

Rhyne, E. and R. Christen. 1999. *Microfinance Enters the Market Place.* Washington, DC: USAID.

Ringold, D, M. Orenstein and E. Wilkens. 2003. *Roma in an Expanding Europe - Breaking the*

Poverty Cycle. Washington, D.C.: The World Bank.

Robeyns, I. 2000. *An Unworkable Idea or a Promising Alternative? Sen's Capability Approach Re-examined.* Cambridge, UK: Wolfson College.

Rutkowski, J. 2003. *Does Strict Employment Protection Discourage Job Creation? Evidence from Croatia.* Policy Research Working Paper 3104. Washington, DC: The World Bank.

Saith, R. 2001. *Social Exclusion: the Concept and Application to Developing Countries.* Working Paper. No. 72. Oxford.

Schneider, F. 2004. *The Size of the Shadow Economy of 145 Countries all over the World: First Results over the Period 1999 to 2003.* IZA Discussion Paper. No. 1431. Bonn.

Sen, A. 1999. *Development as Freedom.* New York: Anchor Books.

Smith, G and A. Wilson. 1997. *Rethinking Russia's Post-Soviet Diaspora: the Potential for Political Mobilisation in Eastern Ukraine and North-east Estonia.* Europe-Asia Studies.

Surdu, L. and M. Surdu. 2006. *Broadening the Agenda: The Status of Romani Women in Romania.* Budapest: OSI.

Szelenyi, I. 2000. *Poverty, Ethnicity, and Gender in Eastern Europe During the Market Transition.* Greenwood Publishing Group.

Tomova, I. 1995. *The Gypsies in Transitional Period.* Sofia: IMIR.

Tomova, I. 2005. "Konstruirane na Romskata Identichnost" (Constructing A Roma Identity). *Sociologicheski problemi.* No. 3-4. pp.187-214.

UNDP. 1994. *Human Development Report 1994.* New York. Oxford: Oxford University Press.

UNDP. 2002. *The Roma in Central and Eastern Europe: Avoiding the Dependency Trap,* Regional Human Development Report. Bratislava: UNDP.

UNDP. 2004. *Unleashing Entrepreneurship: Making Business Work for the Poor.* New York: Commission on the Private Sector and Development.

UNDP. 2005a. *Faces of Poverty, Faces of Hope.* Bratislava: UNDP.

UNDP/Ernst&Young. 2005b. *Employing the Roma: Insights from Business.* Bratislava: UNDP.

UNECE. 2001. *Declaration on Small and Medium-Sized Enterprises at the Dawn of the 21st Century.* (http://www.unece.org/indust/sme/cei-decl.htm).

UNHCR. 2006. *The State of the World's Refugees: Human Displacement in the New Millennium.* Oxford: Oxford University Press.

UNHCR/OSCE. 2000. *Update on the Situation of Ethnic Minorities in Kosovo.* Period covering February through May 2000. UNHCR/OSCE.

UNHCR/OSCE. 2001. *Assessment of the Situation of Ethnic Minorities in Kosovo.* Period covering October 2000 through February 2001. UNHCR/OSCE.

Williams, R.C. 2004. "Post-Conflict Property Restitution in Croatia and Bosnia and Herzegovina: Legal Rationale and Practical Implementation." *Forced Migration Review.* Vol. 21. September 2004.

Women's Commission for Refugee Women and Children (WCRWC). 2001. *Refugee and Internally Displaced Women and Children in Serbia and Montenegro.* New York: WCRWC.

Woodward, S. 1995. *Balkan Tragedy: Chaos and Dissolution After the Cold War.* Washington, D.C.: Brookings.

World Bank. 2001. *Attacking Poverty: World Development Report 2000/2001,* Washington, D.C.: The World Bank.

World Bank. 2005a. *Growth, Poverty and Inequality. Eastern Europe and the Former Soviet Union.* Washington, D.C.: The World Bank.

World Bank. 2005b. *Poverty, Social Exclusion and Ethnicity in Serbia and Montenegro: The Case of the Roma.* Washington, D.C.: The World Bank.

World Bank. 2005c. *Public Opinion Research Sheds Light on Roma Attitudes.* Washington, D.C.: The World Bank.

World Bank. 2005d. *Doing Business in 2005: Removing Obstacles to Growth.* Oxford University Press.

Zhelyazkova, A. 2001. "The Albanian National Problem and the Balkans". *Urgent Anthropology.* Vol.1. Sofia: IMIR.

Zhelyazkova, A. 2005. "Bosnia: Tolerant Hostility", in: Moulakis, A. (ed.) 2005. *Root Causes of Instability and Violence in the Balkans.* Lugano: Institute for Mediterranean Studies.

Zivkovic, J. 2001. "The Destiny of Romanies from Kosovo", in: *Series Philosophy and Sociology.* Vol. 2. No. 8. pp.527-538. Nis: Facta Universitatis.

UNDP is the UN's global development network, advocating for change and connecting countries to knowledge, experience and resources to help people build a better life. We are on the ground in 166 countries, working with them on their own solutions to global and national development challenges. As they develop local capacity, they draw on the people of UNDP and our wide range of partners. World leaders have pledged to achieve the Millennium Development Goals, including the overarching goal of cutting poverty in half by 2015. UNDP's network links and coordinates global and national efforts to reach these Goals.

United Nations Development Programme
Europe and the CIS
Bratislava Regional Centre
Grosslingova 35, 81109 Bratislava, Slovak Republic
Tel: (421-2) 59337-111
Fax: (421-2) 59337-450
http://europeandcis.undp.org/